THE DILEMMA IN INDIA

Owing to the antiquity and rarity of this book, certain pages are regrettably absent, and readability is compromised due to the blurring of the original text. If you possess any insights regarding the availability of these missing sections, kindly inform us. Your assistance is crucial in ensuring the completion of this significant work for the benefit of future generations.

THE DILEMMA IN INDIA

SIR REGINALD CRADDOCK

GYAN

Published by

Gyan Publishing House
5, Ansari Road
Daryaganj, New Delhi-110002
Phone: 011-47034999, 9811692060
E-mail: books@gyanbooks.com

Distribution Network
gyanbooks.com
India, USA, Canada, UK, Australia

ISBN: 978-93-7014-581-8 (PB)

First Published, 1929

2nd Impression 2025

Printed at: Gyan Press, Delhi.

THE DILEMMA IN INDIA
Arthur SIR REGINALD CRADDOCK

THE DILEMMA IN INDIA

THE
DILEMMA IN INDIA

By

SIR REGINALD CRADDOCK, G.C.I.E., K.C.S.I.

LONDON
CONSTABLE & CO LTD
1929

PREFACE

I CAME to write this book at the suggestion of a friend, who has great experience of India under the reforms, and many other friends have kindly helped me with information regarding those parts of India with which I am less well acquainted and in respect of events since I last returned home. The book is an attempt to lay before such of my fellow-countrymen as are interested in India such facts and deductions from the facts as I have been able to observe and draw from a long experience of the country and of its people of all classes from the polished lawyer to the wild aboriginal. As I am asking for a hearing, I am bound to state what my experience has been. I began my work in the Indian Civil Service before I was twenty-one, and had just turned sixty when I left India for the last time. I served there under nine Viceroys, from Lord Ripon to Lord Reading, and on retirement revisited the country as a member of Lord Lee's Commission on the Higher Civil Services. I was singularly lucky in the matter of early promotion, and thereby enjoyed special opportunities for becoming acquainted with Indian problems from many sides, first in the District and Division, and then as the Head of two Provinces, and as a member of the Executive Council of the Governor-General. I have visited every Province in India except Assam, some of them several times, and on my last tour in India with the Royal Commission I had special opportunities of gaining information about the working of the reforms. I fear that I cannot, like some of my colleagues in the Indian Civil Service, claim to have specialised in any particular studies, but I found my day-to-day work in a varied range of appointments of absorbing interest because it was a study in itself of men and measures, and their reactions upon each other.

The ordinary stay-at-home British citizen is either totally apathetic about Indian questions, or applies to her problems only the experience that he has gained in his own immediate environment. Only very few have the time or inclination for deeper study, and superficial knowledge is a dangerous thing. The late Mr. Keir-Hardie was misled into voicing a spurious grievance of landlords in the honest belief that he was championing the cause of the tenantry, and the greatest danger in India to-day is that by conceding political ascendancy to a few ambitious men reckoned in hundreds, we shall deprive ourselves of the power to protect the downtrodden reckoned in millions ; thereby undoing all that we have achieved during a century of impartial rule.

We British who have served in India are often accused of lack of sympathy, but with whom should we sympathise most ?—with the millions who are poor and helpless ? or with the few who have always exploited them ? The British democrat is so occupied with his concern that the demands of lawyers and politicians should be gratified that he forgets all about the interests of the masses, and is rash enough to believe that these lawyers and politicians will prove better custodians of the welfare of the poor than those who have spent the best years of their lives in using their power to hold the balance even between all sorts and conditions of men. At any rate we retired officers of the Indian Services have no axe to grind ; and if, as one amongst many of them who retain a keen personal interest in the country, I place the results of my experience before the British public, I trust that I may be given at least as patient a hearing as is accorded to the Indian politicians who seek to delude both themselves and the British people into the belief that British rule in India has been a curse to the country, and that her salvation lies in the committal of complete power to a few over the lives and fortunes of toiling millions. Is not the greatest happiness of the greatest number an objective more worthy of sympathy than the gratification of the ambitions, however intelligible, of a narrow section of that vast community of human beings?

The Labour Government stands for the succour of the "under dog." The only true friends of the "under dog" in India have been the British, and if that Government were to relax British control in deference to the clamour of a small political section, it will merely be tightening the chains round the "under dog." I would urge upon the Labour Party that before they shout, they should make sure that they are shouting for the right dog.

Among the intellectuals of India there are a few who are sincere in their expressed desire to improve the lot of the poor: the insincere largely outnumber them, and by parting prematurely with our controlling supervision we shall merely usher in a new era of oppression, for, sincere or insincere, the task is beyond their power. In the pages that follow I have endeavoured to make this plain. I have tried not to burden the story with more figures and statistics than are essential to explain the argument. The problems discussed in Part I. of the book might each form the subject of a separate volume to itself, and there are many other problems which are not touched upon at all, for I have concentrated upon those which have the most bearing upon the political issues now under investigation. I can honestly say that throughout my service I have stood for progress in India, but it is balanced progress for which I have striven. The standard that the Services have tried to follow, whatever the short-comings of fallible human agency, has been the standard of "Justice, Equity and Good Conscience," involving a just balance of the claims and interests of all classes of men. Attempts at unbalanced political advance will mar that ideal.

The Dilemma in India is grave and difficult. The way out is not to be found, as some suppose, by a mere bargaining of politicians seated round a table; for that method rests on the wholly fallacious assumption that the men round the table hold the mandate of a sub-continent. Whereas those men cannot even command the obedience of the section to which they belong, and will be ready to make promises which even had they the will they will not have the power to redeem. If a British Government, no matter what the party in power, is induced to sacrifice the interests of the silent many to the demands of the noisy few, the verdict of history will be that it deserted its post.

I MUST express my acknowledgments to the *Times*, for kindly allowing me to reproduce, in Chapter XXXII., a letter which appeared in its columns in 1928 from a correspondent, Mr. Dumasia, who is, I am informed, now on the staff of the *Times of India*, Bombay.

I also desire to acknowledge the courtesy of Mr. C. Vijayaraghovachariar of Salem (and through him of the *Hinda* of Madras), for permitting the republication in Appendix IV. of his article, "The National Demand," which was first published in the *Hindu* of March 3rd, 1929.

Lastly, I must record my special obligations to Mr. Rudyard Kipling for readily according his consent to the use that I have made in Chapter XXVII. of one of the famous stories contained in his *Second Jungle Book*.

R. H. C.

CONTENTS

PART III. THE PRESENT IMPASSE

PART IV. THE DILEMMA: REFLECTIONS AND SUGGESTIONS

APPENDICES

INTRODUCTORY

OF THE IMPORTANCE OF FACTS

In this dull and prosaic age there are no longer inspired prophets to tell us in sonorous if cryptic language of the things that shall come to pass in some undefined future. If there were we should pay no more heed to them than did Noah's contemporaries when he was building the Ark. But in the absence of inspired prophecy we fall back upon such terms as "vision" and "imagination," and these faculties are quite properly pronounced to be the attributes of all true statesmanship. But we must feel sure that we understand these terms aright, and are not mistaking dreams for imagination, and mere visionaries for men of vision. Imagination, in the correct sense, must be based on an understanding of the feelings and impulses of the human material with which we are concerned, and vision, in the desired sense, is the correct deduction from existing facts of the course and possibilities of future developments. It is on these two things that the statesman hazards a forecast of events, and bases his measures; but if the facts are not as he imagines them to be, or if he is ignorant of the facts or ignores them, his forecasts go astray, his measures fail, and he himself proves, however well-meaning, to have been but a visionary. The old story of the Greek merchant whose Armenian servant ran off with his master's property has a moral. The merchant and a friend started in pursuit of him. After a while they came to a hostelry, over the door of which was inscribed that the place was for Armenians. The merchant said "we shall certainly find him here," and wanted to go inside; his friend said: " On the contrary, he will know that we should look for him here, and would certainly not go in." They lost much time in arguing. But the fact was that the Armenian, not being able to read, had naturally not noticed the inscription at all, and had passed on. They had forgotten the simple fact that he could not read. How many people remember that over 90 per cent. of the population of India cannot read at all, and over 99 per cent. cannot read English?

All problems require for their solution that the intending solver shall use the correct data, and the problem of the best system of government in any collection of territorial areas can only be solved by applying to them the data special to those areas. Everything else is mere analogy often diluted by weak optimism. The Meteorological authority who tried to forecast the course of the Indian monsoon from observations made in the North Atlantic would be dismissed with ridicule; but the political soothsayer who forecasts the future before India from the data of Westminster may find himself hailed as a far-seeing statesman. Yet the currents of thought that pass through these vast masses in India differ far more widely from the thought currents of the British democracy than do the currents of air in the Bay of Bengal from the air currents of the North Atlantic. In India there are problems to be solved of the first magnitude, on their correct solution depends the fair name of Great Britain and the happiness of millions of the King's subjects in India. Yet the tendency is to neglect facts and worship phrases. The Constitutional theorist is listened to with the greatest respect, while the men who have the facts are contemptuously brushed aside because their facts will not support the theory. The golden maxims of this or that political leader, uttered in respect of one situation or one nation, are apt to be regarded as Holy Writ, applicable to all situations, and all races, and all times, and those who will not fall down and worship before them are consigned to the burning fiery furnace. And so we go on "exploring avenues" and "making gestures," and talking about "new angles of vision," "changes of heart," "self-determination," "responsible government," "making countries safe for democracy," all of which phrases mean something at some times and in some places, but are perfectly meaningless in others. When the people of Ephesus shouted for the space of two hours "Great is Diana of the Ephesians," they shouted a slogan which meant something, and they knew what they meant, and from their own point of view they were perfectly right. On the cult of the goddess depended the welfare of their city and their own prosperity, but the slogan was worthless elsewhere. And so are many of our slogans and catchwords. They may be wisdom under the pine, but they are mere futility under the palm.

The British people are anxious to do their duty; they wish to be fair, to keep their promises, and to do justice between man and man, but their conception of their duty is circumscribed by these phrases, and they do not know either the facts or the factors which govern the facts. The vast majority are quite naturally immersed in their own pursuits and interests. India is a long way off. Where their own immediate interests are concerned they like to have a say, and they are not backward in saying it. Where their own interests are not conspicuously involved they are content to leave things to the politicians. And so it comes about that only one man in a thousand (and that is a liberal allowance) takes any serious interest in India, or cares very much about what happens there, or thinks it worth while to study the facts.

But among those few who think about India at all there are two wings, the left and the right. The left either spread or swallow the fantastic tales of a nation oppressed and enchained by brutal British Imperialism squeezing out the life-blood of a starving people. By these the men in the Indian Services are regarded as harsh and domineering, and the men of commerce merciless exploiters. To the men who spread these lies, knowing them to be lies, it is useless to speak. To the men who swallow them credulously, but repeat them honestly believing them, the truth if demonstrated may appeal.

Then there is the right wing, consisting of the men who have lived in India, served India, and who know India, as also some people who have really learnt India by visits and by diligent and impartial study. These men will know whether what is said in this book is true or not. India is a vast country; no man can know it all equally well. The experiences of one man and another may vary in degree, and every man must form his own conclusions from the facts as he knows them. But there is a certain Oriental mentality, an atmosphere, only understood by those who really know the country.

If the British people were made up entirely of these two opposite sections they would fight it out and there is little doubt that the truth would prevail; but neither of these sections has any real voice in the decision. They are both narrow fringes of the inhabitants of this country. In between them is the vast bulk of the people who do not care because they do not know, and do not know because they do not care. The fact that this attitude of indifference is natural does not make it less dangerous; it is dangerous to the Empire, but much more dangerous to the inhabitants of India. The mass of the British people, treasuring their own political maxims, based on their own experiences in their own country, though they may reject the calumnies on their fellow-countrymen which are spread by the left wing, yet discount the opinions of the men on the right wing, as those of worthy and well-meaning persons who have by their very experiences sunk into a groove so deep that they cannot extricate themselves. There are grooves in India, but are there not also grooves in Westminster? And there is a difference. The Englishman in India is not a complete stranger to the institutions of his own country, or the thoughts and literature of his own people; does he not read English books and newspapers during his sojourn in the East? Does he not periodically on his furloughs refresh his contact with British problems and British psychology? But what contact has the average stay-at-home Englishman with the real peoples of India? their thoughts and their sentiments, their joys and sorrows, their beliefs and their prejudices, their aims and ambitions? How, not knowing any of these things, can he say what should be done or left undone? But the highbrow wraps himself up in the virtue of his theories, and with his little hoard of political maxims preaches down the hearts of those who love India and have worked for her all their time. And the business man, after a few desultory remarks, goes back to his Stock Exchange quotations or his own particular interests, and dismisses from his mind problems that do not seem to concern his own prosperity. And the Man-in-the-Street skips the article concerning the Indian Empire that may on rare occasions find its way into the popular Press, and devours the latest news about football or racing. For the Man-in-the-Street and the business man I have every respect; they are trying at least to mind their own business, or are enjoying their favourite amusement, but the highbrow rouses one's sense of mischief. I wish that somebody would disturb him from his own pathetic contentment with himself and his maxims before it is too late.

India empties the House of Commons, and Indian subjects are boresome to the ordinary reader. Verily, India is a long way off. When "Truthful Tory" wrote the following in an article in *Truth*, he was more than ever truthful:

"It was an amazing blunder," he wrote, "to make Lord Birkenhead Secretary of State for India, to lock up the wittiest and most dashing Parliamentarian of the day in a Department in which nobody but a few retired civilians takes the slightest interest, to drown him in details which have never yet been mastered by anybody save Permanent Officials, to force him to read a long statement once a year amidst the yawns of specialists on empty benches, was surely a waste of the best political material. There is no one, not even Mr. Churchill, who combines in an equal degree of perfection, the arts of platform and parliamentary speaking. But what the deuce was F. E. to do in that Indian galley?"

What refreshing candour, and how true a reflection of feeling! To the vast majority Sir John Simon is just performing a tiresome routine duty in a remote part of the Empire. And the leader writer of an evening paper, commenting on the decision of a Lancashire cricketer to retire from his Parliamentary candidature in order to captain his Lancashire Eleven, commented on the "obscurity" which had befallen the once-famous Sir Stanley Jackson, Captain of the All-England Eleven, by his relegation to "a humdrum" Indian Governorship. This is exactly how it strikes the Man-in-the-Street. What is the glory of governing forty million Bengalis compared with that of the Captaincy of the All-England Eleven? It is all very natural, and I am making no complaint; I am merely citing press quotations in support of the statement that India makes no appeal to people who have not been there.

I was present at a meeting of a very old Debating Society in London, in which the question of reforms in India was the subject of debate. After an excellent speech by the Vice-President, who had got up his facts and figures admirably, though he had not been to India himself, a member of the Club was persuaded, with some apparent reluctance, to intervene in the debate. He freely confessed that he had never given much thought to India, but made the point that as the great mass of the British electors, upon whose decision the issue depended, was like himself, it was obviously clear that the Indians must know much better than the British elector what the situation required, and therefore the only safe course was to give them all they asked for. He ignored entirely the history of India during the last two centuries, or the fact that there might be some few of his fellow-countrymen who knew something of the country. Whether he was in earnest, or merely indulging in banter, which as a stranger I could not say, he was voicing what a great many electors might be tempted to do, viz. being too lazy to study the facts, just follow the line of least resistance.

I happened to ask a man, whom I met by chance in the smoking room of a Golf Club, whether he took any interest in Indian affairs. He said that he was afraid he did not, but afterwards, recollecting, added: "I had at one time some money in Indian Loans and Indian Railways, but hearing that sedition there was on the increase I sold out." That, of course, settled the matter.

Some five years ago I was staying at the same hotel with a former Liberal M.P. for a Lancashire constituency. He was lamenting the decline of the Indian demand for Manchester cotton goods. I asked him whether he had been in the House of Commons when the Bill introducing the Indian Reforms was passed. He admitted that he had voted for the Bill, but said: "We did not know; we did not understand what the scope of the Reforms was, or what exactly they portended."

Yet it is not all apathy. Sometimes, in unexpected quarters, one finds interest. On the last occasion that I came back from India, in 1924, having collected my heavy luggage, I was taking it down to the country, and at the London terminus found an elderly man, dressed like a porter, who was giving receipts for the money due on excess luggage. As he seemed rather surprised that I had so much luggage, I said to him: "I don't always travel with so much, but I have just brought these back from India." "India," he said, "it will soon go the way of Ireland, if we don't govern it properly. Them Sikhs," he went on to say, "will never consent to be governed by them Baboos." "Very true," I said, "but how do you come to know anything about it? You must have served in India." "No," he said, "I haven't." Then I said: "You must have a son or a near relative there, or at least some friends." "No," he said, "I haven't." "Then how do you come to take so much interest in these things?" I asked. "Sir," he said, "I am an old Guardsman, and I also have a vote, and as I have a vote I think it my duty to read up about things, so that I may be able to exercise my vote wisely."

I shook hands with him as being a model elector.

It would be unreasonable to expect that any large proportion of the British electorate should be well informed about Indian affairs, but it is essential that they should not be misinformed. It is so far to the good that the great daily papers and the Reviews are sparing more space for Indian news and the discussion of Indian questions. Not so long ago the London papers, with the exception of the *Times*, published no Indian news, except stray Reuter's telegrams about some special or sensational happening. The improvement in this respect, so far as it indicates serious thought among an increasing number of readers, is a good omen. It is absolutely essential to counter the calumnies so sedulously spread by Bolshevik agents, and repeated by the extreme left of the Socialist Party. These men are anxious to convert India into a question of party politics. All classes of the British people, and most of all the working men of England, are, if they only understood it, deeply concerned that a false step should not be taken. But few realise what a critical period in the history of the relations of Great Britain and India we have arrived at.

Particularly does it behove all members of Parliament, of whatever party, to realise that whatever right of interference they may have surrendered during the progress of the instalment of reform granted in 1919, yet, with the expiration of that period of experiment their responsibility returns, in full measure, for any step that may be taken on the report of the Simon Commission. Those steps may have most momentous consequences to the great mass of mankind comprehended within the term "Indian." Above all is it important that the true facts should be understood. Generous gestures are good only when they are accompanied by understanding. There is no generosity in beckoning men to a fool's paradise. Whither are we leading the people of India? The sanguine theorist will say that we are leading them to a land flowing with democratic milk and honey, but people who know India well know that the theorists are merely directing them towards the same wilderness from which we ourselves once rescued them. The theorists shouting directions through their megaphones are a poor substitute for the cloud by day and the pillar of fire by night. They do not know where the promised land is situated, nor if there be such a land. In the end it may after all prove a mirage.

I will now try to set out in the succeeding chapters, for those who care to read, the facts as I know them, and I will take them through all the great problems which must be solved before the democratisation of a unified India can even come within the horizon of hope. Much of what I write will seem elementary to those who really know India, but there are some who have visited it, some who have even lived there for a time, but have not even begun to understand it. There are large numbers of thinking men and women in England to whom it is really a sealed book. The supposed major problem of a constitution for a self-governing India is not the major problem at all. It is these other problems which the Constitution-maker comforts himself by ignoring, or by fondly hoping that they will solve themselves. These are the major problems. If they can be solved, then the problem of a self-governing India will be simplicity itself. Until they are out of the way, if they ever are, the future of India remains an enigma, but it will not resemble in the least what the theorist fondly imagines.

PART I

THE PROBLEMS

CHAPTER I

THE PROBLEM OF DISTANCES AND RACIAL DIVERSITIES

Is there any Reason why India should be a Nation?—Comparisons between Europe and India

An Indian Nation, if such be possible, has to be created before it can exist. It never existed in the past, and it does not exist now. Do we flatter ourselves that we have created it? If so, it is sheer flattery. There is no word for "Indian" in any vernacular tongue; there is not even any word for "India." Nor is there any reason why there should be an Indian Nation. The only bond of union among the races to be found there is that they have for the last century and a half been governed in common by a Foreign Power. If that Power abdicates its authority, the bond of union goes with it. It is we, the people of England, who began calling the inhabitants of the sub-continent "Indians." Europe generally talks about the East Indies, the Dutch East Indies, the West Indies, and large numbers of people on the American Continent have been called, or miscalled, Indians. We ourselves in India are generally called Europeans, and speak of ourselves as such, although there is no single European nationality. The term "Indians" only began to be used during the last twenty years. British people used to call the inhabitants of India "Natives." The educated Indian no longer likes to be called a "Native," though by a slip of the tongue he frequently used the term himself. The objection to "Native" used as a noun is intelligible—the objection to the word as an adjective is ridiculous. Uneducated Indians never call themselves by that name; they call themselves by their racial or caste name, and if they want to distinguish themselves from us they will say: "We dark men do this or think that, and you white men think that or do this." They are not at all ashamed of their colour, for which we can certainly respect them, but the difference in complexion is the most obvious distinction between themselves and ourselves, and they use it unaffectedly. The whites have not the monopoly of virtues, nor the browns of vices, nor *vice versa.* Fairness of skin is esteemed in India as a mark of beauty; as brown complexioned people, however, they look down upon people whom they call "black," such as the Aboriginal. There was a man serving under my orders once who was extremely learned in both Sanskritic and Arabic languages. His complexion was unusually dark; he was engaged upon work that was unpopular at the time among the politicians, so they nicknamed him derisively "Habshi," or the Abyssinian. It may sound a paradox, but it is British rule and the English language alone that have suggested the idea of Indian nationality. It has no real substance. What passes for it is the Anglophobia of a proportion of the intelligentsia, and the colour consciousness which is not shared in by the teeming masses of the country. There are certain qualities we have which they admire in us, and there are also certain things we do which they dislike, but the colour of our skins has nothing whatever to do with either feeling. We cannot well expect that self-respecting Indian politicians would accept such unpleasant terms as "Anglophobia" and "colour consciousness" as a correct description of their feeling. Indian nationalism sounds so much better, and is infinitely more valuable for impressing Western thought, so that is the term they prefer. I do not blame them, but let us at least know what the words really cover. I come back to the question: "Is there any reason why there should be an Indian Nation?"

India belongs to the Old World, and we must therefore put out of consideration for any comparison countries of the New World, such as the U.S.A. and the great British Dominions beyond the seas. There is not a solitary feature which India shares with these new countries. But Europe and Asia really form a single vast continent, of which Europe and India are two of several sub-continents. The races which inhabit both of them are races whose forefathers in prehistoric times roamed over the whole, some Eastwards, some Westwards, to the North or to the South, until they finally settled in their present habitats. The days of great waves and invasions of humanity in the mass have passed away, but they have left their separate diversifications like so many claims pegged out over the enormous tracts which these migrations covered. Pristine tribes who came from no one knows where were driven into the hills and the forests, and the invading hordes occupied the level plains and the fertile valleys, each successive wave fighting with the last-comers for supremacy. Thus were formed the races and countries of Europe; thus also those of Asia; and thus, too, those of India. During all the centuries, in the course of which nationalities became localised in particular areas, constant wars were waged. There were wars to acquire, wars to recover, and, as a consequence, wars to retain. The great nations of the world are now at last hoping to ban wars to acquire and wars to recover, but war to retain must still remain the rightful defence against any breaker of a Peace Pact. All these kinds of wars were chronic in India from the oldest days until the latter part of the last century, as this or that race or creed sought to acquire hegemony over the rest.

Then ensued the Pax Britannica and closed down all this turmoil, and the land had peace at home for seventy years. It is only by the interposition of some paramount power that divergent peoples, warring races, and jarring creeds can ever be governed in common, and warfare between them restrained. The Power that governs separate countries and nationalities, and keeps them united, has almost always been autocratic in its nature. The Chinese, Russian, and Austrian Empires were kept in this way in a state of comparative stability. In the case of Russia, Soviet tyranny has merely taken the place of Tsarist despotism, but, even so, certain nationalities have broken away. Germany has lost her non-German races; Austro-Hungary has split into many parts; Finland, Poland, Latvia, Lithuania, Esthonia, Austria, Czecho-Slovakia, Hungary, Jugo-Slavia, Albania, have appeared on the map of Europe. Some countries have been enlarged by additions, and others made smaller. These separate nationalities may perhaps prove themselves able to govern themselves, though some of them are still very shaky, but if one thing is certain it is that these countries, either solely or jointly, cannot govern each other, and here are we calmly building on the hypothesis that there is one Indian Nation, merely because British rule, the most benevolent despotism that the world has seen, has been able to impose peace among a collection of heterogeneous races and creeds who are always ready to fly at each other's throats. Even China, which has had a single national record for several thousand years, has, with the fall of autocracy, been convulsed by anarchy during the seventeen years since the Empire fell.

Travel a thousand miles in Europe and how many races and countries do we come across? And yet do we really expect to travel double that distance in India and find a single nation? from Bombay to the Wild Was on the borders of China, from Cape Comorin to Chitral, from Darjeeling to Victoria Point? But if we know too much to expect this, do we expect that a few eloquent debaters in Delhi will enforce the writ of an Indian Commonwealth over millions of turbulent men, and will be able to raise the down-trodden and subdue the unruly? It sounds too much like the millennium.

It is very difficult to make the stay-at-home British citizen comprehend aright this problem of races and distances in India. He will hear it, just as a man hears the fact that the distance of the sun from the earth is ninety millions of miles. It might be nine millions or ninety thousand for any practical effect on his mind or his actions. Even so, does he think of India's millions as just a nation of dark people for whom the solid political maxims which he himself loves must be equally suitable, and whether there are three millions or three hundred millions or how many different languages they speak he does not stop to think.

In the hope of making it easier to visualise the problem I have placed in Appendix I a comparative statement of the independent countries of Europe with the Provinces and States of India, balancing the areas and populations as well as it is possible to do. It is commonly said that India is the size of Continental Europe, excluding Russia, but we can go a little further and include, on the European side, Finland, Poland, and the new Baltic States. When one compares the two group by group the correspondence is very remarkable.

Thus, Bengal and the Central Provinces with the States attached to them are a fifth larger than Germany, but have much the same population, 63·64 millions as against 63·18 in Germany; France is larger in area than Madras, but her population is slightly less, 40·74 millions against 42·31, but add Germany and France together and compare them with these three Provinces, and the areas are 394,000 and 358,000 square miles, and 103·92 millions and 105·96 millions respectively. In this way we may compare Italy and the Province of Behar and Orissa and its States; Spain and the Bombay Presidency; Portugal and the States of Gwalior and Baroda; the Netherlands and Belgium with Luxemburg and the Nizam's Dominion. It will then be found that France and the other countries of Western Europe correspond with the three Provinces and the three large Native States mentioned to make total areas of 582,000 and 558,000 square miles respectively, with the respective populations of 121·62 millions and 124·80 millions. In Central Europe I have already set off Germany against Bengal and the C.P.; Austria, Hungary, Jugo-Slavia, and

Czecho-Slovakia have a much larger area than the United Provinces and the States attached to them, but the total populations are 40.84 millions and 46.63 millions respectively. Poland balances nearly with the N.W. Frontier Province and the Punjab and its States; Roumania with Rajputana; Bulgaria with Mysore; Greece, Albania, and Turkey in Europe can take their places alongside Assam and the Manipur State. The three Scandinavian countries, Sweden, Norway, and Denmark are a balance to Burma; Finland to Beluchistan and the States and Tribal Areas on the N.W. frontier. The three new Baltic States of Latvia, Lithuania, and Esthonia cancel out with the Central Indian and Madras States, and the small territory of Ajmere-Merwara. The enclave of Delhi and the new city State of Danzig are not dissimilar. After contrasting all these areas I am left with Switzerland in Europe and the Kashmir State in India (the latter much larger), having populations of 3·96 and 3·32 millions respectively. On the whole total Europe (Soviet Russia excluded) is just 90,000 square miles to the good, and India exceeds in population by 5,000,000. I have, however, left out Nepal because it has been declared independent in return for its wonderful services in the War, but it is still geographically as a Himalayan State and politically from its special relations to India and the Indian Army properly included in the Indian sub-continent, while its Hindu religion makes it part of real India. If we also add in the Andamans and Nicobars, and the small Himalayan State of Bhutan, which is also under Indian political relation, the area superiority of Europe is reduced to 15,000 square miles only, or 1 per cent., and the population superiority of India is raised to 10,000,000, or 3 per cent. Europe has twenty-six independent States, not counting the separate States of Germany, or the three tiny States of Monaco, San Marino, and Andorra, India has Provinces as large as the larger countries, and several States larger than the smaller countries of Europe, and yet some people persist in thinking of India as a young nation ripe for democracy.

Race and language are the great dividing features in India, as they are in Europe. The history of Europe has precluded the emergence of a single European nation; the same cause has the same effect in India. The tendencies of the time are entirely fissiparous and emphatically not coalescent. Coalescence, possible under empires and powerful monarchies, is impossible when men of various races and languages become democratic in their outlook. Every few hundred miles, and the race and language changes, whether you wander about Europe or roam about India. The only difference between them has been the superimposition of the paramount power. Had there been such a power in Europe for a century and a half, artificially uniting the different nationalities of Europe, and had this power then abdicated, can it be supposed that the democracies of Europe would have remained united under one single central government? To expect such union in a self-governing India is to fly in the face of history, experience, and human nature. The allegory of the Tower of Babel is still with us.

The principle which underlies the difficulty of the democratic union of divergent races is surely plain. Race divisions differ from all other class distinctions. When political parties consist of different racial entities, one race will dominate the other in a democratic combination by reason of its numerical superiority. When divisions are merely class divisions within a race, political parties run athwart them; otherwise democracy could not succeed anywhere. It would not be national rule by a majority representing the nation, but class rule by the class forming the majority. I am speaking, of course, of genuine not sham democracy, in which anything may happen, Bolshevism, or complete anarchy, or absolute tyranny. But, taking democratic countries, if Norway and Sweden could not keep together, if Ulster and the Irish Free State could not be got to combine, how can it be expected that the infinitely greater diversities and divergent racial elements to be found in India can be welded into one self-governing and democratic whole. Indian politicians were wont to point to China under Swaraj; they have had their answer. China as an empire had a record of antiquity unequalled in the world, but China as a republic has for seventeen years been disintegrating into chaos, under the effects of civil war waged by military adventurers and ex-brigands, until corruption and anarchy have robbed it of all semblance of unity, people terming themselves Nationalists, Socialists, Communists, Soviets, and pseudo-Soviets have been contending for mastery, while its unhappy citizens, whose thrift and honourable trading capacities are surely worthy of a better fate, are ravaged by pestilence, flood, and famine, relieved only by battle, robbery, extortion, torture, and sudden death, until its fabled four hundred millions must by this time have been decimated. And the intellectuals go on uttering the maxims of a democratic copybook and proclaim new constitutions which they have not yet shown that they possess either the power to enforce or the genius to apply.

Surely, in China and Russia, we have serious warning of what may happen in these colossal countries from the ill-judged confidence that a little top dressing with constitutional spray will cause a wilderness of thistles to put forth a bountiful crop of the choicest democratic figs. India is not just a nation of budding democrats; its distances are too great, its area too vast, and its racial diversities too many.

Railways, telegraphs, and the Post Office, we may be told, have worked miracles of unification. They have stimulated trade, they make strangers better acquainted. They may in these ways soften antipathies between individuals of different races who have more chances of meeting each other. They may do all these things, but they cannot turn aliens into blood relations. They have failed to do so everywhere in Europe; why should they be expected to succeed any better as between Bengal and the Punjab? In India, communications have helped to create the fiction of an all-Indian nation, but the creation of the reality is entirely beyond their power.

Some of my friends tell me that I underestimate the growing "National" feeling to be found among the young educated Indians. I do not under-rate this feeling; it is at the bottom of all the political troubles. But we must call things by their proper names. There are a good many Indians who are genuine "Nationalists," that is to say, persons whose desire is that there should be an Indian Nation. But until the Nation, the noun, comes into existence, the adjective, National, does not represent facts. Thus a Burmese, a Bengali, a Sikh, a Pathan, may all four be Swarajists or even Nationalists, but there is no common bond of united nationhood between them, for no one of them would readily accept the condominium of the others with and over himself. The Prohibitionist and the Bootlegger may together prefer a "Dry" Law, or the Nonconformist and the Bookmaker may combine to resist the Betting Tax, but for nothing else will they be found in combination. So it is with the Indians. They may champion the East against the West, but no true Indian nationhood is involved in this championship. And even such Nationalist aspirations as exist are confined to a trifling percentage of the whole population.

The politicians of the North and the South may take counsel together and combine in wordy warfare directed against British supremacy, but racial jealousies are much stronger than racial affections. The latter cannot for long stand the strain of the former. It is indeed difficult for man to join what God has put asunder.

CHAPTER II

THE PROBLEM OF RELIGIOUS ANTAGONISMS

Hindu and Moslem—Religious Strife aggravated by Historical and Economic Causes—Reasons why Conflicts less Common in Native States—Effect of Political Jealousy

PROBLEMS arising from religious differences should *prima facie* be more tractable than those of race. They have existed in some form in most countries as between Christian and Jew, and between Protestant and Roman Catholic, but in the last century or two we have witnessed in most Western countries a steady diminution in the antagonisms due to religious differences, though every now and then there is evidence that some of the old fires are still smouldering under the surface.

But in India the differences of religion are accentuated and exacerbated, because they are also in considerable degree differences of race, while the separate Hindu problems of caste complicate their relations with other creeds. Further, while religious differences in Europe between Christian denominations or between Jews and Christians are more on a parallel with the differences that exist between distinct sects among Mahommedans or Sikhs, there is absolutely no parallel elsewhere to the basic antagonism that divides Hindus and Mahommedans. Hinduism, with its love of images and symbols, and its polytheism, and Islam with its strict Unitarian faith and its strong iconoclastic principles, are at opposite poles. The sacrifice of a cow by Mahommedans or the procession of an idol near a mosque to the accompaniment of loud music by Hindus may at any moment cause an outbreak, leading to bloodshed and murder. Let but a pretext arise, and men who were yesterday working side by side in apparent amity, will be bludgeoning and knifing one another to death. Temples will be burnt and mosques desecrated, and every insult or injury inflicted by one side evokes reprisals in kind from the other. It is only the strong arm of the British law that keeps these animosities within any bounds at all. Once they break out, each outbreak leaves behind it bitter memories which go to perpetuate ill-feeling, and sow the seed for fresh outbursts of hatred. And the pretext for the outbreak need not be religious at all—it may be purely secular or political; anything, in fact, that happens to cause bad blood between members of the two communities, and when the bad blood begins to boil, chance scuffles may be magnified into religious assaults, and an ordinary dispute between a shopkeeper and a customer may cause a whole bazaar to be wrecked. The Mopla Rebellion in 1920 showed the terrible savagery and outrage with which such outbreaks will be accompanied if they are once out of hand. In a certain district during the War, when a Hindu cultivating caste responded readily to the call for recruits, and were complimented by the Collector for their loyalty, the remark they made was "We are not allowed to kill Mahommedans in this country, but we are told we shall be able to kill as many as we please in the country we are going to." When the Emperor Aurungzebe razed the great Hindu Temple at Benares to the ground and built upon the site a great mosque, he left behind ineffaceable memories, and Hindu temples with the images defaced by Mahommedans are to be found in many parts of the land.

But apart from the antagonism due to conflicts between the two religions, there are other causes at work producing perpetual jealousy between the two communities. The Mahommedans never forget that they once ruled the country, the Hindus that they were ruled with a rod of iron. There are strong economic causes to keep up the perpetual feud, for the Hindus now enjoy most of the education and the wealth, and the Mahommedans most of the ignorance and the poverty. Usury is forbidden by the Koran, but the Mahommedan has to pay usurious interest to the Hindu moneylender. It is only on the Northern half of the West coast that Mahommedans of special race and sect can compete successfully in the rivalry of commerce. Over the country at large it may be said that the Mahommedan antipathy to the Hindu is largely due to economic causes, and the Hindu antipathy to the Mahommedan is mostly due to historic, but with religious fanaticism always present to come to the surface merely because this side there are Hindus and that side Mahommedans. Be the bone of contention what it may, political or economic or personal, any dispute is sure to assume a religious complexion. The whispering galleries of the East spread incitements as well as rumours; the number of mischief-makers is legion; their cunning wonderful, and their opportunities unlimited. Every happening in India is sure to take on a religious twist. Religion in danger becomes the universal cry. In the Mutiny it was the greased cartridges intended to destroy caste which formed a rallying point. Over the partition of Bengal, Hindus and Mahommedans took opposite sides, and the Bengali Anarchist Press, attacking the British Government, was full of invocations to the Goddess Kali. The Khilafat Agitation was purely political, though served up in a shape calculated to arouse Moslem fanaticism. Proposed laws to protect minor girls from a life of infamy were invasions of religious custom. The Rowlatt Bills enabling the law to deal more effectively with anarchical conspirators were translated to the populace as a measure which would enable weddings and funerals to be interfered with and the confiscation of wedding and funeral robes. The people of Delhi, Lahore, and Amritsar would never have broken out into murderous riots over the sorrows present or future of Bengali anarchists. Religion is the certain reagent calculated to infuse white heat into the coldest secular dispute, whether that dispute arise between two communities or between one or more of them and the British Government. A letter found at a search in

Bengal from a well-known Bengali politician to a local pleader during the partition trouble exhorted him to cloak his sedition under the guise of religion. It is an ancient game, of which the players never tire. A permanent dam across the Ganges at Hardwar to replace temporary ones so as to ensure early irrigation to a large area of crops started the religious cry that a barrage would destroy the sanctity of the great river; the fact that a similar barrage had existed for many years at the head waters of the Lower Ganges Canal without a thought of this objection was completely overlooked.

And yet, with all this, Hindus and Mahommedans have often lived as neighbours in kindly amity. I have seen this many a time during my twenty-seven years in the Central Provinces; I know places where Hindu processions with music playing have passed mosques when none forbade, or stopped playing at a polite request. There Hindus and Mahommedans took part in each other's festal days, until the mischief-maker came along and replaced harmony by discord. And then the Hindus began to clang their loudest music when they passed a mosque, and pseudo-worshippers collected stones to stone them with in passing. I have known a house opposite a mosque turned into an improvised temple, with a hastily imported idol continuously worshipped with loud music simply to annoy Mahommedans at prayer. And I have known an improvised mosque started on the route of an ancient Hindu procession merely in order to furnish the excuse for interrupting the route. So are bogus pretexts created by both sides when a real one is entirely lacking. There are always the agents provocateurs.

The two questions most often asked are why these conflicts should be more frequent in British India than in Native States, and, secondly, why there should have been such exacerbation of the relations between the two religious communities in the last ten years. The answer to the first is that there is much greater liberty to be used or abused in British India. In the Indian States the religion of the ruler has a powerful effect. If beef is proscribed and cow slaughter a criminal offence in a State ruled by a Hindu, his Mahommedan subject will have to content himself with the sacrifice of a goat. Nor, if the ruler is a Moslem, will the Hindu subjects offend the co-religionists of the ruler by impeding religious sacrifices or playing deafening music in front of a mosque during prayer time. In addition to this, there are more ways of punishing recalcitrant subjects in these States than in British India. There is no law of *Habeas Corpus* in the Indian States, and no Court which would enforce it against the ruler if it existed.

To the second question the answer is that there are two factors which operate—one which is at the root of dissensions, and the other that has facilitated their finding their manifestation in violence. Unwittingly, benevolently, and with no shadow of malice, we have thrown an apple of discord between the two communities by holding out to them a hope of self-government. We thought to offer liberty, but our proffered liberty became a sword. Those who offered it thought of Hindus and Mahommedans as one people, governing jointly Mahommedans and Hindus, but to Hindus and Mahommedans the question was, as one must dominate the other, which is it to be? So long as the British Government was governing both impartially, there was comparative concord. The great Mahommedan leader, Sir Syad Ahmed, bade his followers keep aloof from the National Congress and all politics pertaining thereto, and concentrate their own efforts on educating themselves, and thus reducing the inequality between them and their Hindu fellow-subjects. With political contest, he foresaw, would come strife and a set-back to the progress of both. His oft-quoted saying that Hindus and Mahommedans were like the two eyes of a beautiful woman, and that to injure one would injure the other, was applicable only when both were equally protected under the impartial aegis of a benevolent ruling power. Both could then continue to progress, but if they both attempted to contest the supremacy of that power, they were bound to fall apart. During his lifetime and for several years following his death, this advice was treasured and followed by his co-religionists, but the very moment that the first steps towards the bestowal of political power on India came within the horizon, the spell was broken. The famous Moslem deputation to Lord Minto and the promise that he made of separate Mahommedan representation on a generous scale in the Legislative Councils became a binding pledge to us and a source of friction between Hindu and Moslem, ever growing in volume and bitterness, until their rival claims have become well-nigh irreconcilable.

And then there is the second factor. Not long ago there was real fear of breaking the peace. Heads were broken at times and stones thrown, but mobs were less easily moved to violence and more easily subdued. Outbreaks which were mild and sporadic have become violent and epidemic; the mob violence of the crowd has been supplemented by murders in the back lanes. Excitement that was evanescent has been turning into hatred that is lasting. For a time, but for a very short time, there was a rapprochement between Hindus and Mahommedans directed against the Government, when Hindus drank water at the hands of the Mahommedans, and Hindu orators were invited to occupy Moslem pulpits. Hindus had to pretend to be interested in the Khilafat, and Mahommedans to be followers of a misguided Hindu saint. The reconciliation was too hollow, the union too ill-assorted —it could not endure—the combination became explosive. But the prolonged passivity of the Government in face of this combined attack upon its authority so weakened its respect that from that day to this it has not yet recovered. Whether the rioters be Hindus or Mahommedans, ragging students, or labourers on strike, the law grows more timid and the crowds more audacious. Hindus and Mahommedans may cry peace, peace, but there is no peace, and there cannot be peace while each is struggling for mastery over the other, and the sound of the referee's whistle is drowned in the uproar. But it is political ambition that moves the classes, and not religious fanaticism. That is used to sway the multitude.

Over all India, Hindus outnumber Mahommedans in a ratio of three to one. In Bengal, the Punjab, the North-West Frontier Province, Beluchistan, and Sind, Mahommedans are in the majority. Even in provinces where they are few over the whole area, they are an important section in the cities and towns, where they settled in the days of Mahommedan rule. In Northern India are the largest number of Mahommedans who are descended from the original Moslem invaders; in Central and Southern India they are more frequently the descendants of Hindu ancestors who, some forcibly and some voluntarily, embraced Islam. The Saiyads are probably the best educated and the most peaceful; the Pathans are easily the most turbulent.

There are many other religions in India, of which several are offshoots of Hinduism, and the "All India Hindu Mahasabha" (Grand Association) comprehends among Hindus the Aryas, Brahmos, Jains, Sikhs, and Buddhists (no doubt excluding the Burmese Buddhists who, by no stretch of definition, could be called Hindus). In any Hindu-Moslem controversy all these creeds would incline to the Hindu side. There are in the Punjab bitter memories between Sikhs and Mahommedans, and some points of conflict between Sikhs and Hindus; the Sikhs being a militant religious clan which has ruled the Punjab, do not relish the idea of domination by Hindus and still less by Mahommedans. They are proud of their ten Gurus and their Granth-sahib or Sacred Book, their Gurmukhi script, their martial traditions, and the fact that they have ruled. The only kind of Swaraj they regard as worth having is Sikhraj. Home rule to them is Sikh rule.

Christians number 4¾ millions, of whom 4½ are Indian Christians; then there are the Parsees following the Zoroastrian Faith, which they imported with them from Persia whence they fled from Mahommedan persecution, and again, among Mahommedans themselves, there are the two great divisions of Sunnis and Shias, the former being in an overwhelming majority. Between the adherents of these various religions and sects there might at any time arise acrimony or fracas, or even rioting, but these are not likely to give rise to conflicts on the grand scale so often resulting from the antagonism of Hindu and Moslem, at least not so long as British authority remains supreme. After that had gone, if it went, no one can say.

There have been several small rebellions among the animistic aboriginal tribes, provoked generally by attempts to restrict their liquor, or by the tyranny of Hindu money-lenders, and these tribes would certainly take to raiding expeditions upon peaceful Hindu villages near their hill fastnesses, as they used to do of yore. Educated Indians forget these things after years of peace and order, but the memories of ancient feuds and raids are handed down from father to son among these rude peoples, and should the opportunities once more offer, robber chiefs will soon arise to take them.

Thus we have in India powers of conflict and disorder so long kept under restraint that few people realise that they are still there under the surface in case at any time the forces of law and order should be weakened. For the Mopla dreams of a new invasion and the loot of Hindu Malabar, and the Rajput noble in his cups boasts of the number of Mahommedans that he will slay to his own sword on the day that the spoil is once more open to the spoiler.

CHAPTER III

THE PROBLEM OF CASTE

The Wonderful Survival of Hinduism—Social Reform must come from within—Hinduism the Soul of India—What will replace it?—Not the Ballot Box

THE Hindu system of caste enforces social distinction by means of religious ostracism. It has grown out of an original classification of persons by occupation, and the Brahmins, who no doubt made themselves the first or highest class as the depositories of all learning, secured for themselves an ascendancy that has endured for some 3000 years. Caste is the most anti-democratic of all social and religious systems, in contrast to Islam which is in religious matters entirely democratic, though in ordinary life social status is recognised, and birth has its privileges. Hinduism, of which Brahminism is the corner-stone, has survived the attacks of Buddhism, Islam, and Christianity, and to this day the proper method of addressing a Brahmin is "Maharaj, or Great King." The warrior caste of Kshatris, the second caste, supplied most of the Hindu rulers and the fighting men, and the third caste consisted of the Vaisyas. These were the men engaged in commerce and moneylending, who were necessary both to priests and kings and were held in high esteem. These were the three great social compartments mapped out by the early oracles of Hinduism, and all the rest of the people were Sudras. Following the traditions of their superiors, the Sudras also divided themselves by degrees as the years passed according as their occupations were dignified, or manual, or menial. The land and the loom and the pen had their lower as well as their higher branches. The water-carriers and the sweetmeat sellers carry exemptions from bans, and in respect to their particular occupations are ceremonially clean. It was convenient to make them so. There may be similarities of race and antipathies of creed, or antipathies of race and similarities of creed, which bring men together for some purposes and place great gulfs between them for others, and within the castes are sub-castes, and sections, and septs, and then there are those beyond the pale who still call themselves and are called Hindus, though they are denied the use of the well and the temple and the school, and in Southern India even the road, whose touch or even proximity is pollution. Then again, there are the aboriginal tribes of animists, of whom great numbers have been Hinduised, still only on the skirts of civilisation, some like the Gonds who ruled Hindu subjects for several centuries; others mere wild denizens of hills and forests. Over all these 220 millions of Hindus, Brahmins numbering 14 millions have had religious sway and enjoyed social domination. They have been the ministers and high officials of Hindu kingdoms, and the power behind the throne, reserving for themselves the benefit of the clergy. There are Aryan Hindus, Dravidian Hindus, Mongolian Hindus; there are Deccani Brahmins, Gujerathi Brahmins, Tamil Brahmins, Telegu Brahmins, Bengali Brahmins, Hindustani Brahmins, Kashmiri Pundits, between whom is a freemasonry of caste, but they make neither one nation nor one language. There is no Hindu nation, though Hinduism is the most remarkable survival of a social system unique in the world. Other races have had their aristocrats, their middle classes, and their working classes, between whom are social distinctions, but never were there the barriers between class and class across which intermarriage or talents or wealth could not find a way. But among the Hindus no legal intermarriage could cross this barrier, and an illegal union only produced yet one more caste. And each caste, new or old, however so high or however so low, has its own social rules, its own outcasting, its pains and its penances, and its purification ceremonies, and in all these matters the *caste punchayat* is a tribunal from which there is no appeal. Power and wealth may obtain its exemption and dispensations, as it has done in many other parts of the world; but neither power nor wealth can buy a man a passage from one caste to another, and not all the wealth of a Croesus can make a man of lower caste a Brahmin. Into that select fold the greatest monarch that ever lived could not buy admission. All these wonderful things separate Hindus from one another and from all outside the fold. The closer the union of the caste and its privileges, the greater the disunion from the rest. And yet, with all the things that seem to us Westerners so strange, so inexplicable, and even horrible, here is a religion and a social system which is older than any other extant faith and still survives with unabated vigour. Miss Katherine Mayo's book, *Mother India*, faithfully recounts social and sexual evils which one would think must long since have destroyed any race or religion which even permitted them to exist, much more one that gave them the cover of religious obligation. Under all modern Western ideas of eugenics, hygiene, and sanitation, there could not, one would think, be to-day 220 million followers of a religion which admits no proselytes but lives under these conditions.

Yet, side by side with these things, Hinduism has produced its sages, its men of piety, its great Sanskritic learning, its reformers and saints animated by high ideals, its wonderful sense of filial duty, its self-sacrifice within the family circle, its veneration for the old, its charity, generous if undiscriminating, its subtle philosophers, its theories of life and death, its "Dharma" and "Karma," its religious duty, and its good and evil destiny, earned by good or evil deeds, perhaps in this life, perhaps in a former existence, to find expiation or degradation or elevation as compensation in the next. The daily life is a series of sacraments; its ideal of marriage is an ideal of chastity; its ideal of *suttee* was one of wifely devotion to accompany her lord to the other world. Such are the arcana of Hinduism. No Western mind can understand them. There were, amongst others, three ideas which had been the most preservative of the Hindu system—the hereditary purity of stock, and the hereditary principle of property bound together by the division of caste and the institution of the joint family, and the final committal of these principles to the chosen interpreters of all ordinances, the Brahmins. But human passions and human infirmities have made a travesty of the ideals which attracted the ancient founders of Hinduism. Just as the basic supremacy of the Hindu Trinity, God the Creator, God the Preserver, and God the Destroyer, has been overlaid by thousands of gods and godlings, saints and heroes, incarnations and reincarnations, tribal gods, village tutelary deities, *lares* and *penates*, crude idolatry, animist propitiation of *Bhuts*, demons and nats, superstitions innumerable, and practices outwardly obscene however inwardly they may in origin have been considered spiritual: so also have these basic principles suffered under the stress of human infirmities and human weaknesses. Yet so closely intermixed are religion and social custom that all these incrustations upon principle have spuriously attached to themselves the claim to be reckoned as religious obligations, to which they may even have become the absolute antitheses. In these climates there is earlier development and earlier decay; the age of puberty is advanced, the passions are stronger. There is no confidence in either male or female continency. Male incontinency did not affect the purity of the family stock, therefore it does not matter, but female incontinency would destroy the purity of that stock, and must be strictly guarded against. Hence arose child marriage and the earliest possible consummation of that marriage. Along with fatalistic belief attributing diseases to the displeasure of a grim goddess and placing ceremonial purity before physical hygiene, the ends and the means have become so transposed that religious practices wholly inimical to health have been substituted for the simple sanitary regulations of the primitive Hindu society, and the suffering thereby entailed on innocent women and children has become tolerated as inseparable from the penalties and obligations of sex and the paramount importance of the maintenance of a pure lineal male succession to the hereditary line.

Miss Mayo's courageous book, however dark its implications and inferences, however stressed the shadows and but dimly perceived the lights of the Hindu system, has rendered a remarkable service to the Indian reformer, for it has shown him how customs which have grown up as excrescences on a system which he had learnt from his childhood to revere as designed for the protection of society, strike an unprejudiced American lady who held no brief for British rule. The book has hurt his feelings by its bluntness; he knows that it is in substance true, though in effect unjust to the high ideals which inspired the original founders of Hinduism. It is a valuable support to those thinkers who had already raised the cry " Back to the Vedas," just as among Christian society there are the men who call us to go " Back to the Sermon on the Mount." And Gandhi, the impracticable saint, calls for a return to the simple life of a self-contained Arcadia.

But what about social reform? Earnest ladies who are social workers in England are eager to help, but they cannot thrust this aid unsought, for social reform of this magnitude applied to millions of ignorant men and women can only come from within. Unasked advice from a foreigner is never palatable to any race or in any country. Only educated Hindus can deal with the problem, and the men can do but little until the women also are educated. The West may set the example, but the East must follow it of its own initiative. If you want to convert a man, the last thing you should do is to abuse his ancestral faith. They must be convinced by what they see, and not by what you say, for to preach at is to patronise, and to patronise is merely to confirm the obstinate in his obstinacy. It is given to very few of the laity to preach without patronising. One dislikes the man who tells you you are a miserable sinner, but if you realise it untold you are halfway to conversion.

But the progress must be gradual. Centuries cannot be crammed into decades, or decades into months. If the movement gains momentum it will be because it comes from within.

I have touched on this book because it has aroused a wider attention through the world than any other book on India, and to us administrators, who have spent the best years of our lives in endeavouring to minister to the betterment of India, it is of absorbing interest. We know the difficulties we ourselves have had to encounter, and we know, at all events better than the home-staying British zealot, the difficulties which face the genuine Indian reformer himself.

It is time, however, to revert to the dry facts about caste. Only the principal castes, viz. castes of which the members form a substantial element in the population, were separately tabled by the census of India, and these alone filled ten closely printed pages of foolscap. There are, besides, large numbers of minor castes to be found in Provincial tables or relegated to the category of "others." Educated Indians who are politically minded and like to think of an Indian nation, are fond of telling us that caste restrictions are disappearing—certainly strict observance of caste is weakening among the English educated, the higher intelligentsia, especially those called the Europe-returned,—but the impression made on caste observances among the great masses is almost nil. You have to convert not a few Europe-returned but 160 million of caste Hindus before all these bans and taboos can be lifted. Even the educated Indian is one man outside and another at home. In the family circle he is obliged to conform to the family custom; out of it he relaxes himself in the matter of food and drink. It is because in these matters he finds caste restrictions irksome to his comfort and convenience when he is travelling abroad. An elderly Brahmin magistrate who, with a twinkle in his eye, confided to me that he did not despise a whisky and soda in strict privacy, complained that if he had ever to travel to Bombay he always tried if possible to go alone.

If his wife went with him, however hot the weather, he must not allow himself even a soda.

It was nearly forty years ago that, as a young district magistrate, I was asked to give police protection to a courageous Brahmin judge who was arranging the remarriage of a girl widow in his family, but, after all these years, how many Brahmins of to-day have followed that bold example? This very year the press has reported a case in which, in a district of the United Provinces, eight Brahmins were convicted of bludgeoning a ninth to death because he had accepted food from a low caste man. Railway travelling has weakened to some extent prohibitions of physical contact, but I remember a Mahommedan of low status who said that he always secured plenty of elbow room in a crowded third-class compartment by the simple expedient of giving out that he was a sweeper. Evidence given before the Lee Commission in Madras in 1924, relating to the treatment of the depressed classes, was to the effect that in Courts in outlying places far from British supervision, Hindu judges would not allow a party or a witness of untouchable caste within the Court precincts, and their interrogation was conducted by means of a messenger, who asked the questions and came back with the answers. Yet I heard a Brahmin in responsible office boldly tell a British audience that the British had done nothing for the depressed classes—a beautiful example of how educated India passes on Indian shortcomings to the debit of British rule. India is so permeated with caste that you may find even Mahommedans continuing their caste designation, such as Mussulman Rajputs, though centuries have elapsed since the conversion of their ancestors to Islam, and caste Christians, as distinct from pariah Christians, are to be found amongst converts to Christianity in Madras. For indeed by continual caste inbreeding, castes have given themselves artificially quasi racial characteristics, thereby strengthening the divisions to be found in India. Good cultivation or bad cultivation are not merely different personal qualities, but distinct caste attributes—some are well known as thrifty or hardworking, others are notoriously slovenly or extravagant.

Thus to the great barriers of distances and diversities of race, climate, language, and mentality, which are really the work of nature and physical environment, by which, under a Mendelian law, widely divergent racial characteristics have become fixed and well-nigh immutable, have been superadded the man-made barriers of religious antagonisms and social partitions, maintained as in no other country on earth by rigid endogamy, by cash fines, and severe religious penances. And thus many millions of humble folk have been condemned to humiliation under the accepted belief that their subjection is due, not to the arrogance of their oppressors, but to their own sins in some previous existence. An Anglicised politician, secure in his Brahminical privileges, may talk magnanimously of the equality of all, and of his fervent sympathy with the woes of the depressed classes. How could he stand before the British democracy and claim equality for himself and deny it to these? There are a good many high-minded reformers who are ready to defy custom and show the courage of their professions, like the gallant Maharaja of Kolhapur, whose struggles against Brahmin oppression have won him a special place in the hearts of his people, but in the majority of cases these are mere conventional phrases which the depressed classes refuse to take at their face value, and doing so dread the loss of such protection as British rule has been able to give.

And one wonders what shall replace this remarkable system of caste that has grown up in the course of thirty or more centuries. Will all the cherished traditions of Hinduism go with it? We see in caste all the evils and restrictions that it entails upon the lowly, but there are and there must be compensating advantages which we do not perceive, for no institution so rotten as many Westerners might regard it could possibly have endured as it has done without many redeeming features. The fortress of caste cannot be taken by external assault. Its walls will only crumble when the garrison within ceases to repair them. The only real discipline that India has maintained is the discipline of caste. If you really could create genuine democracy in India it would destroy caste. If it destroyed caste it would destroy Hinduism, and if it destroyed Hinduism it would destroy India, at least the India that has existed for so many thousands of years. Hinduism is the soul of India. And it may not be the Christ that would replace Krishna. It might even conceivably be the Bolshevist anti-Christ that would step into the vacancy—*sans* faith, *sans* hope, *sans* love, *sans* everything. Far, far better that they should remain good Hindus than become rampant atheists! And the theorist thinks that the ballot box will solve this problem too!

CHAPTER IV

THE PROBLEM OF POVERTY

Vast Territories under Small Farming may be Prosperous but not Wealthy—Ancient Wealth and Present Poverty both grossly exaggerated—Great Progress in Prosperity under British Rule

PROBABLY a hundred million of the total present population of India would never have existed at all if British rule had not come in to close down wars, suppress crime, relieve famines, construct irrigation works, make railways, fight epidemics, supply waterworks, and thus open the way for better health and for investment of capital in larger industry. But this very increase in population makes a heavy charge upon the additional wealth produced, and especially must this be the case where 230 million of the total of 320 depend upon the land for support. For the land cannot rapidly be coaxed to increase its produce in strict ratio to the extra mouths to be fed. India is, of course, a poor country, but it is neither as poor as it was nor as poor as it sounds to European ears. After all, a peasantry engaged in small farming may be reasonably prosperous, but it can never be in any country rich as the world now counts riches. The "Kulaks" of Russia (of whom we have heard so much lately) have, however, their counterpart among the Indian ryots; and the tales that the anti-British press spreads of the ryots poverty are grossly exaggerated. After many years' close acquaintance with the ryot in his village, much closer acquaintance than most of the town-bred writers to the Indian Press have ever enjoyed, I can certainly testify to the fact that the condition of the Indian cultivator has much improved. His credit and his power to resist the effects of crop failures have wonderfully increased, and over the greater part of India he enjoys a degree of protection from exorbitant rent or arbitrary ejectment which many farmers in other countries might well envy. Within my own observation agricultural wages have risen fourfold, while rents have not increased in anything like that ratio. The value of land has gone up by leaps and bounds, and the prices of agricultural produce have trebled since the advent of railways. It is after many talks with village elders spread over many years that one learns how brick houses have begun to replace mud huts; tiles have replaced thatch; gold ornaments have replaced silver; and silver base metal; brass vessels have displaced earthenware; clothes have increased both in number and quality. All these things are true; they are borne out by the comparisons of reports made fifty and sixty years ago with those of more recent times. Nevertheless it is an uphill task, for the fine division of holdings as families increase, the absence of cheap credit, heavy expenditure on wedding and other ceremonies, the severe vicissitudes of seasons, the exactions of the moneylender (useful as he is in rural economy), the love of litigation—all these things have been countervailing influences.

And yet again there are compensations. The cultivators in an Indian village pay rent for their land at a rent per acre which a British farmer would regard as a fleabite. There is no rent for the house or the hut, or the land on which it stands; there is no duty on country tobacco; no income tax on agricultural profits, and no death duties as a holding passes by inheritance. Many of the cultivators pay no rates at all; a great many not more than 5 per cent., and few more than 10 per cent of their rent. Grazing for cattle and fuel for cooking, animal manure for the fields, are obtainable either free or at a trivial cost. The tax on salt means a few pence a year per head. The prosperity of a village depends mainly upon the fertility or poverty of its land. In light soil villages or in hilly and forest areas the village community, often largely aboriginal in race, must naturally be poor. Their grain food is supplemented by forest fruits and roots. In a village of average or special fertility you will meet with many degrees of relative prosperity or relative poverty. In what community is it otherwise? Thrift or idleness, benevolence or oppression by a landlord, extravagant display involving indebtedness, or particular misfortunes will have differentiated this man from that. After a long study of the subject in some thousands of villages, and perusal of many reports of different provinces, and after excluding permanently settled areas for which less accurate details are available, I should estimate that about 20 per cent. of the peasantry are in comfortable and often flourishing circumstances, and about 20 per cent. are poor or heavily indebted. The rest may be described as in average circumstances. Thus, if we take a fifth each to represent the extremes, and three-fifths for the means, over any considerable tract of country, we shall not be very far wrong. In the richest tracts, unless very highly congested, the results will be somewhat better. In the poorest areas they will be worse. Men pass from class to class, some upwards some downwards in the scale, some backwards and again forwards, from agricultural labourer to small tenant, from small tenant to a larger one, or *vice versa*. The variations of seasons entail a constant ebb and flow, except where irrigation or soil advantages give special stability. When the prices of a crop are world prices, they may be highest when local crops are good and lowest when they are bad, thus meaning unwonted wealth or unaccustomed tightness; or it may be the other way when good prices compensate for short yields, or a good yield for low prices.

It will be asked, what has British rule done to improve these conditions? Less perhaps than the maximum possible, but always infinitely more than any previous authority that ever ruled the country. And as time has passed defects have been remedied. More and more moderation in assessment; more and more concession in collection of the land revenue when crops are poor; land cesses reduced; large estates saved from ruin by the Court of Wards; small tenants helped by loans for seed and cattle; larger ones by loans for land improvement; co-operative credit societies, model farms, demonstration plots; protection against famine, relief in famine when it comes, legislative measures to protect tenants against landlords and to prevent land passing out of the hands of deserving cultivators, special measures for specially distressed tracts; every man's holding is mapped and numbered, its area recorded, the name of the tenant, his tenure, and his rent. Look back to the career of a Revenue Officer charged with the administration of the land, and you will find that his whole energies have been engaged for years on end in compassing the improvement of the peasantry and striving to protect them as far as possible from loss. I myself passed through two terrible famines in the Central Provinces, as well as several severe crop failures of less wide extent. In the first we were late in our measures, and it was a long time before we could catch up with distress; cholera, dysentery and privation, and aimless wandering by people who came in from neighbouring States where measures were inadequate, laid a heavy toll on life and health. But thirteen of our own British officers lost their lives in that struggle.

In the second famine, only two years later, our measures were prompt and so comprehensive that relief was excessive and indeed demoralising. In the huge Raipur District, at that time 15,000 square miles in area, with a population of 1½ million, in the height of the rains, when relief works could not be properly carried out, no less than 640,000 people were being fed twice a day at kitchens scattered over the length and breadth of that large tract, and over the whole Province, then numbering about 10,000,000, at the maximum period of distress, the 2,000,000 mark was nearly reached of people receiving relief in one shape or another. Never had prospects looked blacker than in the closing months of the great famine of 1900. The recovery was so rapid as to be almost miraculous. All the money poured out like water had not been in vain, and the people set to work with remarkable courage to make up for lost time. Hope succeeded despair, and almost in the twinkling of an eye the whole position changed. Finances improved, private enterprise became active as never before, public funds became available on a much larger scale for roads, buildings, railways, and irrigation. After chronic unemployment and privation amongst the poorest of the labouring classes an unsatisfied demand for work was converted into an unsatisfied demand for labourers. In this renewed flow of prosperity at a higher level than before there were only partial and local setbacks until the Great War and its aftermath once more upset all ratios and disturbed all standards.

The village artisan and the agricultural labourer are, as a general rule, poor, though the agricultural labourer will often rise to the status of tenant with land of his own, and the artisan will frequently make a comfortable living. I have even known village watchmen who have become well-to-do and taken to money-lending. It would be the sign of a fool to assert that there have been no failures or blemishes in our administration of the land, but the man who accuses British rule of being responsible by its neglect for the comparative poverty of India's cultivators is either a knave or an ignoramus.

Such then are the peasant classes—the backbone of the country's stability—the most lovable element of the whole population, clinging to their lands, patiently bearing adversity, courageously repairing their losses, cheerfully enjoying their weekly markets and their festivals and domestic ceremonies, faithfully fulfilling the ceremonial prescriptions of their religion, burying their little hoards, or investing them in ornaments which they can pawn or sell when times are hard, giving of their charity to the deserving aged and crippled poor of their villages, and often, I am afraid, to the wandering beggar and mendicant who are totally undeserving, loving litigation for its excitement, thanking God for the rain, propitiating their local deities when skies are brazen or rain excessive, or when disease comes among man or beast, regarding their calamities as sent from heaven. The incongruities one sees are very striking. I remember a village of some 4000 souls, with a large proportion of market gardeners, the landowners were at feud and the tenants, though peaceful, were for ever pestered with the factions and bullies of the landlords, there was the usual Primary School, a Mission School, and a Middle School, and a small town fund for petty improvements. On the walls of the schoolroom, amongst the usual oleographs of the Royal Family, were some exciting pictures, cut out from some old copies of the *New York Police News*, which must have found their way in packing to this village miles from the railway. The village was on a stream, and one day in the rains there occurred some cloudburst in the catchment area, and the flood came down and washed away a few huts, and the whole place was in danger. Then the people began throwing goats and kids into the torrent, and when the poor animals struggled to the bank they were thrust in again, to serve as an offering to propitiate Devi. And presently the flood abated, and the village was safe!

This huge peasantry are contented with their lot, so long as they have their beloved land, their house in the village, their cattle, and the small pursuits and excitements of their gala days. Are we correct in calling their contentment pathetic? Is there anything that we can do to make them really happier? The things that we have done, or tried to do, have been to teach them to respect each other's rights, to learn to read and write, so that they may not be cheated by a harsh landlord or a cunning moneylender, and may understand the bonds and the deeds, and the accounts which are inseparable from people who have money and grain to borrow and always require credit for their farming. We have tried to teach them the value of thrift by co-operation and by Post-Office Savings Banks; we have tried to teach them to improve their land, their seed, and their cattle, by better and more economic methods; we have tried to teach them the value of pure water, and the necessity for better sanitary surroundings; we have taught them respect for the law, and they know that the humblest complainant can get justice so long as he can put forward true evidence of the wrong. People may ask why we have not succeeded better, why in spite of all the schools are vast multitudes still illiterate? Why do they still seem to prefer dirty water to pure? Why do they still go on with old methods of agriculture? These are some of the problems of poverty, and in the next Chapter on the Problem of Ignorance and Illiteracy I will return to these questions.

These people cannot, however, be judged by Western standards of comfort or Western rates of wages, for if a pay of 15 Rs. a month only went as far as 22s. 6d. in England (9d. a day) and the cost of living in India was equally high, the population would have died of starvation long ago. India in the mass is poor, because India in the mass consists of small peasantry, farm labourers, and small artisans. But its alleged extreme poverty now is just as fabulous as its alleged former wealth in olden days. Its emperors, and its princes, and its nobles, and its larger merchants accumulated treasure and jewellery and created a market for silks, gold embroidery, and fine raiment, but the peasant and the labourer saw none of these things. He lived his own frugal life in poverty, none cared if he died in famine. When the great ones built their fine buildings they were made by the blood and sweat of the poor, fed like the bullocks they drove, but without wages and under compulsion. Skilled artificers were held in repute for their artistic skill, and poets and painters received honours at the courts, but the rank and file were mere pawns to be sacrificed without remorse. If one of this class did manage to accumulate some cash or ornaments he had to hide them away lest someone should rob him of his little store. Now and again there were good kings who did good in the sight of the Lord, but the other kind were as plentiful as among the kings of Israel and Judah. With the entrance upon the scene of law and order and justice under

British rule India's total wealth has increased and multiplied exceedingly. Still are there violent contrasts between the rich and the poor, but the share of the poor man has steadily increased and is increasing. The Labour M.P. who visits India in the cold weather exclaims because the poor peasant or artisan lives in an Indian hut instead of in an English cottage, and squats on the floor instead of on a chair, and consumes his rice or his chupattis instead of his bread and cheese, and beer, and bacon. The M.P. takes his facts from some Swarajist romancer, and his figures from some Indian paper of which the sole occupation is to besmirch British rule. These peasants and artisans are persons who believe that fingers were made before forks, and the floor before chairs, even such as, in the Gospel story, took up their beds and walked. In that old India, in its so-called golden days, the wealthiest preferred a seat on the floor amidst their rugs and their cushions, and spread their dishes on the ground, the sacred ground to which the dying Hindu is lowered from his cot so that he may draw his last breath in contact with Mother Earth. To this day only the Westernized people, or the Parsees, have in their houses use for knives and forks, and tablecloths, and European furniture. Some even of these, when they return back from Europe, love to go back to eating their food with their fingers, and their own spicey fare beside which our English diet seems so insipid. And the Hindu strips to his waist to eat his food, and is infinitely happier thus.

I was travelling one bright moonlight night on a construction train on a narrow gauge line not yet opened for traffic, and they gave me a chair in an open goods truck. At a halt I took a stroll along the train, and looked at the sleeping forms on the hard floor of the other trucks. It was very hot weather, and the sleepers wore nothing but loin cloths. I stopped before one truck, and asked my clerk who accompanied me who all these people could be, and he pointed out one and said: " Sir, that is the District Judge, and the man next to him is the messenger of his Court," so

I passed on, for it would have been embarrassing to the Judge, in this almost nude state, to be talking to the Commissioner. Yet that man had a salary of at least Rs. 500 a month, and could have had a chair for the asking. Why worry about the villager and his lack of chairs and tables?

In the large cities conditions change. It is only in the very largest that the "Chawl" and the tenement, the importations of Western industrialism, have played havoc with the open air habits of the labourer in his hut, and have imposed on the wages of the factory hand the burden of exorbitant rent and expensive fuel from which elsewhere he is free. But even among the factory hands there are many, perhaps the majority, who have a share of a field in some rural tract, with members of the joint family to receive them there, where they are fed for a time and refresh themselves from the atmosphere of the factory or the "Chawl," back to the land for a season or even for good, while others from the villages go into the cities for work at docks or mills in their place. But it is uphill work improving the lot of these labourers. Raise their wages and they will not raise their standard of comfort. Rather will they lower their standard of industry, work four days instead of six, and loaf about the bazaars, spending more money on the idle days. Only 10 per cent. of the whole population were in 1921 engaged in industrial pursuits, and out of these again only one-tenth were employed in organised industries, mills, factories, and mines. These labourers are the overflow of congested agricultural areas, or of villages temporarily depressed by crop failures. They come and go. But gradually the railways and the mines are attracting a more permanent labour force. That there is surplus labour in India vainly seeking employment is nowadays a myth. There are large seasonal migrations for harvesting, and for special agricultural work at the due seasons, and the surplus labour from Madras and Behar and Orissa finds its way into Burma, Ceylon, and the Straits Settlements, for the open season, after which they come back to their own fields with their accumulated earnings. The railways and the river steamers, and the coastal steamships, carry them to and fro, as also the pilgrims, Hindu and Mahommedan, by the hundred thousand.

With an overwhelming population of peasantry, the wealth per head over the whole sub-continent must necessarily be small, but the Indian-owned Press repeats day after day obsolete *per capita* estimates of income, and persists in treating them as *family* income of the present day, and ignores entirely the actual progress that has been going on, or the fact that the figure that it takes as the average income is less than the lowest pay of the poorest labourer. The Press writes as if all exports were a loss to the country, grain taken out to feed Europe at the expense of the people who are already starving on only one meal every other day. These fables and fabrications will pass muster among the ignorant and the half-educated, while the land-owner who sells his harvested crop at a high price, and spends the proceeds on imported luxuries, rejoices at the bargain he has made. The Press loudly deplores the British capital that has been sunk in the country, although it employs Indian labour, swells the earnings of Indian railways, and develops India's industries at returns which fail to attract the Indian money-lenders. The two measures of a country's material progress are its trade and its public revenue, and these tests the Press disregards and falsely alleges that India is growing poorer every day, plundered and exploited by foreign parasites.

True that cottage industries and the great hand-weaving industries have declined or are struggling. That is the charge which the politicians bring against British rule. But all these industries have gone down before machinery, Indian as well as British. It is not only Gandhi who deplores this feature of modernism. Our British administrators and the missionaries have constantly striven to sustain and revive the arts and the crafts and the cottage industries. They have done good here and there by organising exhibitions and by starting schools of weaving and handcrafts by introducing improved hand-looms, by grants in aid to industrial schools, by special help to weavers in famine times. Yet what would have been the condition of India to-day if she had had no railways, no factories, no mines? Economic laws will have their way and trade will not be denied. British administrators are guiltless of the one blot on England's management of Indian affairs, the Cotton Excise Duties. They condemned their imposition and always worked for their abolition.

The production of wealth is the first condition if a country is to attain to prosperity. For this you require first peace and security, the improvement of every facility, and the removal of every obstacle. The second and more formidable task is to secure or to encourage its more even distribution, so that each man may receive due recompense for what he earns by his toil, and no section of the community shall be sweated by another. But all the time it is wealth you want to distribute, not poverty, as the Soviet Government is busy doing, and therefore the production of wealth is a condition precedent to its better distribution.

British rule has, more than any rule known to India before, done more in its efforts to attain both these objectives, so far as anything can be done by legislative and executive measures, and administrative policies. In its principles and practice it has been far ahead of the understanding of the vast populations over whom it has held sway. No government in the world has solved the question of the equal distribution of wealth, and no government ever will until all men are equally competent. But in impartiality, in its efforts to redress inequalities, the Government of India will bear comparison with any government known to history. The unsophisticated Indian has been more shrewd to perceive this than the ambitious politician who takes credit to himself for all success attained, and blames the British for his own shortcomings as well as theirs. The illiterate man remembers the tales told him by his grandfather, which he too had learnt from his grandfather. That is why British rule has continued. The Labour M.P. expects European standards on a revenue of 6s. a head[1]; let him take charge of a district for a couple of years and his eyes will be opened.

India is poor, very poor on Western standards, but it has progressed, is progressing, and will continue to progress so long as politicians, British and Indian, do not gamble with its progress in their zeal for political theories.

[1] The Provincial Revenues aggregate 6s. per head of the population concerned; District Funds add 10d. a head more.

CHAPTER V

THE PROBLEM OF IGNORANCE AND ILLITERACY

Myths and Facts about Mass Education in India—Literacy a Question of Occupation—Lapse into Illiteracy of Millions—Obstacles in the Way of Rapid Improvement

We in England in the twentieth century find it difficult to understand how anyone can get on without being able to read and write. And yet people do manage to do it. I was in a chemist's shop the other day in London, a very respectably dressed woman was purchasing a bottle of medicine. She spoke English fluently, and repeatedly asked the chemist about the dosage and the time for taking the medicine, and the chemist said more than once that there were plain directions on the bottle. Then the lady said she could not read, and asked him to repeat the instructions once more. After she had gone I expressed surprise to the chemist at so well-dressed a person being unable to read. He said " She is a Russian, and there are several like that about here." Yet she had learnt to speak English fluently. And so it is in India. There are by the last census about 296 million people who are illiterate, as compared with 22½ million who can read and write. But a great many of these, too, are only nominally literate, and would certainly fail at any dictation test. Yet these people manage to carry on their occupations. For people who are literate do not realise what wonderful memories the illiterate have. Afghan pedlars will sell their wares in the very centre of India on credit, and at a credit price calculated to yield them about 120 per cent. per annum. They will only make oral enquiries about their borrower's solvency; they will not have a scrap of paper as evidence, and they will go back home across the N.W. frontier, and in two years perhaps come back and remember the village and the man and the debt, and recover it from him or from his heirs if he be dead, by virtue of their memory, their formidable physique, and the fear they inspire. We have forgotten that it was once the same in England, and when we hear the Swarajist orator laying the blame for India's illiteracy upon British shoulders, we might stop and ask ourselves how long it was between the time that 90 per cent. of our people in England could not read and the introduction of compulsory education in England in 1870. The Swarajist has been able to persuade well-meaning but gullible English ladies who declaim before British audiences that it was British rule that destroyed education in India, and that before we went there there was a school in every village, and, further, that if we gave them self-government the problem of illiteracy would be speedily solved. It is a marvel how otherwise intelligent persons can swallow such foolish tales. There were schools in India before we went there; there were seats of Brahminic or Islamic or Buddhist learning, as there are to-day. These were supported by the religious orders, who themselves depended on the offerings of the pious. There were also small schools in a good many villages where parents of the privileged class combined to pay small fees to an indifferent teacher. The Koranic schools, where pupils learnt to recite Arabic texts from the Koran, and the monastic schools in Burma were more catholic in their efforts, but the Hindu masses stood altogether outside the scope of education, while females were expected to be content with being drudges if poor and playthings if rich. The secular education imparted at these petty schools was of very little value. If schools of this kind have diminished in number it is because our system of District Board Schools has largely taken their place. I remember some survivals of them which earned small grants from District Funds, and some were still unaided. These paid the teacher 4 Rs. a month, which was occasionally supplemented by small gifts in kind from better-to-do parents. One of my clerks met with a tragic death, and on making enquiries as to the means of the family I found that his father, a man in a somewhat advanced state of leprosy, kept a small private school of ten or twelve pupils; and this was in the heart of a big city, and he lived on the small fees.

There was no State system of education before our time, no public schools, no public funds available to support them. One wonders whether these English ladies who repeat these myths of an imaginary golden age have paused to consider how brief were the interludes of peace in the centuries of wars and raids and forced labour and insecurity, which made men bury their money if they had any, when grain rotted in good years and men died of starvation in bad ones, when cities, towns, and villages might be laid waste, the inhabitants robbed or massacred, and whole tracts made desolate. In the Nimar District of the Central Provinces efforts have been made during the last thirty years to re-colonize land covered with jungle and highly malarious, though very fertile in character. Amidst this jungle are seen the remains of villages and temples, for the tract was devastated by Sindia's army, and the following year ravaged by a famine (the Mahakal), of which traditions remain amongst the people. These events took place in 1803. It is recorded that the price of flour rose to R.1 a lb., at that time at least one hundred times its normal price. The people fled or died, and the land became desolate. Such things could not happen under British rule.

The idea of State secular education is a purely British introduction, but the earlier administrators had neither the men nor the money to do more than make a beginning. The protection of life and property, the establishment of law and order, and of courts to administer criminal and civil justice, added to the settlement of the land, were tasks surely more than enough to absorb the energies of a handful of civil and military administrators, and to tax the resources of a vast country suffering from many centuries of misrule.

Literacy had been the privilege of the Brahmin, the professional accomplishment of the scribe, Hindu or Mahommedan, and the business necessity of the moneylender and the high-class trader. The rest of the people, occupied in manual or menial work, had no interest in it at all—it was not for them. It was naturally also from these limited classes with whom literacy was an hereditary occupation that British administrators were obliged to appoint their officials, and clerks, and school teachers, when they inaugurated the first stages of the campaign against illiteracy. To this day it is still these classes that supply the major portions of literates in India.

We cannot see a true picture of the illiteracy of the Indian masses unless we eliminate Burma, where the monastic system has produced special results, and also those races and classes which, for various and particular reasons, have enjoyed a greater advance in literacy than all the other elements in the population. The special classes to be thus eliminated are Europeans and Anglo-Indians, the Parsees, the Indian Christians, the Brahmins, the Jains, and two or three special clerical castes among the Hindus. All these exclusions count for 38 millions out of the whole population, and 9½ millions out of these 38 are literate, leaving 280 million people, of whom only 13¼ millions can read and write. The percentage of literate in the former is about 25, and that of the latter less than 5. The desire for education by the masses has also varied greatly in different parts of India. In Madras, British administration began earlier, and the great missions did notable work. In the South, besides Roman Catholics and Protestants, converts since British rule, there were large communities of Nestorian and Syrian Christians, and the Christians descended from the Portuguese converts. Literacy was also much more advanced in the trading areas near Surat, and in parts of Bengal. In all of these parts a substantial start towards diffusion of education had been made from an earlier time, but over the rest of India it cannot be said that the State educational system became at all established until after the Mutiny. Since that date there has been continuous progress, but it was very uphill work among those who had no aptitude or taste for book learning. At the last census the Census Superintendent of Mysore, himself an Indian, wrote: "What determines literacy in any community is, in the first instance, the nature of the occupations it usually follows, that is whether they are such as require a knowledge of reading and writing, and, in the second instance, whether there are any special facilities within reach which attract the members of the community to learn though there be no great need for the learning. The pursuit of letters purely as a means for intellectual growth is mostly a figment of the theorists." The Census Superintendent of the United Provinces wrote of the large proportion of boys who leave primary schools before they have really learned to read and write: " The parents of such a boy," he states, "never seriously intend that he should be educated." They send him to school under pressure when he is very small to keep him out of mischief; "or perhaps in case he shows a special aptitude for learning. He does not desire education for his children for its own sake, but only as a means of obtaining employment. There is no motive for educating the boy who is destined for the plough."

There is indeed no atmosphere favouring reading in rural areas. There are no books in the villages, no advertisements, no newspapers, no shop-fronts with labelled goods, and in fact nothing to induce the boy who did sums and read little stories from text-books in his early childhood, to practise reading. This boy went back from his books to the plough, and never opened them again, and thus in a large number of cases we have been pouring water into a sieve, and the proportion of literates amongst these masses has made very slow progress. The War certainly stimulated the desire for reading as nothing else could amongst returning Indian soldiers, who had seen for themselves in France the difference between a literate and an illiterate country, but the effect of this enlightenment has been of importance mainly among the virile people of the Punjab, which supplies most of the men for the army. I will, however, go further, and say that the infant and primary classes of a village school, though of course the necessary preliminary for those who pursue their studies further, whether in secondary schools or in some occupation in which reading is required, are of very little use by themselves for raising the intelligence of the population. For those early and soon-forgotten lessons droned out in the village class-room are almost destitute of effect on the bucolic mind. The railway and the road have proved themselves far better stimulants to the intelligence, and the street arab in the town who has never been to school is infinitely more quick-minded than the rural boy who has stumbled through these primary classes. The average Indian politician loves to think in numbers, in quantity rather than quality. If there are so many schools, and so many pupils on the roll, he is proportionately pleased. He would like to add to the schools and to the pupils in them. Whether the schools are good or bad, the teachers trained or uncertificated, the classes overcrowded, the low castes relegated to so much of the lesson as they can catch from outside the school-room window; whether the attendance is good or bad; all these are things he does not seem to care about. And so, when the total resources are small, he will prefer to multiply indifferent schools rather than improve the existing institutions. There are some 158,000 primary schools for boys and 26,000 of such schools for girls in British India, and their numbers are progressively better. These schools teach, but they do not educate. They take the masses up to the threshold of education in increasing numbers, but those who really cross that threshold are few. As the people begin to learn that the cultivator is a better cultivator and the artisan a better artisan when he can read and write, real progress will be in sight. For the present the right atmosphere is wanting, and if the cultivator or the artisan takes to books, his ambitions become clerical, and he is lost to his natural avocation. Female education lags hopelessly behind. Here again there is movement, but only when the grandmothers and mothers have learnt to read at home will the problem of ignorance be in the way of solution. In 1921 the number of literate females was 2,782,000, or 21 per mille excluding infants, 20 per mille aged 20 and over, but Christians and Parsees, and Buddhists in Burma swell the total. Hindus showed only 16 and Mahommedans only 9 per mille. There is lack of desire in regard to males, but there is positive objection in regard to females. It must take years before this objection is overcome. It is only the more cultured Indian women who will press the education of girls, and they are very few. Those literate in English are only 18 in 10,000—7 among Hindu women, 5 among Sikhs, and 3 among Mahommedans—and the highly cultured outside Europeans and Parsees are limited indeed. No wonder that the progress is slow.

In the meantime the cultivator and the village artisan will keep his oral tradition, his memory for events, his hereditary aptitudes, and the shrewdness born of his experience within his own narrow sphere. The doings of Legislative Councils in distant capitals, which he may never visit, are no more intelligible to him than were the mysteries of Isis to the Egyptian peasant of that day. You must not hustle the cultivator too quickly out of his habits; make his village more attractive if you can, but once let the man on the land come under the fatal lure of the town and learn to despise the close contact with nature that his forefathers prized, and you have taken the first steps to the ruin of India. By giving him at this stage a vote, you only add one more method to the many by which the most nimble-witted will exploit his simplicity. He is totally unripe for democracy.

Mr. Brayne's remarkable effort at "Uplift" in the Gurgaon District of the Punjab deserves all praise. But the work needed an apostle who could devote his whole time to it. He had material to work upon among men with whom he had served in France, no large town in his district with its carping critics to crab his motives and minimise his efforts, and a wife who had the ability and enthusiasm with which to second his work with the women, and yet a district not far from the capital of India, traversed by the railway, and possessing therefore a groundwork of some intelligence, without the opposition of any jealous local politicians. There is scarcely any district in which Mr. Brayne's great campaign could have had so good a chance of success, but he himself is the first to admit that without the powers and authority which he enjoyed as District Magistrate, enabling him to command the services of his official subordinates, he could not possibly have done what he did. It is really one more striking testimony to the truth of the statement that in India the rule of a personality is the only rule that really commands respect. But we cannot have a Civil Service composed entirely of apostles, or guarantee them wives of equal apostolic zeal, or make districts light enough to give them time. Nor in a country of changes and chances can we guarantee a man a seven years' tenure of a district. Nor, in these days, can control over local funds be centred in one authority. Will it endure when the prime mover is no longer there? We may hope so if other workers are sufficiently infected with enthusiasm to keep it going, but it is doubtful. I myself saw a strong total abstinence movement among the Gonds of the Satpura Uplands. It was originated by a leader of these people, and Government helped it and encouraged it by every means in their power. It was based on the undoubted fact that Gonds had been steadily deteriorating in their circumstances from habits of drink. It looked at first like lasting, but in two or three years' time it faded away. Yet, all honour to this brave reformer who tried his best to uplift his jungle kinsmen. That was a genuine temperance movement and not only a plank in political agitation.

How then are we to solve this problem of illiteracy? In crude parlance, "You cannot feed a child's mind while its stomach is empty." You must go on improving the material welfare of the people, and, as this improves, their desire for literacy will develop itself. The better off the tract, the better educated it rapidly becomes, and the better educated, the better equipped for still more material progress. The problems of poverty and illiteracy are really one and the same, and their solutions lie along the same route. What we want in India are more vernacular middle schools, the institutions which are perhaps the least popular among the people. The ambitious parents can think only of English education, while what we want are tens of millions educated in their own tongue instead of tens of thousands in English. It is these latter that cost the money, not the former. But the demand of the intelligentsia for English learning knows no bounds. Universities, colleges, and high schools are constantly increasing, and when the peasant's son becomes an "Entrance Fail," he turns into the wasted raw material of education. It is only the vernacular middle schools that can give to primary education its proper sequel and its full value. It is futile to over-educate the dull-witted sons of poor parents. It is the clever sons of poor parents that require all our attention. The rich can educate their sons, clever or dull-witted, as they choose, and can pay high fees for the luxury, but in India the fees at these English Schools are too heavy for the poor and too light for the wealthy. We want cheap schools for primary and middle vernacular standards, and after that scholarships and freeships in great abundance, awarded solely on the ground of merit, to the brighter lights among the poor man's children.

These are the considerations which apply to those who want to educate or over-educate their children. There remains the case of those who want their children's services for help in their fields or their looms, and who do not want to educate them at all. Compulsory education is the reply that most people will give. Yes, but where and for how long, and for what ages, and for girls as well as boys? In England there might be no difficulty in answering these questions, but in India there is. Schemes for compulsory education have been and are being tried here and there and left to local option. At present compulsory education for girls has not been established anywhere, and between the ages of six and ten for boys is about as far as it has been possible to go. It will require more schools, enlarged schools, many more teachers, and more normal schools to train the teachers, and it will require huge extra expenditure if it were to become universal throughout India. Then there is the question of the girls. In some provinces in the absence of any local keenness for female education, Provincial Governments provided the whole funds for girls' schools because local funds were not forthcoming. There was a complete lack of female teachers, and old men of sixty were generally employed. A few parents, keen on educating small girls, would send them to the boys' school, but these were very few and the girls were very small, and were soon removed. British critics are very impatient, but just as it would be ridiculous to blame all British statesmen from the time of the Plantagenets up to 1870 because education was not made compulsory centuries before this step was taken, even so, is it unjust to blame British rule in India because there is not universal, free, and compulsory education for boys and girls?

How can you find a parallel in England for the conditions obtaining in India either during or before the period of British rule? In the Middle Ages in Europe education was the special care of the Church, and among the laity there were pious benefactors who provided facilities for students of ability, no matter how humble their origin. The poor students who found entrance to the medieval universities prove the existence of elementary education, and great numbers of these were of humble birth. Literacy was not the prerogative of the rich or highly placed. Far from it. Nor did it continue long to be the monopoly of any religious order or a priestly class.[1]

[1] In Oxford alone there were in the fifteenth century five grammar halls for schoolboys. (St. Edmund, Archbishop of Canterbury—Edmund Rich of Abingdon—is a typical historical example of a poor university student, whilst Chaucer's

Compulsory education was nominally put in force for boys in the Baroda State in 1906. Six years later I saw in the

"Clerk of Oxenford" provides a representative from creative literature.) In later times the existence of grammar and other schools all over the country, and not in the towns alone, proves that in those days the benefits of education were not reserved for the rich. Turning to Shakespeare, Sir Hugh Evans, in the *Merry Wives* kept a day-school at Windsor in which the children of middle-class folk were grounded in their "accidence." Holofernes in *Love's Labour's Lost* is a village pedant, to whom the curate, Nathaniel, bears grateful testimony. "I praise the Lord for you, and so may my parishioners, for their sons are well tutor'd by you, and their daughters profit very greatly under you: you are a good member of the commonwealth." Nathaniel's parishioners, we may take it, were simple people, but their children, girls as well as boys, went to school. The ministrations of the village dominie in the reign of Elizabeth seem to be exactly the same as those of the village teacher a hundred and fifty years later, as he is described in Goldsmith's *Deserted Village*, and as he (or she) is shown in paintings and drawings of the first half of the nineteenth century, in which the pupils painted or drawn plainly belong to the working classes. Statistics of school accommodation and attendance do not seem to be available until well on in the nineteenth century, but some, to be found in *Social England*, vol. vi., and in the *Enc. Brit.* article on Education, show that the education of the people was fairly widespread long before the legislation of 1870 made it compulsory. Many years before 1870 the system of grants-in-aid to educational bodies working on a voluntary basis had been the rule. In 1816 a Commission (Lord Brougham's) was appointed to report on Education, and found that there were in England 19,000 infant and day schools of all kinds ("day," *i.e.* as distinct from Sunday Schools, which at first provided secular as well as religious instruction). These 19,000 schools were attended by more than 600,000 pupils of all classes. It was stated, however, that the number of children for whom education ought to be provided was more than 2,000,000. Nevertheless, 30 per cent. of the children of school-going age in England at the beginning of the nineteenth century received some sort of education.

In 1833 the number of pupils under daily instruction belonging to all classes had reached nearly 1,277,000; but of course many of the schools in which they were taught must have been very inefficient. The population of England and Wales was then 14 millions.

In 1861, when the population was 20 millions, a report on education was issued by the Newcastle Commission. It stated that at that time there were 2,500,000 pupils attending day schools of sorts, or, in proportion to the population, 1 in 7, as compared with 1 in 8 in Holland, 1 in 9 in France, and 1 in 6 in Prussia, in which last-named country education was compulsory.

It emerges from these facts and figures that the spread of popular education in England by no means dates from the institution of a compulsory State-supported system. Voluntary agencies, either definitely religious or merely charitable, had been at work centuries before, and the part played by legislation was at first, not so much to extend the educational field, as to improve facilities already in large part provided, to introduce order and system, and to secure, by financial support, regular inspection and the like, a greater measure of efficiency than was possible in the absence of State regulation and control. Thus education in England was almost universal ten years before it was made compulsory. India can offer no comparison.

annual report of that State that some Rs.30,000 had been imposed on parents for failure to send their boys to the school. I happened to see a responsible authority of the State and asked him whether these fines had not been felt as an intolerable grievance by the poor among the parents. The answer he gave was that the fines were imposed but never collected.

Many of those politicians who call loudest for compulsory education of the masses do so merely as a sign of their own enlightenment. They have no idea of imposing, much less paying, greatly increased taxation to secure this benefit, and are like the Provincial Legislative Councillor who exclaimed that it was high time that more money was disgorged from the Treasury and less taken from the taxpayer. The politicians do not understand that free education, though it may be free to the parent *quâ* parent, is very far from free to the same man in his capacity as a tax-paying citizen. If you start compulsion in advance of the means of the country, the result will be that more children will struggle through the lower primary classes and then go back to their ordinary work, forgetting all that they learnt. And the masses will remain illiterate. It is on improvement of the schools, not upon the multiplication of evanescent teaching, that we should concentrate efforts and resources. It will not be until secondary vernacular education is more widely diffused that illiteracy will really give way.

The aborigines of the Bustar State rebelled in 1910, and one of the first things they did was to burn all the schools. When the rebellion had been suppressed, and they were addressed regarding terms of surrender, they wanted the schools abolished. The Hindu schoolmasters, they said, extorted money and grain from them and did their children no good. They were, however, willing to concede that it was a good thing that one man in every village should be able to read and write, so that he might explain any notice or orders that came from the State Government.

We can hardly expect to solve by a stroke of the pen in India problems which were not solved in England until less than sixty years ago, and the mere registering of people as voters will not teach them to read and write. If we now confer votes upon masses of ignorant people they will make their marks against the ox, or the tiger, or both, on their voting paper, and go home wondering what it is all about. Some foolish fad of the Government!

CHAPTER VI

THE PROBLEM OF THE INTELLIGENTSIA

The Problem analysed—The Differences between the Indian Intelligentsia and the Intelligentsias of Other Countries—The Old and the New—The Limited Nature of the New—The Complete Irresponsibility of the Press

THE title of this Chapter may seem a strange one. Why should the intelligentsia of a country constitute a problem at all? It might conceivably be an economic problem if the brain workers became too numerous for the occupations available. It would then be a problem of unemployment. There are signs of this in Bengal, where the rush for English education drives excessive numbers to the High Schools and the Arts Colleges in their struggle for dignified employment. But that is not the problem I am examining.

In Russia the intelligentsia became a stumbling-block to the so-called workmen and peasants, who were egged on and deluded by certain followers of Marx into the belief that the gates of a workman's paradise were open before them. That problem was solved by the massacre, flight, or death by starvation of the flower of the intelligentsia, the remnant who escaped being compelled to share the misery of the population, which is slowly discovering that the gates through which they passed led into inferno and not into paradise. That problem might yet arise in India if the ignorant masses should haply find themselves faced with starvation which they recognise to be due to the folly and ambition of the intelligentsia. But this problem, too, I am not examining; not directly at all events, for I hope that the British people will not be guilty of the folly which would bring about that ultimate result.

The problem of the intelligentsia which I am examining is almost, I think, *sui generis*; for I do not believe that history can provide an exact parallel, certainly not on the gigantic scale that the situation in India offers. Here is a population, larger probably than the population of the world at the time the Christian era began, composed of many races and languages, out of which a few thousand individuals have been, as it were, projected forward by some Wells' "Time Machine" into contact with a state of society many centuries on in time, and after there acquiring a modern veneer, whisked back again to their own century, and finding themselves once more in their old environment. Here they are back again with all their old hereditary and traditional characteristics, but speaking fluently a foreign modern language, not understood by their own people, and daily repeating sentiments centuries in advance of their own fathers and grandfathers, exotics to the soil. Now in India they have had foreign guides and instructors with them to keep up this new contact, but if they lose these guides, and they are trying to get rid of them, who can say what will happen? Will the call of the blood prevail and the new veneer wear off? Will art triumph over nature, or nature over art, or will there be a compromise between the two? A Hindu may sometimes be the son of two fathers, the natural father who begat him and the adoptive father who adopted him, but by the fiction of Hindu law his natural father is no longer his father, and his adoptive father has become his natural father, yet the call of the blood will be the stronger. But these two fathers are both of the same generation, while the English-speaking "Europe-returned" has a natural father of one century and an adoptive father of another, and many centuries divide the two.

Let us apply a few tests.

The intelligentsia of a country should be a body of highly-educated people to which every class of a nation has given its contribution. It is not so in India. There this new English knowledge is the peculium of a few classes.

The intelligentsia of a country should be the product of indigenous evolution. It is not so in India. There its learning is imported, foreign to its soil and its environments.

The intelligentsia of a country should be merely the top layer of its intelligence, with layer upon layer below it, each layer nearly approaching the layer above, and only just a little better than the layer below. It is not so in India. The English-knowing intelligentsia is just a thin crust that has cooled, and if the seething volcanic forces below it should break through and belch out their lava the crust will vanish.

The intelligentsia of a country should be the voice expressing the thoughts of the people, which they can understand, even though they might not so well express themselves. It is not so in India. The language they talk in is not understood by the people, and the sentiments they express are not the people's thoughts, nay, they are often the exact opposite of the thoughts that the people think.

The political intelligentsia of a country should be honestly trying to guide the people right. It is not so in India. There the political intelligentsia are perpetually misleading them, often wilfully and of malice aforethought, and when they tried to persuade them that the British Government was "Satanic" they not only said the thing that was not, but the thing that they knew was not. It was not merely the outpouring of Oriental hyperbole, it was "the cold calculated lie" that once brought so severe a reproof from Earl Balfour against a political opponent. The saintly character of the slanderer is no defence.

This political intelligentsia can sway the people for evil, but their influence for good is either *nil* or is not exercised. They can influence them by falsehood, but they cannot influence them by truth. If they could the social progress of India might have been differently writ. They can raise storms but they cannot allay them. They can dupe the ignorant by dishonest promises of an imaginary millennium, but they cannot or will not explain to them the things that are good. When plague was raging did the intelligentsia exhort rat killing? No, they encouraged the idea that it was irreligious. When inoculation was urged, did they help? No, they did nothing to contradict the report that plague was due to wells poisoned at British instigation and that inoculation led to impotence and was designed to reduce the population. When efforts were being made to induce people to camp out in the fields they concealed their own infection and bolted, spreading the disease themselves. The brilliant exceptions are few, and among the politicians fewer still.

All these characteristics of the intelligentsia, except the last, which is unhappily the attribute of the politically-minded, are not their fault, but arise from the circumstances of their origin, and one must be fair to them and not lay to the charge of them all the follies and fatuities which characterise the few who are daily striving to wrest from the British the supremacy which they covet. Even on these it is still possible to be too harsh in our judgments, for the new wine has gone to their heads. They are imitating and exaggerating just the worst traits of the politics of Europe, while lacking and failing completely to discern, much less to imbibe, those traditions of fair play which in the West neutralise and compensate for the effects of the wildest tirades of politicians, and thus save to the conduct of a nation's affairs a spirit of reasonableness which dilutes, and in the long run overcomes, those excesses of speech. It is this spirit which makes for a high standard of public life in a country. To this question I must revert later on, but in the meantime I will analyse the materials of which this intelligentsia is composed. And I must begin by indicating that there are two intelligentsias in India, the old and the new, the indigenous and the semi-Anglicised, or semi-de-Indianised, the men who speak English thoughts but only half believe them.

There are people who are learned in India, people of high intelligence, who scarcely know a word of English and who take no interest in politics. There are learned Pundits, and

Maulavis, and Buddhist monks, who are the indigenous product of an ancient civilisation. The highly orthodox among Hindus, deeply versed in philosophy, the strictest Moslems, full of Arabic learning, and the leaders of the Buddhist Church in Burma, all have had little affinity with the English-speaking, whom they regard as mere imitators of western materialism, and not very far removed from heretics to their religion. These people are highly conservative in their outlook, but for the most part they are well affected towards British rule, because it has left them their religious liberties, confirmed to the Hindus their temple lands, and to the Mahommedans their *wakfs*, or religious trusts. It is true that there are wandering mendicants and ascetics (Saniyasis, Bairagis, Gosains, and Fakirs) who may have been used as the instruments for spreading sedition, but the solid elements of orthodoxy have never been numbered amongst the seditious, and they still carry an influence with the masses not equally enjoyed by those who think and talk and write in English. Again, there are among the landed aristocracy and the ancient ruling families thousands of men with little or no English who regard the rant of the English-speaking agitator as an unmixed nuisance to the peace of the country. And these wonder in amazement at the ridiculous tolerance (as they regard it) by which a great and mighty Government allows itself to be abused and bullied by a number of nobodies (as they would term them), who if the lion only roared would scamper away into hiding.

And there are highly-polished and highly-respected bankers and traders whose treasure chests and commercial prosperity depend upon the stability of credit secured by British rule. It is all these who make up the old and indigenous intelligentsia of the country. Some few persons out of these sections have been won over to the side of the agitators, and among the traders in particular the higher income tax and the super tax, and the much-increased strictness in assessment and collection since the War, have helped to alienate their cordiality towards the Government, but should a crisis arise the wealth and capital of the country would find its way to the side of law and order.

In the midst of the sedition of 1919 in the Punjab there came to a British Officer in charge of a certain area an old moneylender in dirty raiment carrying a battered old tin box, and he sought audience in private and said: " Take the contents of this box and if the Sirkar has need of it I will bring an equal sum again." And the box contained half a lakh of rupees in notes, the mark of his gratitude to the power under whose protection his wealth had come to him. The money was gratefully returned.

To all these old and solid elements in the society of the country this new-fangled English-speaking intelligentsia are the *nouveaux riches* of intelligence, with a foreign veneer. And it is not upon them but upon the rock of British security that they regard their safety and prosperity as founded. These people, representing the old intellectual wealth of the country, have a clearer insight than the new intellectuals, whose pride and ambition obscure their judgments. That is the old intelligentsia, now for the new.

In all India, including Burma, there are altogether 2½ million people who were returned as literate in English in 1921, viz. people who were said to be able to read and write a simple letter in English. Of these there are, of course, many thousands who may have a smattering of English, but could not possibly be included in the intelligentsia of this or any other country. But for the moment we can take these 2½ millions literate in English as a basis, and analyse their composition. The numbers are reduced to 2 millions by the exclusion of the Indian States; another ¼ of a million has to be deducted for Europeans and Anglo-Indians, whose mother tongue is English and who have no desire to be ruled by Indians. There are thus about 1¾ millions only of Indians in British India who could, under this qualification, be included in the English-speaking intelligentsia. Their distribution is exceedingly uneven. If we look at them by the provinces, of the 2 million in British India we shall find that

$1\frac{2}{5}$ millions are concentrated in Bengal, Madras, and Bombay, leaving only 600,000 for the whole of the rest of India and Burma. That is to say, that in the three Presidencies thirteen people in a thousand are literate in English, and in the rest of British India only four in a thousand. Take again the whole $2\frac{1}{2}$ millions by races and creeds and we find that 70 million Mahommedans contribute only 315,000, against five times that number from the Hindus of the higher castes. Again, out of the innumerable castes and tribes included among Hindus those literate in English are concentrated in a very few. Thus while about 1,600,000 Hindus know English, the Brahmins numbering $14\frac{1}{4}$ millions contribute 600,000; the Kayasths, a clerical caste, 340,000; the clerical castes in Madras 80,000; and Baidyas in Bengal 26,000; the Khatris of the Punjab and North-West Frontier Province 27,000. Thus Hindu castes, numbering only 20 millions, contribute two-thirds of the whole total of English-knowing Hindus, leaving about $\frac{1}{2}$ a million among the remaining 200,000,000. These 20 millions thus yield 500 per 10,000, and the 200 millions 25 per 10,000.

As a contrast we may cite castes like Chamars, in the United Provinces, who comprise nearly 6 million people, with only 239 persons who know English. The Mahars, of Bombay, Baroda, the C.P. and Berar, and Hyderabad, together number 3 million people, and among them are only 845 people who know a little English. These two humble, untouchable castes show scarcely 1 per 10,000 who can understand English. Indian Christians, thanks to missionary efforts, number about 150,000 English literates, and Sikhs and Jains about 45,000 between them, while the Parsees show as high a proportion as 39 per cent. But it is the Brahmins and the few clerical castes that I have mentioned, with a sprinkling of Mahommedans, who fill the Government offices and hold the highest civil appointments.

Again, the vast majority of the English-knowing Indians, with the exception of the rural converts to Christianity, are to be found in the cities and towns, and as 10 per cent. only of the whole population of India is urban the number of English-knowing people living in the rural areas is necessarily insignificant.

It is thus clear that knowledge of English is concentrated in towns, is the accomplishment of a few special races and classes, and that a quarter of the Indians literate in English belong to the Brahmin caste. This proportion is raised to a third if we include the few clerical Hindu castes. Thus out of the total population 316 millions are innocent of English.

Again, taking the 2½ millions, persons aged twenty and over number only 1,745,000, of whom 1,127,000 are Hindus, 220,000 Mahommedans, 60,000 Indian Christians, 39,000 Parsees, 37,000 Buddhists, 15,000 Jains, and 14,000 Sikhs. The Brahmin caste alone produces more adults literate in English than all the non-Hindu Indians put together.

The Brahmins in Central, Southern, and Western India easily hold the supremacy in English-speaking. In Bengal the Kayasths and Baidyas are serious rivals to them; in Behar and the U.P. they may even be said to overshadow them. In the parts of India nearest to the seats of Mahommedan rule the Brahmins evidently lost some of their ascendancy, and it is noteworthy that the Kayasths in particular were forward in learning Persian and writing the Urdu script, and thus made themselves useful to the Mahommedans, and secured most of the clerical employment. Furthermore, in the U.P. and Behar there are large numbers of rural Brahmins who cultivate land and have no claim to learning. Nevertheless, though overshadowed to some extent in these ways, the English educated Brahmins have come up to the top as leaders, and the Kayasths can never enjoy the prestige that the Pundits and the priests command in the eyes of the people. The Kayasths have latterly laid claim to belong to the original Kshattriya caste, but the claim is not admitted by other castes, and they have not the characteristics of the Rajput. They are really clerical people who under British rule have come to the front, but they have no ruling tradition. If there were to be a pure trial of wits in a Swarajist India the Brahmins would be at the top, and the Hindus of these clerical castes would find a level many degrees below them. In Bengal, where the Kayasths and Baidyas are at present specially advanced, I feel little doubt that the Mukerjis and Chatterjis and Banerjis would show themselves the masters of the Boses and the Ghoses and the Sens. In Madras and Bombay, the C.P. and Berar, the provinces where a non-Brahmin movement is particularly strong, the other Hindu castes would not stand a chance against the Brahmins.

Among English-knowing Indians the true higher intelligentsia is strictly limited. There are thousands of English literates so classed consisting of clerks and minor officials who have read only up to Middle and High School standards. Their interests are centred in their families, their desks, and the price of provisions. Many of these may be called politically minded in that, like the callow students, they catch up the phrases of the politicians, and like to take part in political demonstrations, but they carry no weight in the country, except such as owning land or the caste to which they belong may confer upon them in a private capacity.

Among the Government clerks, on the railways, and in the post-office, there are some who *sub rosâ* are ardent Swarajists. Some notable bomb conspirators were drawn from this class, and they constitute a large element in the *Bhadra log* of Bengal, but among this class again there are thousands too occupied with their daily routine, and too much concerned with their pay and prospects, to trouble about politics.

Similarly, it would be a great mistake to class the flower of the intelligentsia as all politically-minded or as extreme politicians. Some of the finest intellects among the Indians recognise the difficulties of the situation, and though just as anxious as the politician to see the country advance are sane and sober in their outlook. Thus so eminent a man in law as Lord Sinha, and in commerce and industry as Sir

Rajendranath Mukerjee, the most trusted Indian in the business world, are naturally scarce, but the Bench and the Bar and the Indian Civil Service can show many moderate men of high capacity who find the perpetual jingle-jangle of the politicians tedious and futile. No one could accuse the late Mr. Gokhale of being a laggard in promoting the welfare of Indians. He was a very fluent and effective debater, but he had always with him that strain of common sense and moderation which saved him from the pastime of winning the cheap applause of the semi-educated by an uncontrolled violence of language. He recognised the limitations as well as the aspirations of political advance, and freely pointed out to his audiences that while there might be individual Indians in every way the equal of the best Europeans, the average of the Indian was deplorably lower than the average of the British citizen; and he recommended them to raise that average before they could expect to rise to higher things. The pioneer of Indian industrial enterprise in India was the late Sir J. N. Tata, a man who would have been remarkable in any community. Madras, Bombay and Bengal have produced many notable men, whose contributions to the welfare of the people were of the greatest value, but none of these men ever thought of corrupting the inexperience of students, or pandering to the passions of ignorant masses, for none of these men were "politically-minded," like the Swarajists of to-day.

Perhaps the greatest problem of all about the political intelligentsia is their Press. The editors of the best conducted Indian-owned papers have it in them to take a high place in journalism if they did not worry to death that perpetual King Charles' head of British rule. A late Presidency Governor described this Press as " Seldom just and never generous." This is really a mild description of the anti-British propaganda in which they now engage without ceasing, magnifying the trivial, belittling the good, wearying the flesh with their perpetual jeremiads, turning Indian beams into motes and British motes into beams, clever in the turn of a phrase, yet adepts in the spoiling of a cause; taking in the ignorant and the foolish, disgusting the fair-minded, for their lapses into virtue are few and far between. Why are men capable of so much better things content to be just "wandering stars and clouds without water?" And below them again are the less reputable organs, a few English but mostly vernacular, living on cant, and rant, and platitudes, distorting facts and confusing issues, and the salutary restraint of the Press Act was light-heartedly discarded while youth is corrupted, hatred inspired, and treason disseminated. These are really busy building their own funeral pyres, for if the British with their indulgent toleration departed from the country these papers and their editors would go up in smoke. In sterner times the writers of this sort of paper would prove to have been but a flock of sheep masquerading as a pack of wolves. But the British public know none of these things.

There have been just a few papers that have made brave, but, alas, puny efforts to stand up against the avalanche of prejudice. The gallant little *Indian Mirror* and some papers in the West. Their efforts have been unavailing.

How can a Press like the Swarajist either elevate or educate? What can one say of an editor of one of these who described the murderous activities of bomb conspirators as "the foolish pranks of a few hare-brained youths," and in another article hailed these same youths as "the saviours of their country?" Or of a newspaper which, reviewing the All India Sanitary Report, ascribed the total deaths, some 9,000,000 in a year, to starvation, and then proceeded to write a leader on " Nine million victims of starvation?" In a word, the Press of India is utterly irresponsible. A sense of responsibility is the missing quality which you will look for in vain. By their Press ye shall know them. That is the real problem of the Swarajist intelligentsia. They are totally and utterly irresponsible.

CHAPTER VII

THE PROBLEM OF THE BRITISH SERVICES

The Essentials of a Public Service—The Effect of Public Opinion—British Public Servants controlled by British Public Opinion—The Disastrous Effects of the Loss of that Control—The Great Difficulties of Indian Public Servants—The Effect of an Atmosphere—The Various Services Examined—The Absolute Necessity of British Services as long as British Troops defend India

Every State, despotic or democratic, must have its officials. On their honesty and efficiency the welfare and happiness of the subjects or citizens will largely depend. We in England are proud of our Civil Service, though at times we speak scornfully of them; we are proud of their honesty and sense of duty, but we are wont to gibe at their red tape and their alleged narrowness of outlook, and to contrast them to their disadvantage with the servants of large private concerns. The comparison is quite unjust, but let it pass.

There are certain main essentials about the public service. The personnel selected must be reasonably competent; their employment must be secure; provision for their old age assured. Honesty and hard work must have its recognition, brilliancy its special reward. There must be periodical rises of salary and prospect, but seniority must be tempered by selection, and selection by seniority, while absolute probity must be the condition of all these benefits. All these public servants will be under the head of the Department in which they are working, under the orders of a Minister of State, who in his turn is responsible in autocracies to a royal master and in democracies to the Prime Minister of the Cabinet of which he is a member, and through him to the Parliament and the people. But the whole tone and standards of a service are governed and determined not so much by rules and regulations but by the tone and standards of public opinion prevailing among the people from whom the service is drawn, and if that opinion is lax and venal the chances of the service being honest will depend mainly upon the personality of its chiefs, and on the degree of supervision which they can exercise; even so the good that an honest and diligent chief can accomplish is of necessity limited, but the mischief that an unprincipled head can do is infinite.

Now the system which has prevailed in most Oriental countries offers the exact antithesis to the main essentials described above. The official secures both his original appointment and his promotion by the favour of somebody or by paying somebody something for it, his qualifications often being a secondary consideration. He can never feel secure; he works in a hotbed of intrigue. If his superiors are themselves dishonest his own honesty will be a positive handicap to him; he will always need some patron to recommend him. His pay will be low in proportion to his responsibility, and often irregularly paid, and he will be as much expected to take douceurs as any waiter at a hotel. If he manages to rise he will become arrogant to those below him, or to the humbler members of the public whom he is supposed to serve. Lack of security accompanies such an one through the whole of his career. I was once down inspecting a distant tract on the borders of an Indian State, and my local Revenue Officer in that tract had a brother similarly employed just across the border. He described to me how his brother was always in dread of what the midday post might bring. In his work he had to make enemies, and any day he might find that one of them had succeeded in securing his downfall. Some of the best officials under the old rulers in India were those who held hereditary office. When the incumbent became old and infirm his son or his nephew received the post, and was expected to provide out of his emoluments for the retired incumbent. These men at least had some security, and there were some fine old men among them with a sense of chivalry and honesty, but they were the exceptions that proved the rule. So sagacious a sovereign as the great Emperor Akbar might collect around him men of ability and character, but how many Akbars were there in the history of India? A David who won by war might be succeeded by a Solomon who consolidated by the arts of peace, but a Rehoboam was sure to follow, who flouted the elders and was led by worthless favourites. The relatives of a low-bred mistress have been the worst enemies of honesty. Even if they cannot pervert the man they will ruin his reputation.

But some will certainly say, surely there are many high-minded Indians, men who follow a high standard in their own lives and who try to create an honest public opinion. There are many high-minded men; there are many more also who would prefer to be honest, but public opinion cannot be created in this fashion. The masses admire honesty but they do not expect it, nor are they in a position to encourage it. *Vident meliora probantque deteriora sequuntur.* How often have I said to the villagers: "You can trust so-and-so to deal with your case, he is an honest man," yet how often do they answer: "Sahib, you do not know our people like we do. You may never have heard what he did in the case of 'X'; you will find him out one day." And sometimes I have.

A very famous Indian administrator, now dead, used to tell a story of how when he was a District Officer some litigants applied to him to transfer a case from the Court of a very experienced Indian officer to that of a very inexperienced young Englishman. He demurred to making such an order, saying that the case was one in which the Indian's special knowledge and experience would enable him to make a right decision in a very intricate matter, while the Englishman, having very short service, would be "quite at sea." "Yes," they said, "we know all that; we know that the young Sahib is a fool, but he is honest, and God helps him, let him try our case."

There has been immense improvement in the honesty of our Indian magistrates and judges, which better education has brought about in the last forty years. Even when I joined the Service there were a few men whose reputation not even the worst bazaar scandalmonger could assail, but the majority were not trusted, and a great many fell into the category "notoriously corrupt." There were quite a number who took bribes from both sides, decided the case on its merits, and returned the money to the unsuccessful party. There was one man so ingenious that he managed to keep both, though at the expense of his own reputation for judicial ability. He decided the case so wrong-headedly that the Appellate Court reversed his decision. To the one party he would say: " I decided in your favour"; to the other, that he did not like to make it too obvious that he had been bribed, so he had decided the case against him but in such a way that he was bound to succeed in appeal, and so he kept both bribes. How can you prevent these things? You cannot, you can only check them. Not one in a hundred cases can be brought to proof. The bribe-giver is equally guilty in law with the bribe-taker. If you give him a pardon he is still a tainted witness. The bribe is given through secret intermediaries, to whom some of it clings on the way—these men will never split. The accuser will generally, therefore, concoct false evidence of the actual handing over of the money, and his case breaks down. Yet everyone knows of judges and magistrates who have always been extravagant, and yet are surprisingly well-off when they retire. It is very seldom that a bribe is taken to convict a man, but the bribe not to convict is common. It is easy to write a judgment of discharge or acquittal. There are always some discrepancies in evidence, and a Court can always write that it disbelieves it or gives the benefit of the doubt. It is impossible to convict a man of corruption merely on inferences from his decision, however useful these may be as confirmatory of positive evidence of bribe-taking. Higher education, as I have said, has produced much improvement, but it has by no means extirpated the evil. In the great famine we were obliged to enlist the help of Civil Judges during their vacation in the distribution of famine loans and charitable grants from the splendid generosity of the British public. These grants were restricted to those cultivators who were absolutely broken. It scarcely seems credible that a judge with the University Degrees B.A. and B.L. should have been detected in the despicable meanness of deducting commission for himself from the recipients of this charity. But so it was. Indian society has no effective condemnation for acts like these. I prosecuted a Brahmin money-lender for forgery of the basest description, by means of which he nearly succeeded in depriving a poor cultivator of his land. The forgery involved a set of completely fabricated accounts carried over two years, and a false bond at the end of it. So base was the forgery that the sentence was seven years. When discharged after serving his term he was met at the jail gate with the offer of an appointment from a very large firm of Indian bankers.

But there are many other influences involved besides mere vulgar corruption. There is the influence of class or creed partiality. A Mahommedan in the Indian Civil Service, himself a Sessions Judge, held land in another province, and he told me that his difficulty was that he could never get fair treatment from the Hindu Civil Judges before whom he had litigation in connection with his land. His suspicions may have been unjustified, but that a man of his status, himself holding a high judicial appointment, should feel like this, is highly significant. The pressure exerted by considerations of caste or creed or race is not easily realised in England.

I have put into an Appendix II a story of my own personal experience which is typical of things that may occur in outlying places. It has its humorous as well as its serious side, and I have called it "The Story of the Cow that shied.[1]"

[1] That animal's shy caused about twenty people to commit perjury, the dismissal of one and the punishment of two Government servants, and the locking up for seventeen days of two men on a false charge.

That story is an indication of the extent to which the law is invoked in India to punish an enemy or a member of a rival faction. Witnesses can be hired for very small fees, and involving your enemy in a lawsuit or a criminal charge is much more interesting and less dangerous than using force to him. Moreover, it gratifies cunning. It is for this reason that the Indian public servant is constantly faced with difficulties from which British officers are almost entirely saved. He has a pressure on him which we do not realise, and temptations from which we are free. British members of the Services in India are bred and trained on British standards. It is another way of saying that they are the product of British public opinion, and British public opinion does not tolerate things which are regarded with indifference or complacency in ordinary Indian circles. The sporting instinct which helps an Englishman to be fair is deficient in the average Indian. The Indian Assistant Magistrate, or Subordinate Judge, may have had these traditions impressed upon him by his British superior officers and colleagues, but he was not bred in them, and under the stress of pressure he is liable to backslide. The whole atmosphere in which he works is different and very difficult to resist. Indians are by nature emotional and sentimental, and while these tendencies will often make them generous and sympathetic they will also frequently destroy the sense of proportion when personal inclinations will get the better of commonsense. It is given to very few of these Indians *to feel themselves above suspicion*, and this is one of the reasons which make them timid in taking prompt decisions.

It is upon these characteristics of the Indian mind and Indian public opinion which cannot shake itself free from caste and class that the necessity for a strong British element in all the higher public services is founded. British public opinion is a constant check upon the British officer, and the British officer is a constant check upon the Indian. But if Indianisation became complete, British public opinion would cease to feel any responsibility for the conduct of affairs by a service of which the personnel was entirely Indian in a self-governing India.

The Lee Commission's proposals contemplated the gradual reduction of the British proportion in the Indian Civil Service and the Indian Police, the two security services, to one half. This was deemed the absolute limit of security. As an abstract proposition, educated Indian witnesses in some cases pressed for the immediate cessation of British recruitment. Most of them would have been very sorry to have seen that proposal accepted in the concrete, and the same Indians who were ready to press for wholesale Indianisation will be found to call loudly for British officers to be sent to this district or that charge when trouble of any kind occurs. Since the Lee Commission's enquiries communal feeling in India has grown in intensity, and the increasing violence of town mobs has been an object lesson of the necessity for greater caution. I have known many Indians in the I.C.S., several of whom were under my own observation. There have been some who have had a brilliant record. I have never heard of any corruption among any of them, but many of them have been of a colourless type, and there have been several great disappointments. In scholastic honours they can hold their own, but in the stress and strain of an official life they fall below standards. A district which has been for any length of time under purely Indian control seems as if all the strings had become loose.

In the various provincial Civil Services the best Indian officers are very good, but they tail off badly, and there are more cases of corruption among them than ought to occur in these days when the personnel is more highly educated. The subordinate Civil Services are very unequal. Some of the men are wonderfully good; others deplorably bad. Indians succeed best on the judicial side, or in such Departments as Accounts and the Post-Office. On the Executive side, where driving power, initiative, and rapid decision in an emergency are essential, they do not hold their own with their British colleagues. Indeed, I have found these qualities better developed among the less well-educated Indians who were to be found in these services formerly than among the better-educated men of to-day.

In the police the necessity for a large proportion of British personnel is even more urgent than in the Indian Civil Service. The Service does not attract the best Indians; it involves a hard life, constant abuse in the Press, and special opportunities for corruption, and though hundreds of individual policemen show gallantry and devotion to duty of a high order, it is only under vigorous and impartial leaders, whom Hindu and Moslem can alike trust, that this Service can be relied upon. There are unfortunately many black sheep among them, and it may be imagined if weaker vessels are found among educated and well-paid Indian officials, how futile it is to expect the lower ranks to resist temptation. One of the hardest things is to induce the constable to be pleasant and considerate to poor people. The villager in uniform and clothed with this considerable authority is apt to be hectoring in his manner and rough in his handling with humble folk. But the police must partake of the nature of the population from which they are recruited, and I have never ceased to wonder that educated Indians who are so lavish in abusing the police are so dull as not to perceive that they are framing an indictment against their own people. Nowadays it is rare for the police to concoct a totally false charge against a completely innocent man, but their mode of thought is this: We are sure that "A" is guilty and ought to be convicted, but there is a small link missing in the chain of evidence against him, and so we are quite justified in forging that link. Many true cases have failed because of this forged missing link that broke down under cross-examination and discredited the rest of the true case. It is only by forceful and sympathetic leading, by condign punishment of the offending members, and by constant encouragement of the honest man that the Force can be purified. Under these influences there has been immense improvement during the last fifty years, but with the withdrawal of impartial leadership the *esprit de corps* and the advance towards cleaner work will likewise disappear. Bribery will recrudesce on a wholesale scale, and the work of fifty years' effort will rapidly disintegrate.

The Indian Medical Service: There have been Indians in the Indian Medical Service for a great many years, but their contribution to the outstanding work of that Service has been disappointingly meagre. Private medical practitioners in the large towns are to-day numerous; in rural areas they scarcely exist. The people at large have some belief in Western surgery, but very little in Western medicine. They do not understand qualifications, and anyone who calls himself "Doctor" can attract patients. They have a strong preference for their own ancient systems of medicine. The practitioners of these systems have often an inherited aptitude, and an empirical knowledge of the action of simples and drugs, but not much science. As to the ordinary village quack, the most important elements in his pharmacopoeia are charms and invocations. I have knowledge of cases in which British doctors have been called in only to find that their treatment has been rendered nugatory by the patients being induced to take other specifics or religious charms, such as cow's urine. In one case the patient so treated was rich, with an English education. The quantity administered was nine bottles. The patient died!

Indian patients and their friends, rich and poor, will mix up the treatment of different systems regardless of consequence. There are many Indians with high medical degrees who are excellent surgeons and a credit to the profession, and among the Subordinate Medical Services I have seen some wonderful work. Nevertheless the profession in India is likely to go to pieces if it is not constantly reinforced by the best British products of the great British Medical Schools. The organisation and maintenance of a great hospital requires high administrative talents as well as professional skill. A Government Medical Officer has very responsible duties in medico-legal work, and there is no branch of the work in which bribes are so often offered. The charge of the large jails is also a highly responsible duty. The most efficient Indian I.M.S. officers that I have personal knowledge of happened to be Parsees by race, and Parsees are of course in a category by themselves. But, apart from the medical needs of the country, as long as there are Europeans in the army, the Civil Services, or in commerce, they will prefer medical attendance, especially for their wives and families, by doctors of their own race. There are a few individual Indian specialists whom Europeans consult, but not generally in cases involving those intimate and confidential relations that should prevail between doctor and patient. So long as British Services are retained in India, the continuance of British Medical Officers is a *sine quâ non*. And for this, even if there were no other reason, the Indian Medical Service must be included among the Security Services, and not left to the control of ministers dependent upon legislative bodies, of whom the members are frequently adherents of the Ayurvedic or Yunnani systems of medicine. Even some western-trained Indian medical men revert to these systems.

The Public Works Department of India, though often the subject of adverse criticism on account of its departmentalism, has a wonderful record. Civil Engineers in the past have had to perform the duties of engineers, architects, and clerks of the work, all rolled into one, and the effect of the scattered nature of their works, and the great size of their charges, is not known to people in this country, and its significance not appreciated by many people in India. The large sums of money to be spent, the great temptations to favour this or that powerful contractor, or to pass inferior work, are so great as to be well-nigh irresistible to all the subordinate agencies (and there are many who have fallen to temptation among the Indians holding higher ranks). These considerations demand the most stringent supervision. It is idle to suppose that efficiency will not seriously decline if the livest wires, the ablest engineers, and the most conscientious supervisors are to be rapidly eliminated. More especially in the Irrigation Department, where the issues are vital and the interests of thousands of poor cultivators are at stake, is this supervision necessary.

Again, if we take the Forest Department, the public interests involved in the good management of the enormous forest estates are of the highest importance, both to the present and future generations, and to the agricultural welfare of the country, but the town-bred politician cares for none of these things. The best educated Indian has no liking for the hardships and solitude of the Forest Officer's life. To him, consequently, service in the Forest Department is a mere *pis aller*. It is not easy to find men out of this material who are fitted to rise to high office. The landowner with some private forests will ruin his forests for ready cash; the vast agricultural community would like to have their forest produce free, and to graze down and hew and hack at their pleasure. The contractor for timber and firewood naturally seeks to make as much money as he can out of his contract, but the conservation of forests to the best economic advantage does not weigh at all with any of these, and the town pleader or politician looks upon the unpopularity of forest administration as a mere stick with which to belabour the British Government.

Then there is the Indian Educational Service. Lack of funds kept back the development of this service in the last century, and it was only during the last twenty years that the Department was really put on good and strong foundations. Just as it had settled down to its task came the Reforms, and the so-called "popular movement" for eliminating British agency, and since the War there has practically been no British recruitment. Yet all the best Indians of the older generation were the product of early teaching by notable missionary principals of colleges, as well as by a few outstanding men in Government service. I have often heard them express their gratitude to these old principals and teachers, and they do not approve of the door being closed as it has been to men of like talents and character, but they are powerless before the tyranny of the Swarajist Press. Surely when you select western lines of advance, the last step in folly is to exclude all western exponents of that which it is sought to teach. The Press talks nonsense about the "slave mentality" which has been introduced into Government colleges and schools. If that is what the politicians learnt when they were educated at these schools they have a very curious way of showing it. They are certainly very rebellious slaves. The politicians have tampered with the discipline of students, and the old Oriental respect for the teacher—so great a feature of Indian life and tradition—has been undermined. There is a strange irony in the fact that when these men are remodelling the East they have kept so much that was bad and have been bent on destroying so much that was good. They may find talent in Indian lecturers perhaps, but few like the old principals who were builders of character. By this short-sighted policy are they merely pushing back the course of true progress. The unbalanced boys and youths are being fed on the froth of political extravaganza instead of on solid nourishing thought. How can nation-building, of which they are so fond of talking, be achieved by means such as these?

Agriculture is still at the pioneer stage. This great Department was created by Lord Curzon so recently as 1903, and many of the best men then imported to be founders of the new Service have resigned prematurely because they could do no good under irresponsible Ministers. The Department has done wonderful work, and just as it was beginning to make a real impression on the country it finds itself in process of disintegration in favour of the new alumni of Indian Colleges, who, though they may be able to obtain the necessary diplomas cannot possibly fill the shoes of the founders of the work of the Department, or persevere in that policy of research, initiative, and drive without which the Department will fail to retain the ground won and is unlikely to conquer fresh fields. The alumni of these new colleges naturally deserve to be given a chance in the higher work of the Department, but not to the exclusion of the best products of British Schools of Agriculture. Science can only thrive with the most scrupulous fairness in calculating the results of an experiment. If results are coloured to suit theories, instead of theories being modified in accordance with the result, however disappointing these be to the investigator, the value of the Department is prejudiced at the very start. The spirit of true science is deficient, not I would say on account of deliberate dishonesty, but simply for the lack of that infinite patience to obtain accuracy or to exercise supervision over subordinates, who are quite ready to cook results to please a superior, or to vitiate them by carelessness in order to save themselves trouble. These people are just like the cultivator who will water his cotton to secure a higher weight, regardless of the fact that the deterioration in quality of his staple must soon recoil upon himself by a reduction in the price which it can command.

The Royal Commission on Agriculture has made it quite plain that the country cannot do without imported scientific agriculturists, but the transfer of Agriculture to the charge of Ministers in the Provinces has prevented them from making the one recommendation that might enable their well thought out policy to be carried out, viz. the restoration of the Indian Agricultural Service with a proportion of at least 50 per cent. of British Officers.

I have dealt with most of the principal Departments of Government. There are others in which, to a greater or less extent, the same consideration will apply, notably the Railways, the Telegraphs, and the Customs, and the best way for Indians to make good in these Departments is to have by them the support and steadfastness of British colleagues who have no axe to grind in the country, but are trying to do their duty in a spirit of equity and good conscience. British officers will be loyal to principles—the Indians only to men, and if the men that lead them are themselves for various reasons unstable the instability of those who follow is magnified and multiplied.

One hears the theorists say that the British administrator in India makes a fetish of efficiency. There is such a thing, they say, as "too much efficiency." The theorists are quite wrong, for they are confusing efficiency with red tape or the routine of the martinet, or a soulless driving of Robots. So far from doing this, the British administrator is perpetually compromising with the weakness of human nature; he is perpetually making allowances for prejudice, and sympathising with difficulties. Only while in the Secretariats does he for a while lose his contact with men and things, but the personnel of the Secretariats should be, and generally is, shifting, so that the men who serve there may constantly refresh their contact with facts to correct their theories. But the man in the districts is roaming or has roamed the highways and the byeways, the field, the forest, and the villages, and the lanes of the cities, and he knows the men that dwell therein. He has seen them in famine and plenty, in drought and in flood, in peace and in riot, in all the moods of humanity, and in all the moods of nature. He is for ever striving after honesty, clean standards, even justice. In the words of the litigants which I quoted before: " He may be a fool, but he is honest, and God helps him." And this is the way in which he has won the confidence of millions of simple, unsophisticated men. Anything less like a Prussian drill-master, or a red-tape clerk, it is difficult to imagine. The real fetish worshipper is the theorist sitting comfortably in his armchair, laying down his theories and contemptuously labelling the men who have borne the burden and heat of the day as sun-dried bureaucrats.

I may be told that all this has changed, that the young Indians in the Services coming on are on a very different level, and that the past is behind them, but I do not believe that the characteristics of races are going to alter in five years. By all means try out this young blood, give it its opportunities, treat it fairly, but I have seen young men of this type, eager, smart, and conscientious, but as they grow up towards middle age their keenness abates, their smartness is replaced by slovenliness, and their consciences are becoming dulled; they are gradually succumbing to the atmosphere, as we British ourselves might also succumb if we were not constantly fortified by our leaves, by our renewed contact with western environments, and, above all, by the continual influx of fresh blood amongst us. And thus it is true that the majority of Indians fail to fulfil their early promise and lose their fitness for leadership just when they reach the age at which they should be ripe to assume it. Even among the British there are men who do not last the course, and who become stale and unprofitable. With them it is the exception; with the Indians it is common. They cannot stand up against the atmosphere around them.

The efficiency for which we stand in India is honesty in public dealings, honesty of purpose, honesty in the Courts, honesty in success, and honesty in failure. In our patient and plodding way we have laid the foundations on rock, and were commencing the superstructure, and now has come the political theorist to tell us that we builders are no longer required, that our buildings and sites should be abandoned in favour of a new building founded on sand and inscribed with a big notice "Democracy." "A plague on your plodding views," they say, and yet let them look round Asia—the only nation that has risen to great national heights is Japan, the only Asiatic nation that has cultivated efficiency; and nations and peoples that disregard efficiency will surely perish. You may instil Western doctrines into the minds of these Oriental people; they may alter their form of speech, but they do not alter their actions and reactions. Kemal Pasha in Turkey and Amanullah in Afghanistan were men in a hurry, and *more orientali* they pursued despotic methods, and thought to change men's heads by forcing them to change their head-dress. In India the reforming despot has not been our rôle. We have not asked the people to change their raiment; it is the constitutional theorist who bids them wear the garments of democracy, and thinks that this will change the men within.

There is yet one more consideration and it is paramount. British troops will be required in India until its feuds and its jealousies and its lack of thoroughness have passed away. No one, theorist or practical man, can honestly think that the British Parliament and nation will send out British troops to fight on the frontier while their communications and supplies are at the mercy of Indian politicians controlling Indian railwaymen, telegraphists, engineers, doctors, police, and district officers, without that strong leaven of British men in the British Services and the Indian Army which alone can ensure that British forces defending the country will not be stabbed in the back by treachery or starved by inefficiency. The man who will not provide that leaven can only belong to the school of "Perish India."

These are the problems of the British Services. How can an united India progress without them? She can not.

CHAPTER VIII

THE PROBLEM OF DEFENCE AND INTERNAL SECURITY

The Efficiency of the Indian Army dependent upon British Leadership—Its Constitution—Its Disintegration under Congress Politicians—The Foundations of Internal Security

MANY better-qualified writers have written on the subject of the defence of the land and sea frontiers of India. There is plenty of material available to those who seek to study these questions as expounded by experts, military and political. I am only concerned to state a few salient and elemental facts which are sometimes overlooked.

So long as India remains British the British Navy will see to it that she is not invaded by sea, and so long as the British Navy keeps the sea routes and the Suez Canal secure for transports she will be able to reinforce the British and Indian armies now in the country with sufficient strength to defeat attempted invasions by land. But the moment that India became a Dominion she would have to depend entirely on her own military forces and resources for preserving internal security, and largely also upon them to repel an invader by land. And the moment that she threw off her allegiance to the King, as a section of her politicians wildly talk of doing, she would lose the protection of the British Navy, the value of which would only be realised when it was lost. But the talkers of the Congress, and of the various parties and leagues which have been formed by the politically-minded, are so lost in admiration of their own and their neighbours' daring that they cannot spare serious thought to the commonplace fact that with the withdrawal of British troops not only will the problem of external defence prove beyond their capacity, but the rupture of internal peace will wreck all the optimistic forecasts of Kashmiri Pundits, Madrasi and Bengali Brahmins, Kayasths and Khatris, Naidus and Pillais, regarding the golden times in store for India, when once the domineering British have packed up their trunks and departed. While the British control the Indian Army—and they can only control it by a strong backing of British troops—it is reasonably certain that the whole of the Indian Army, as well as the forces of the Indian Princes, will, when they fight, always be found fighting on the same side. If the control of the Indian army passed to a congress of lawyers and journalists, drawn from small sections of the population, with no military traditions behind them, the Indian Army would become a house divided against itself, and might speedily split up into as many sections as those of which it is composed. Some might flock to the standards of Mahratta, Rajput, and Sikh princes; Nepal might very well find uses for the Gurkhas; the Pathans and the rest of the Mahommedan troops would find leaders of their own, and disintegrated groups of Sepoys would very soon begin to live on the country. It is no reflection upon the splendid loyalty and fine discipline of the Indian Army to predict that without the accustomed leadership the whole organisation would break up entirely. The discipline of an army depends upon its leadership, and if that leadership were to change the soldiers would certainly prefer to find new leaders of their own particular race, or caste, or creed, rather than obey groups of non-martial lawyers, pundits, and Lalas.

It is impossible to build up traditions round a central loyalty of a century and a half's duration and then remove the bond of union and expect the traditions to stand firm. If the Congress politician does not see this he is purblind—if he does see it and is merely bluffing he is playing a dangerous game. In either case he completely destroys his own reputation for political sanity. The Congress politician is seeking rapidly to Indianise the officer ranks of the Army, but if he succeeded it would do him no good, for Indian officers of the martial races would be no more willing to follow his beck and call than the ranks are now, while if he found the officers from the non-martial intellectuals the men would not follow their officers. If one looks at the constitution of the Indian army one will find that it is drawn from the best fighting material of India. It would be a wicked waste of money if it were not. The Indian Army List shows that nearly a quarter of the infantry is made up of twenty battalions of Gurkhas, and there are a few battalions composed entirely of Sikhs, Dogras, Garhwalis, and Kumaonis. All the rest of these classes are divided up as separate companies in mixed regiments, and consist of Punjabi Mahommedans, some few Hindustani Mahommedans, and Mussulman Rajputs. There are also Rajputs of Rajputana, Dogras, or Hill Rajputs, again from the Punjab, and there still remain three companies of Garhwali, or Hill, Brahmins, being the only Brahmins now left in the army. There are some twenty-four companies of Jats, equal to six battalions, and the Sikhs are equivalent to fourteen battalions; the Madras Pioneers and the Madras Sappers and Miners are all that remain of the old Madras Army. There are also the equivalent of some five or six battalions of Mahrattas, drawn from the Southern Mahratta country, and some Deccani Mahommedans. The Pathan element has been much reduced since the Great War.

In the cavalry not more than five or six squadrons out of sixty-three are drawn from Southern India, and Sikhs, Jats, Punjabi Mahommedans, and Rajputs are the largest element among the mounted troops. It is thus clear that almost the whole of these forces are foreigners to the politicians who seek to substitute themselves for the British as commanding officers. They, and their British admirers, are merely flying in the face of facts when they talk of these forces as the "national" army of India.

Sikhs, and Gurkhas, and Pathans, and Rajputs, and Mahrattas will no more follow Bengali and Madrasi officers than the armies of Germany or France would accept Greek or Portuguese leadership. They belong to different races and speak different languages, and to believe otherwise is to deceive oneself once again with the delusion that there does exist an Indian nation, full of national zeal and national patriotism. Men will not follow leaders unless they trust them, and the Sepoys of the Indian army, while they may recognise that the intellectuals have book learning and skill in debate, appropriate enough in its proper sphere, have no respect for them in the novel capacity of company, squadron, or battalion commanders. The regiments set apart for Indianisation of the officers, as the young Indian subalterns appointed to them acquire seniority, are a recent experiment upon which it is far too early to pronounce an opinion, but the scheme is unpopular, both with the young Indian officers themselves and with the politicians. The young Indian officers prefer to be under British command because they think they will be more certain of impartial treatment, that is to say, they do not trust their own countrymen enough. A young Indian officer, who was unwilling to accept transfer to one of the Indianised units, gave various excuses for preferring to remain with his non-Indianised battalion. The excuses appeared to be rather feeble, and upon being pressed further he finally said that if he went to a regiment with an Indian colonel he would never be able to get leave or promotion without paying for it. This may be, and probably is, a libel on any Indian officer likely to be selected to command one of these units, but it shows the ideas prevailing. The politicians also do not like this scheme. Why? They of all people, who say that they want the Indian army entirely officered by Indians in fifteen years, if not sooner, ought to welcome the scheme as affording the earliest possible realisation of their hopes. They, too, do not trust their fellow-countrymen. They are afraid of the test when it comes to action instead of words. They prefer that the young Indian officers should have the shelter and support of British brother officers as long as possible. They fear that the new units may not fulfil their rash boast that the Indian officer will prove himself as good an officer if not better than the British. The young Indian officers themselves, many of them of excellent material now, are far more modest. For my own part I can only give the opinion of a civilian for what it may be worth. If it were only physical courage required we should find it in abundance, but more than this is wanted; we want moral courage, quick decision in emergency, and willingness to take responsibility. For lack of these qualifications some British officers do not qualify for the higher commands, and it is for the lack of these qualities that many Indians in civil life fail to reach the top; and then there is that serious drawback, from which an Indian always suffers and from which the British are free, that fatal jealousy and suspicion that one race or caste has of another which destroys the mutual trust essential between those who lead and those who follow.

There are doubtless among the intellectual people a good many young men who would like to have real martial zeal. During the War this ambition was put to the test. Very little was forthcoming. Even in the Punjab, the most virile province of all, where the literate classes had some fighting traditions, the number who were ready to join the colours was so miserably small that it was exceeded by the boys of a single school, trained and led by Belgian missionaries.

Great efforts were made in Bengal to raise a battalion of the young *Bhadra Log* (the pen workers) and the 49th Bengalis was the solitary response. Recruits, however, were not sufficient to maintain the battalion up to strength on service, and it was found to be of no military value. It is, however, to the credit of Bengal that two or three educated leaders did at least make strenuous efforts, and that some men were forthcoming of a particular class who specially pride themselves on their patriotism, and number some three millions in Bengal. But in the whole of the rest of India, excluding Burma, to which reference is made in another chapter, these literates in English failed to contribute a single fighting unit. Surely they ought to be able to see now how much stronger their claim for consideration to be given commissions in the army would have been if, when they had a chance of fighting for the Empire, they had taken it. In justice to Indians, however, it must be said that on the outbreak of the War a good many students in England volunteered for service with British units under training for the front. Among the Bengalis there are many individuals who have shown great courage and fidelity, and several have lost their lives, as the records of certain Bengali C.I.D. police officers amply prove. These men were in constant danger from the bombs and revolvers of anarchist conspirators. But as a race the Bengalis have no martial instinct at all, and any idea of their being able to compete with such doughty fighters as Sikhs, Pathans, and Gurkhas is quite fantastic. They have many merits in the arts of peace, and some of the younger generation have been trying to harden themselves with sports and games. The Brahmin cultivators of Upper India have fought in the ranks of the Indian army, and are to be found in the armed police, but they do not make first-line troops, and would not inspire the respect accorded to the virile races of the North. It is not the fault of the Southern races that they lack the physique and the stamina of the Punjabis; climatic considerations are against them. And it may be that they may at some future date acquire by effort what they now have not by heredity. But in manning the Indian army the military authorities have to deal with the facts as they are, and cannot risk an army being inefficient merely on future possibilities, which may never materialise.

The first danger, however, that would arise from the withdrawal of British control, which the politicians find it convenient to ignore because it does not fit in with their rash declaration that all India is a united nation, is in regard to the preservation of internal peace. How is this now kept with such apparent ease among all the Provinces and States in India? It all seems so simple. It rests, however, upon the prestige of the British. If you examine it you will find that it depends upon a chain of obedience and co-operation which, if once severed, it might be difficult to join. At the very bottom are the village watchmen and the village headmen, obeying the directions of the police and the district magistrate and his assistants. The police obey their own superintendent, and the superintendent obeys the district magistrate. The police, under 200,000 strong, over the whole of British India, represent one man to every 1250 of the population, and since the largest number of police are concentrated in the cities and towns, the proportion of police in the rural areas is very small. There are only 250 district magistrates and 250 police superintendents in charge of districts in the whole of British India, or one each to every million of the population. But the district magistrate's order represents the King's writ in India. There are, besides, presidency magistrates in the Presidency towns, and city magistrates in the larger cities, the latter being, however, merely the assistants of the district magistrate. In addition to the ordinary police are a few select bodies of armed police, at a few centres, and there are some forces of military police in Burma, Assam, and Bengal. The military police are, however, mainly required for frontier work, and their employment enables a corresponding reduction to be made in the ranks of the army. The armed reserves are used for escorts of large treasure, for the more serious riots, and occasionally for dacoit hunting, but the ordinary police in the districts are not as a rule armed, though a few obsolescent arms, with a very small supply of cartridges, are kept at station houses and at other small police posts. If determined mobs of villagers were to surround these little police stations the whole of the force could be wiped out in a few hours, as the tragedy of Chaura-Chauri so clearly demonstrated.

Behind the police, though only available at a few places, are the troops, Indian and British. If you travel 1400 miles, from Bombay to Calcutta, via Jubbulpur, you will find troops at only three places on that route. If you travel via Nagpur, 1220 miles, you will find them at only one place on the way, but no Indian State dare encroach upon another, or upon British territory, nor British Indian people upon an Indian State. There are concentrations of troops in Northern India and along the North-West Frontier, and in the South only at Poona, Secunderabad, and Bangalore. In the whole of Burma there are only two British regiments. If serious trouble should arise on the frontier, requiring mobilisation, then all these places would be left with only skeleton forces. The auxiliary forces of Europeans and Anglo-Indians, which might have to fill the breach, are in any strength only in large commercial cities and at railway centres. Everywhere else the force is represented by only small handfuls of men.

The new Territorial Force, organised more as a political sop than for their military value, represents an effort to give scope to the supposed martial qualities of the middle-class people, mainly those educated. It was also hoped to enlist men in the ranks who would constitute a reserve to the regular army; it is too early yet to say how far this Territorial Force will prove of real military value. In the Punjab the people who have come forward are the people who already belong to the martial races, and who ordinarily serve in the army, and they include a good many men who have actually served in the army.

In Madras there is also some keenness, because there are certain military traditions of the old Madras Army still surviving. That army deteriorated in military value since the early days of the East India Company because it was not recruited from the more robust cultivating classes from which the old army used to be drawn, but it was filled more from townsmen. Apart from these two Provinces the response is not great and the material differs from that which was contemplated. It remains to be seen whether these newly-organised forces will eventually prove to be a defence or a danger to internal peace.

At the back of all these defensive forces are 60,000 British troops, of whom perhaps 55,000 would represent the number of effectives at a given moment, representing about one man to 6000 of the population. If you consider the area and the population involved it would seem almost a miracle; yet it is accomplished simply because of the universal belief in the power and justice of the King-Emperor's Government. If you took away all your British magistrates and your British police superintendents the whole fabric would be shattered from top to bottom. If you rob them, by slower but insidious means, of their authority and reputation, and their power to protect the victims of violence and extortion, this belief will slowly but surely be undermined. Unhappily this process has begun, to the wonderment and consternation of the many millions who understand where their best interests lie, and to the foolish joy of a few hundred political megalomaniacs who seek to undermine this power. Certainly, if they succeeded, their joy would be short-lived, for they would be the earliest victims of the flood of anarchy that would submerge the peace of the whole country.

In the early months of the War, when British troops began slowly and mysteriously to disappear from one cantonment after another, Indians with any stake in the country became seriously alarmed. They said: "What is to happen to us; if the white troops go the Sepoys will certainly loot us?" They were proportionately overjoyed when, after a short interval, Territorial battalions began to arrive.

To-day, some fourteen years later, Mr. Sriniwasa Iyengar and the younger Nehru throw out a challenge: "Take away your white troops," they say, "we do not want them!" But the challenge would die away on their lips to a faltering whisper if there were any sign of their being taken at their word. Their enemies, if they have any, could wish them no worse fate. A wilderness of ballot boxes will not solve this problem.

The peace of India, both on and within her borders, can only be maintained by resolute men—British and

Indian working together to maintain it. Pacifist Indian politicians sitting in British security may subscribe to the outlawry of war as an instrument of policy, but this will not make the people of India outcast force as an instrument of plunder and revenge.

Let me add one more test to those explained in Chapter VI.

The intelligentsia of a country should be its leaders in war as well as in the lawcourts and in debate. In India it is not so. The pen is theirs; but not the sword.

CHAPTER IX

THE PROBLEM OF THE INDIAN PRINCES AND CHIEFS

The Relation of the Indian States to the People of British India—Their Relations to the Paramount Power—Quandary of the Princes in their Attitude towards Reforms in British India—Subordination of the Princes to an Indian Congress of British India would be Pure Annexation and Futile

THE Indian princes and chiefs can hardly be expected to transfer their allegiance from the British Crown to a collection of political notables drawn from various provinces of British India just to please the ambitions of Swarajist orators, any more than the barons who owed allegiance to the Plantaganet kings would have agreed in those days to bow their heads to a body of burgesses and attorneys. The barons belonged to the same jurisdiction as the burgesses; the princes do not. The political notables, on the other hand, appear to think that the princes are most unreasonable in demurring to this somewhat cheerless prospect. The whole vexed question is at present under investigation by Sir Harcourt Butler's Committee. The importance of the matter cannot be exaggerated, since the States together make up about a third of the total area and contain more than a fifth of the population. Their relative antiquity and status vary greatly *inter se* but not in any close ratio to the areas and populations of each State. Many of the smaller States owed allegiance to former rulers whose territories lapsed to the British Crown for want of heirs. This was the case, for example, with the States of Chota Nagpur, the Central Provinces, and Orissa, and the recognition of some of the petty States in Kathiawar and Central India was probably an accident of their geographical situation rather than a deliberate decision upon the merits of their importance. These petty chieftaincies swell very greatly the number of the States, and had they been all of this description the problem might not have been such a serious one, for their case would not have differed materially from that of privileged landowners holding on a feudal tenure to be found in every province of India. But inasmuch as these petty chiefs have been recognised as falling outside British India, they must be included within the category of the princes and chiefs, and their case has to be settled as part of the major problem of the Indian States. The treaties and engagements made with the various princes and chiefs from the time of the East India Company and onwards require several volumes to contain them, and there are besides other volumes of political practice which enumerate and interpret the precedents according to which their relations with the paramount power have been regulated, from the earliest days up to the present time. To place the great Indian feudatories of the Crown under the kind of government which Indian politicians envisage would not be justifiable on any ground whatsoever—legal, moral, historical, or political—and could only be effected by force, a course of action which, besides being unthinkable in the light of their services to the Empire, would be absolutely futile. Nobody but a Russian Bolshevist would ever contemplate such an action. Individual princes or chiefs may have been unworthy, and some have been deposed, passed over in succession, or permitted to abdicate in order to save themselves from further disgrace. The power to take action against grave and wide oppression, or against serious crime, is a necessary reservation to the paramount power. It never has been, and never will be, exercised capriciously or lightly, but the princes are naturally anxious that their rights should be thoroughly safeguarded against the risk of such action. Whether or not the subjects of these States have detested a particular ruler who has acted tyrannically, the overwhelming majority of the people who live in them have the greatest respect for the ruling house, and would view with deep resentment the humiliation of their ruler by his subjection to a heterogeneous crowd of the lawyer-politicians of British India. As to the princes and chiefs themselves, they are protected against foreign powers, against encroachments by each other and against internal rebellion, and they have absolute confidence in the honour and good faith of the British Crown and the King's Viceroy. With them the expression " The safety, honour, and welfare of our Sovereign and his Dominions" is a phrase that is real. It may be that their loyalty and their self-interest are on the same side, but there are many people in this world with whom the self-interest is supreme and the loyalty nominal. In this matter as aristocrats, whatever their private feeling, they follow the doctrine of *noblesse oblige*; they have no fear of the British Government of India while it is thoroughly British, though they may have their grievances, for which they ask a fair hearing. What they do fear is lest a British Government, ever more and more diluted with the Indian intelligentsia, should find itself slipping so fast down a dangerous slope that it will pull them down with itself. The princes *are*, and are proud to be, part of the British Empire; they are *not*, and they do not wish to be, part of British India.

Their relations to the paramount power, and their relations to each other, are not such serious problems that they are not capable of adjustment. The princes may be asking for more independence and less interference than is desirable in the interests of their subjects. In these matters, with their own advance in education and enlightenment, and with greater contact with the outside world, they have for a good many years past deserved and been receiving increasing consideration, and they would do well to recognise all reasonable limitations on arbitrary or oppressive conduct by individuals of their order. It is indeed in their own interests to do so, since in the world of to-day unchecked enormity of some particular besotted despot might involve in the downfall the privileges and repute which as a body they enjoy.

The real problem of the princes concerns their relations with British India. Though they are outside it, geography cannot be denied, and there are points both of contact and conflict. It is not impossible to provide for joint deliberation reaching agreement between the princes and the Executive Council of the Governor-General. Although the Viceroy has been his own Foreign Minister, yet there have been important matters concerning the States which have been referred to the Executive Council. In my own five years' experience of that Council such cases were rare, nor can I recall any instance in which the action approved by the Viceroy met with dissent in the Council. There were besides a good many cases in which the papers were circulated for information rather than for decision. But to talk of joint consultation between the princes and the Legislative Assembly, or a committee of that body, is quite another affair. Voluntarily it might be feasible, but any such consultation which carried statutory or constitutional authority would be entirely out of place. British India and the princes must meet on a foundation of diplomacy; Parliaments do not negotiate with Foreign Powers, and for the purpose of negotiation, the Indians of British India and the princes are *inter se* on the basis of States foreign to one another. If the Princes or any of them proved so unreasonable or obstructive that the paramount power had to step in, with its authority, it would have to be the Viceroy acting as the King's Foreign Minister in India and appointed by the Crown that would exercise that authority. Directly the Executive Council became responsible to an Indian Legislative Assembly instead of to the British Parliament it must cease to take any part in the control over the princes. There is nothing unreasonable at all in the claim of the princes to be outside the authority of any semi-demi-democracy, or pseudo-democracy that may be set up in India, but the pressure that is being exerted on them to that end is not pressure by their own subjects but by the political intelligentsia of British India, the leaders of which are mainly lawyers hailing from Bengal and Madras, Kashmiri Pundits from Allahabad, and a few other Swarajist firebrands. Neither the landowners nor the commercial classes have any wish to subject the Indian States to their authority, but the agitators of British India, who are so foolish as to take Russia as their model, are busy trying to infect the intelligentsia inside the States with doctrines subversive of the authority of the princes, and it was for this cause that special legislation had to be certified by the Viceroy in order to protect the princes from attacks by the more respectable journals and blackmail by the disreputable. A friend of mine happened to get into conversation with a young Indian in a South Kensington Museum. The young man began to talk rather big about Swaraj, and my friend (who had spent thirty years in India, but did not at first impart this information) listened in wonderment. At last, on the Socratic method, he asked: " But are there not Indian Princes in India, and would they not have something to say about it?" " The Princes," replied the young man, "will not remain. We shall pull them off their thrones and set them to do coolie work." This was too much for my friend, who said: " I think you're mistaken, young man. I happen to know some of the Princes, and I cannot imagine such as you pulling them off their thrones." " Have you been in India yourself?" said the Indian. " For thirty years," said my friend. And the Indian became more subdued. This man was a subject of an Indian State, and the Bolshevist agitator had clearly been at him. Indian politicians have now formed a separate organisation, called The Indian States People, with headquarters in Bombay. How many of the subjects of the several States living in the States are taking an active interest in this new organisation, and whom they represent in doing so, is not clear, but the principal enthusiasts who pull the strings appear to be people interested in similar activities in British India. The general tendency of the Indian Press presents the usual " consistent inconsistency," so characteristic of these organs. The Government of India will be blamed in one breath for interfering too much with the independence of princes and chiefs and in the next breath for interfering too little. As wise people the Government of India have to pursue the straight course, as they see it, without regard to these erratic counsels. There are, however, certainly two points on which the subjects of States, whether they are able or not to voice their grievances, should receive protection. The first is that the princes should limit their private purses to reasonable provisions, and devote the balance of their revenues to public administration, and the second is that they should take measures to improve the quality and independence of their judiciary.

Self-governing institutions of a democratic nature are just as unsuited to the people of the States as they are to the people of British India. A virile and benevolent prince can do infinitely more for his people's welfare than any oligarchy of place-seekers, and the two are incompatible. The prince should have an honest and capable Diwan and a body of well-selected counsellors round him, men who have a stake in the prosperity of the State, and not a body of professional politicians. Certain States have initiated compulsory primary education, but how far the compulsion is real or nominal is open to some doubt. Compulsory education at the last census had been in force for over fifteen years in Baroda, but at that census it was found that there were more literates per mille. in British Guzerat than there were in Baroda. Schoolmasters will put pupils on the school roll who seldom attend except when they are whipped up for the benefit of an inspecting officer, and the fact that education is compulsory is no guarantee either of its excellence or its durability. In any case, something much better than the primary classes in rural schools is necessary before the rural population can become really competent voters. Although a few intellectuals may aspire for political power in these States, there is no emigration from the States into British India such as to suggest that the subjects of the Indian Princes are in any way dissatisfied. Naturally the Marwaris of Rajputana, the greatest traders and bankers of India, have spread themselves all over the country, for it would be impossible for them to find a livelihood, or complete scope for their talents, within the four corners of the States. Again, such industrial centres as Bombay and Ahmedabad will certainly draw people from the States as well as the various provinces of British India. But there are plenty of people who move from British India into the States, and the net gain at the last census from all these movements was only 125,000 in favour of British India. If we look at the vastly greater opportunities for employment that British India can offer the gain is exceedingly small. Further, the people who are best educated in English will also naturally find more scope for their talents in British India.

An exchange of territory is not popular among border villages concerned in such exchange. The villagers on the British side of the border do not sigh for incorporation in the adjacent States because they think there is less security there from official exaction, but neither do the border villagers of the States relish being transferred to British India, for they say: " You may have better law there perhaps, but you have too much inspection."

The innate conservatism of the people no doubt causes them to dislike any such changes, but the notion that anybody outside a few agitators would migrate into British territory in search of political privileges is fantastic. I have myself spoken many times to the people living on these borders, and am speaking from personal knowledge of their attitude. All migrations that do occur are for economic reasons, except in the few cases in which some particular family, having incurred the displeasure of a chief, thinks it prudent to remove itself for a time until the trouble has passed by.

In rare cases, when famine is abroad, or when there has been some local disturbance, people may fly across the border into British territory, but it is those very exceptions which prove the rule, that under all average circumstances the subjects of Indian princes are content with their lot, and there are numberless features about the paternal administration of a good chief which are particularly attractive to the Oriental mind.

It must, however, always be remembered (and this is a point which is sometimes overlooked by princes who complain that their subjects are made to pay taxes to British India through the Customs at sea ports) that the peace enjoyed in these States is no less the result of the Pax Britannica than the peace enjoyed in British India. If the rulers of the Indian States had been subject to foreign attack, or been permitted to make raids upon one another, then the local taxation for military forces and military expeditions would have been infinitely larger than anything the people contribute in the shape of Customs. In that case, also, there would have been serious disturbances which would certainly have led to exodus on a large scale from disturbed States to adjacent British territory.

The princes and chiefs of India are in a serious quandary. Instead of stating boldly that democratic institutions are quite unsuited anywhere in India at all (and that of course is their real opinion) they feel constrained to say that they welcome democracy in British India, but that it is not suitable in their States. There are two reasons for this attitude on their part. First, they hate being pilloried in the Indian press as antiquated despots and Rip Van Winkles, and find it preferable to utter liberal sentiments with regard to other Indians in British India. The second reason is that in order to gain Parliamentary support in their present difficulties it seems good policy to appear as enlightened as possible, by professing a platonic affection for democracy over-the-way. But princes can be enlightened without believing in democracy as an institution; they can believe in justice and humanity; they can preach it and practice it to their heart's content, not merely without forfeiting their claim to the preservation of their ancient status but enormously thereby strengthening that claim. A State administered by a model ruler, who spends his time and resources on the comfort and happiness of his subjects, and purifies his administration, is a much more beautiful thing under the Indian sky (possibly also under other skies) than the wrangling of many politicians for place and power. Democracy as an institution has, so far as it has been tested, succeeded best among the Anglo-Saxons and Scandinavian races, among the French (where, however, it is much tempered by bureaucracy), and in very small countries like Belgium, the Netherlands, and Switzerland. It should find a spiritual home in Germany. Outside these countries and races it nowhere seems to produce stability, and it may anywhere develop into a corrupt and accursed thing. History is always slow in disclosing her secrets; it is only on the day after to-morrow that we begin to understand the day before yesterday. Only a dreamer in an armchair can believe that a peaceful settlement of the Indian States could be attained by making them as a class subordinate to a Parliament of Indian politicians. It would be pure annexation of the States by British India, and just as futile as would be a declaration at Geneva that Greece must be deemed to have annexed Turkey and the Balkan States. It is only the British Raj that can keep the Indian States and British India under a joint control. But what need have we for further evidence, for the princes have spoken with no uncertain voice?

Since this chapter was written, the report of the Butler Committee has been issued; but I leave the chapter as it is.

CHAPTER X

THE PROBLEM OF THE EUROPEAN AND ANGLO-INDIAN IN INDIA

If India could exist as a Self-governing Dominion the Effect on the Europeans in the Services, in Missions and in Commerce—Effect on the Welfare of the Anglo-Indian to whom Education on British Standards is vital to their Continued Existence as a Community

If the British race in India ceased to be dominant there and India were to be self-governing some very serious problems would arise in regard to Europeans and Anglo-Indians. The British element in the Services would virtually disappear, except for a few adventurous people and rolling stones who did not object to insecurity of service if it could be compensated for in other and dubious ways. So different is the Englishman from the Indian that even if India remained in law a part of the British Empire the British in the Public Services there would be virtually foreigners, and the same would be the case with commercial men and missionaries who continued to do business in the country or carried on their labours there.

It can easily be imagined that once the British Government had granted Dominion status to India, and had shed its responsibility for the maintenance of law and order within the sub-continent, it would be extremely chary of interfering with the democracy that it had set up in its own place. Just as other Dominions have restricted the ingress of Indians—and their right to do this has been repeatedly affirmed—so would India as a Dominion insist upon similar restrictions upon white entry into the country. Conditions might, we may agree, be laid down for the preservation of the rights of white British subjects, resident in the country at the time that Dominion status was conferred, but laxity in carrying out these agreements, both to the letter and in the spirit, might be very difficult to prove, and still more difficult to control. The planters in Assam were in a very uncomfortable and indeed dangerous position at the height of the Non-Co-operation movement, and if this were the case when the British Government of India was still in full control over the magistracy, the police, and the army, it is not difficult to see how dangerous would be the position of such planters if these authorities were themselves in a hostile mood. The British Government would make protests, which would be met by fair words and piecrust promises, but the obtaining of redress and protection would become so difficult and costly a business that people like these planters would find it to their advantage to cut their losses and clear out of the country. One cannot live as a stranger among masses of people whose attitude has become hostile; there would be hundreds of men coveting their tea gardens, and even if a civilised system of law and justice nominally existed, men could be so harassed by false charges that their control over their labour force would be gone. Later on, in its proper place, I shall give reasons for affirming my belief that no such democratic constitution could come into existence in India, or, if it did, could survive for more than a very few days; but for the moment I am assuming that India had become a self-governing Dominion and indicating the probable result to the European and Anglo-Indian of any such political development.

The missionaries might for a time continue on the same footing as they do in China, but with the exception of Southern India, where Christianity had a footing long before British rule began, there would be serious risk that their flocks might melt away, and that fair treatment and grants which the missions had enjoyed with a Christian Government in power, might be curtailed or withdrawn on various pretexts. Large numbers of very poor people and aboriginal tribes have been attracted to Christian baptism because in the white padre sahib they had a champion and protector who carried some influence with British authorities, and was ready to help them against unjust treatment by a non-Christian landlord or an overbearing policeman. That particular urge towards Christianity would be lacking, and there would be a steady draw back again to the ancient faith. There have already been Hindu movements to get back into the fold of Hinduism the children of converts to Islam. I have been shown a letter written by a Christian missionary to his father, a parish priest in England, which gives a sad picture of the persecution of his converts by a Hindu landlord in a district where all the higher district officials are Indians. The writer does not accuse them of any direct responsibility in the matter, but makes it clear that unfriendly neighbours with the removal of British supervision have at once become emboldened to adopt a policy of pinpricks and petty persecution, with the result that to avoid such troubles, as having their crops grazed down and their cattle unlawfully impounded, there has been serious defection in his flock, for which he can hardly hold them to serious blame. That letter was written by a witness of truth, it was not the exaggeration of an excited alarmist; it recited sober facts in confidence to the writer's father, and the facts which it told were just those which anybody who knows the country and the mentality of the people would expect to occur.

The wonderful work accomplished by the great Christian missions in India has been accomplished mainly under the aegis of British justice. The Government has taken no hand in proselytisation and Government servants have held deliberately aloof from any part or lot in the Christianizing efforts of these missions, but they have sympathised with and gladly assisted missionary efforts towards education from the village school to the college, in regard to medical relief and institutions for the blind and the leper, in times of famine and distress, and in all the noble work of uplift of the poor, in which the missions, small and great, are perpetually engaged. As long as the missionary spirit prevails in the Christian communities of Europe and America men and women will be found to obey the call, no matter who governs, but it is obvious that the change of the Government from Christian to non-Christian control must have very serious effects on the missions. It is quite true that missions have been shown considerable courtesy and kindness in many Indian States for the good that they have done, but the States are themselves under the influence of British political control, and they would not permit themselves, or be permitted, to outrage the decencies of toleration in respect of benevolent missions. With the departure of British control the whole position would be changed everywhere throughout India. Untoward incidents might have results which involved anti-Christian outbreaks; the missions would be at the mercy of anti-foreign movements. On the other hand, missionaries might find themselves in conflict with Hindu or Mahommedan authorities, and be tempted to encourage their communities to resist orders or actions of which they passsionately disapproved. A few, but very few, missionaries even under the British Government, have been led into the path of Indian agitation inimical to the Government, and their aid in such circumstances is warmly welcomed by agitators, but if, under the change of masters, they were led into any similar trespass upon political ground, the consequences would be disastrous to the welfare of the missions. Accusations of this kind are made at times against Christian missions in China. I do not profess to be able to say whether these were justified or exaggerated, but they are obviously more probable under a non-Christian than under a Christian government, and this position would certainly arise in India. It cannot be denied that the number of Christian converts in India overwhelmingly consists of poor and humble people. The Indian Christian intelligentsia is very limited in numbers, and very few Indian Christians have large possessions, or influence, or political power. Unless something marvellous should occur, such as the conversion to Christianity of large numbers of influential high caste Hindus, it is exceedingly improbable that the community would carry any serious weight in the councils of a self-governing India. At all events, outside Southern Madras, Travancore, and Cochin, it is a great deal more probable that, taking the Christian point of view, there will be more perversions than conversions in all the cases that I have been considering.

Large European commerce is mainly concentrated in the Presidency towns and a few other centres, and it is possible that business and trade would continue to be carried on in such places, as they have been in China, or at the main seaports in foreign territory, but in so far as that commerce is concerned with mines, factories, or plantations in the interior of India it would be subject to all those disabilities and dangers which I have already indicated. In any case, great difficulties would arise in respect to the administration of justice and the working of laws and regulations and customs duties, which commercial men acquainted with China can recognise for themselves.

In all the cases that I have been considering I have been dealing with those who have no permanent domicile in India, and could if they so desired, though not without grave loss or inconvenience, withdraw entirely from the country. I come now to those who have a permanent domicile in it, and to whom the consequences of an unsympathetic government in purely Indian hands would be even more serious. There are, of course, a few people of pure British stock who, encouraged by the protection of British rule, have made permanent homes in India and have settled in good climates, but the great majority of the "domiciled" community, as they are termed, are the people of mixed race who were universally called Eurasians. Since 1911 this community's desire to be known as "Anglo-Indians" was officially accepted at the census. The term [1] is appropriate to men who have British blood in their veins, but it is quite

[1] Owing to the confusion with the older meaning of the word, *i.e.* Englishmen who had lived a long time in India, the revised use of the term has been somewhat inconvenient.

ridiculous as applied to men of mixed Portuguese and Indian stock, most of whom are indistinguishable from Goanese. It is almost impossible to arrive at an exact figure of the true number of Anglo-Indians in the country, for some Anglo-Indians have returned themselves as Europeans, where the mixture of Indian blood has been slight or remote, while, on the other hand, many non-British Eurasians, as well as some Indian Christians, have adopted British names and numbered themselves among Anglo-Indians. The census of 1921 returns the number of Anglo-Indians as 113,000, but allowing for the tendencies towards misclassification, and for census increase, I should say that 125,000 might be a fair estimate of their number, a pitiful little fraction enough among 320,000,000. The number of these to be found in rural areas is quite trivial; they are concentrated in the Presidency towns, Rangoon and a few other big cities, at railway settlements, and at hill stations where the best schools for their children are to be found, the small balance being scattered over the headquarters of districts where they still hold a few clerical appointments. These people of mixed blood were not well treated by the British in the early days when our rule was in process of establishment, but as the consolidation of the Indian Empire progressed, they were extremely useful to the British community, and they have always been consistently loyal to the British Government. They filled a great many clerical posts in the Government offices, and were naturally of the greatest use in the telegraphs and the railways, and as guards, drivers, and workshop hands. Members of this community rendered the finest service in the Mutiny, and in all the strikes and troubles engineered by Indian agitators. Large numbers of them were found in the Volunteer Corps, and are now in the Auxiliary Force, which is the lineal successor of those corps. There are probably only 30,000 male adults all told in the community, very few of them are possessed of any wealth, and they look for employment to Government service and the railways. There is a sprinkling of them in the various provincial Civil Services, and they hold responsible posts in the Opium and Salt Departments, in the Customs, Survey of India, in the Police, and in the Medical Department, and there are many in the Forests and the Public Works. In the large European shops and stores they are employed in considerable numbers.

There are individual Anglo-Indians accepted as Europeans because the Indian strain was somewhat distant and their fathers or grandfathers were of sufficient means and status to send them home for education, where they took up occupations or professions without question as Europeans. A few men like these are to be found among the officers of the Indian army, in the higher services, and occupying other positions in commerce or private enterprise. But apart from these there are a number of Anglo-Indians employed in the various provincial services who have given a very good account of themselves in the charges that they have held. The Indian Medical Department is a Department in which as Military Assistant Surgeons deputed for Civil employ they have shown special merit,[1] both as District Medical Officers and as Jail Superintendents. They have also contributed many excellent public servants as Magistrates, Subordinate Judges, Revenue Officers, and especially in the Forests. But the generality of Anglo-Indians are poor men, who have to content themselves with subordinate positions and with posts in what are called the ministerial services. The competition of Indians has each year become more severe, and it is only by special care of the Government of India and the Local Governments that they have not been shouldered out of this class of appointment altogether. They have been a very valuable asset to the British Government, and though naturally as being a mixed race they have

[1] A Senior Officer of that Department did most wonderful work as a Plague Officer. People flocked to him for inoculation; they brought their womenfolk, expectant mothers, to be inoculated, from distances of thirty or forty miles. Two whole regiments of Indian infantry who could not be persuaded to be inoculated by their own medical officers were inoculated by him to a man, with their wives and their children.

some weak points, their British connection and their religion save them from all temptations to succumb to the pressure of agitators, who are ready to undermine if they can the loyalty of Indians in Government service. Anglo-Indians are by statute and definition "natives of India," and as such are entitled to a proper share of those appointments in the Public Service for which they may be qualified. But would they get these under a purely Indian Government? That is their great fear and anxiety as they see Indianisation increasing year by year.

The Indian politicians say: "If Anglo-Indians will acknowledge themselves to be sons of the soil, children of Mother India, they will be treated with every consideration by us." I have heard Indians in high position say this. I have heard them say that in the matter of education European and Anglo-Indian schools will receive grants on the same footing as Indian schools, viz. the same capitation grant for the Anglo-Indian pupil as is given to Indian schools for the Indian boy. To British ears in England nothing could seem fairer spoken, but Anglo-Indians do not believe these promises and they are not worth what they appear to be. "You are asking for privileges, not rights," say the Indians. "We offer you equal rights, but no privileges." The offer means that these descendants of British fathers, who have shown fidelity to their origin and to the British cause, must give up these loyalties, must Indianise themselves; must abandon their mode of life and their standards of comfort, poor as it is. With all this lowering of status they must nevertheless manage to compete educationally with the Indian, and they must take their chance of being selected for posts on Indian rates of pay among hosts of Indian competitors. No one will deny that the Anglo-Indian community has, like other communities, its faults. As a community they are improvident and too fond of display, because their pride in their British blood is greater than their worldly means can support. They lack energy in the plains, but they do not lack it equally in the hills.

Are their children now to be deprived of the benefits of schools in the hills, of competent European and Anglo-Indian teachers teaching them in their own language and their own religion? If pure-bred British children were always kept in the plains they would languish and die. The indigenous blood of the Anglo-Indian helps him perhaps a quarter of the way to stand the climate, but it stops short at that, and the Kalimpong Homes prove that if the Anglo-Indian child is well trained in a good climate he can make good. It is no wonder that the Anglo-Indian is gravely perturbed at the course of events in India and the prospects looming before him. Will his undoubted qualities secure him in a Swarajist India the position that he holds to-day? Will he have the same opportunities? These are the doubts with which he is assailed. Even now he feels himself slipping; with what possible confidence can he view the future?

You have only to mark the signs of the times to perceive what is likely to happen. Indian legislative bodies are already cavilling at the rates of pay of Anglo-Indian engine drivers and guards, and are anxious to push them out of these employments, in which they shine, and replace them by Indian drivers and guards who are able to live at much lower rates. These bodies have also shown a tendency to restrict the grants already made to European and Anglo-Indian schools. One would have thought that if there was a spark of generosity in these politicians they would have gladly passed the comparatively small sums which these institutions draw from the public revenue. The fees in these schools are much higher than the fees in ordinary Indian schools, and the European community contributes to the taxes sums greatly in excess of that paid by the average Indian taxpayer. Moreover, for considerably over a century the great missions have, with the aid of the parent bodies which support them in Europe and America, contributed large sums for the benefit of the education of Indians. None of the missions have confined themselves exclusively to the care of the children, or the sick, or the poor, of their own communities. The British Government has been scrupulously careful not to use its authority in the past to make lavish grants to Christian educational institutions for the benefit of their own race and kin.

An Association has been formed in London, with a Calcutta Committee to help it, for the improvement of European Schools in India, and these are the facts it gives. (1) There are in India 443 Schools for European and Anglo-Indian children. (2) There are in these schools over 42,000 boys and girls. (3) Of these 42,000 children some 15,000 are orphans or destitute. (4) The schools are maintained from the following sources:

(*a*) Endowments - - - - -	4·4	per cent.
(*b*) Subscriptions - - - - -	26·1	„
(*c*) Government Grants - -	31	„
(*d*) School Fees - - - - -	38·5	„
	100	„

The parents of these children are all poor, for none but the poor would keep their children in India. If European education had not been maintained as a reserved subject these grants might have been seriously curtailed. In the Bishop Cotton School in Nagpur some years ago (and it is probably the same now) the fee per child in the primary classes was Rs. 5 a month. The Indian parent could send his child to a primary school for Indians for the monthly fee of one anna (an eightieth part of the other!) Numbers of the Indian intelligentsia, or if not they their fathers or their grandfathers, have owed their success in life to the education they received in mission schools and colleges, cheaply, efficiently, and to a great extent as a labour of love. Yet some men of this class to-day, aspiring to be called enlightened statesmen, are bent upon cutting down the grants to these 42,000 poor children. One might think that Great Britain had never conferred a single benefit upon India or Indians; that Europeans had never subscribed to hospitals, leper asylums, and famine relief for poor and destitute Indians; that the European and American missions had never poured money into the country for the better education of the Indian boy and girl. Yet I have found Indians as individual men the most generous and grateful of persons for kindness shown to them. And this is only one more instance to show how far Indian politicians are from representing in their politics the virtues of their fellow-countrymen, and indeed their own virtues as individuals. It would be a lasting disgrace to the British name and fame if the British abandoned their own people—and they are their own people—to the tender mercies of those who are seeking to wrest political power and place for their own class and race. The only chance for the Anglo-Indian is a good education under competent European supervision and in healthy surroundings. Then they can make good. But if they cannot have these things then they will go down and down, until they become submerged in the flotsam and jetsam of the great Indian cities.

Anglo-Indians have approached the Simon Commission for special representation on the Councils. No general electorate will ever worry about their rights or their grievances. Theoretically they should be represented; practically the maximum representation they could possibly be given would not turn the balance by a hair in a legislature overwhelmingly Indian. That is the hopelessness of calling things by their wrong names, and mistaking communal ambition for democratic nationalism. British supervision is the only safeguard so long as this communalism lasts. Neither the European nor the Anglo-Indian has any desire to be governed by an Indian oligarchy whose motto they fear is likely to be: "*Parcere superbis et debellare subjectos.*"

CHAPTER XI

THE SEPARATE PROBLEM OF BURMA

The Land and its People—How Dyarchy came to Burma—The Working of the Reforms in Burma and their Results—The Separation of Burma from India—The Complete Immaturity of Burma for Self-Government

(i) THE LAND AND ITS PEOPLE

NEVER was a country and its people more untimely ripped from the womb of political future progress than Burma and the Burmese, when Mr. Montagu, with his magical midwifery across the Bay of Bengal, started to disturb them from their placid contentment. What a country, what a history, what a people!

A country beautiful and varied, rich in its potentialities not yet fully explored, varied in its mountains and its valleys and its plateaus, its mighty rivers, its teeming deltas drenched with torrential rainfalls, its dry zones brown with frequent droughts, its wonderful forests, and rich with its rice, and its oil, and its teak and its timbers, its silver lead, its tin, and its wolfram.

A history, tragic, despotic, sinister, murderous, with its tortures, its outrages, its cruelties, its sieges, its forcible conscription, its forced depopulations, and its forced colonisations; its formidable stockaded towns, to be assaulted with the spear, and the sword, and the matchlock, and to be defended with these and with boiling oil and stinkpots, while those without died in their numbers, scalded and pierced and trampled on, and those within, if the stockade fell, were put to the sword—men, women, children, and holy monks, or crammed into wooden cages and burnt alive. Yet amongst all these horrors the creed of the peaceful contemplative Buddha was diluting animistic passions and gross superstitions, and every height was crowned with a pagoda, and by every village a monastery, and every man went through a novitiate, even if it was only for twenty-four hours. Such was the history of Burma from the time of William the Conqueror and before, and almost down to the Jubilee of Queen Victoria.

From all these centuries of misery and rapine, and kings who interlarded cruel despotism with pious pagoda building, and sometimes irrigation works, there has emerged a people of indolent men and industrious women, merry, laughing, loving bright colours and silk raiment, furiously addicted to gambling and wagers; loving their pony races and their canoe races; never tired of watching their all-night plays, when the star actors come on at two in the morning.

The people are artistic, yet with no small taste for mechanics; hospitable, humorous, squandering any money whenever they make it, a people of cheery spendthrifts, with scarcely a miser among them. They are literate, but with the elementary teaching of the monastic school, filled up with the musty but honourable precepts of old, which they cannot interpret in their daily lives; anxious to "acquire merit" for pious work and by filling the begging bowls of the mendicant Pongyis, but caring little for secular charities; accustomed to a royal court with no aristocracy, to princesses galore, but with no princes to wed, for all the spare princes were massacred like litters of puppies as the strongest prince became king in his turn; accustomed to governors who were given no salaries with the title of " Myosas" or " Eaters up of the Town," and whose minor officials followed the same example. No wonder that they included a government as one of the great calamities, ranking it with flood, and fire, and epidemic. In spite of their Buddhism, fearful of evil spirits and "nats," tattooing themselves against bullets or as charms and mascots to secure to them prowess and victory; torn in a moment with gusts of violent passion, using the *dah* [1] on the smallest pretence, attracted by the novelty of the

[1] The Burman's great knife.

hour, and then throwing it away like a discarded toy. People with no caste and almost no social strata; the women emancipated, pretty when young, neat and bedecked with flowers, excelling as saleswomen, economical as housekeepers; the men loving the excitement of the dacoity, loathing the discipline of the soldier, enunciating high ideals and neglecting to follow them without perceiving the failure, full of dash and boasting, but apathetic in continuity of effort, despising the foreigner, yet imitating his vices, so attractive yet lacking all ballast, so capable of combination and yet so unstable; tolerant of their own and each other's sins, no one trying to be his brother's keeper. And among them all there move austere and holy monks, and some who are neither holy nor austere, for the yellow robe has become too numerous for discipline, and any monk when he chooses can renounce his vows and rejoin the world and become a layman again, free to do all he pleases.

It is wonderful how from such a history there has emerged such a people. Perhaps there have been just two causes—one was the influence of the yellow robe, and the other the attitude born of the troublous times inculcating the principle of " Eat, drink, and be merry, for to-morrow we die," for if the violence of kings comes and goes like a tornado of fire it is best to be merry in the quieter days between.

It is from all these mixtures of causes and consequences that we find the Burmese people as they are to-day. There was nothing democratic beyond the village fence, and nothing aristocratic beyond the capital and the court, and the capitals changed with almost every king, and the inhabitants had to move with them.

As the hush of the Pax Britannica, following all this chaos, gradually extended over the land, from Victoria Point to Mitkyina, and from Akyab to Kengtung, the people gradually settled down to a life of peace, leisure and amusement, tempered now and then with a little toil. Such intervals for quiet had been merely peeps and interludes for a period of nearly a thousand years.

After the annexation of Upper Burma, in 1886, there were some five years of dacoities and guerilla warfare, for Burmese soldiers had always been predatory conscripts, living on the spoils of the land through which they had marched and on the loot of the conquered city, if haply it fell. And after these five years the peace of the country was disturbed only by dacoities, the heritage of the old instincts of plunder, in which the young village bloods often join just to win the hand of a sweetheart, for there are yet girls who will not look at the suit of a young man who has not won his spurs as a dashing dacoit.

For thirty years after the last annexation all the movements and agitations going on in India did not flutter a single Burmese dovecot. What did they care for Indian Swadeshi movements, and politics to them were nothing at all. The old Hlutdaw, the councillors of the Burmese kings, had all been appointed by the monarch to transact such business as the capital required. But if ever they thwarted the monarch's own pleasure they were locked up for the night, sometimes in stocks, till they thought it better to change their minds. It was not till the middle of the nineteenth century that Burmese officials were paid any salaries at all, and the last "regular" massacre of the princes took place in Mandalay in 1879, with an aftermath in 1884. The victims were put to death to the accompaniment of loud music to drown their cries, lest these should reach the ears of the British Resident. During these last thirty years also the only other events to disturb tranquillity were revolts among the tribes on the frontier, and the pathetic, almost comic opera, risings in the name of some exiled princelet, or someone claiming to be a reincarnated hero who tattooed a small following to secure immunity from bullets and marched out with high hopes of conquering the country. The first body of military police that they came across the tattoo failed, and the rising was at an end.

The inhabitants of Burma do not consist only of Burman Buddhists, though these form some 70 per cent. out of the

13 million who live within its borders. These are the only people with nationalist feelings, but they too have amongst them some marked divisions. In Arakan, shut off by the Arakan Yomas, the Arakanese have for many centuries been specially connected with Chittagong, and a great many have an admixture of Indian blood in their ancestry. There, too, the women are less emancipated and there also are remnants of untouchable classes. The Burmans of Upper Burma are the truest Mongolians, and look down on the Burmans of Pegu and Rangoon as too much infected with the ways of the despised Indian Kala (foreigner). Then there are the Talaings, remnants of another Mongolian group. These were known for some centuries as the Peguans. Pegu and Ava were constantly at war, and the Talaings were eventually almost exterminated. Many took refuge in Siam and in Tenasserim, but there are still a good many families left in the Delta, who, under British rule, are able to flourish.

And then there are the Shans, resembling the Siamese, who held dominion over all Burma when the Pagan Dynasty broke up, for the last king of that dynasty brought in the warriors of Kubla Khan from China when he wantonly executed in cold blood all the members of a Chinese Mission which had been sent to his court. It was 170 years before the Burmans recovered their ascendancy, but the Shan chiefs remain in the East of Burma, and though themselves British subjects rule over a country of great potentialities, though with a population too thin for its proper development. These also have their separate language, but between Shan and Burman there are memories of sword and fire.

Then there are the Karens, the Animistic Karens of the hills, of the wild Karenni States, and the Karens who wandered down into the Delta, of whom some have become Buddhists, but most are ardent Christians, and these dread the Burmans and fear them, for they were oppressed and downtrodden before British rule, and these too speak their different languages.

And then there are the tribes on the West and North-West, and to the North and North-East, the Chins, the Kukis and the Nagas, in the Upper Valley of the Chindwin, and the Kachins, the Marus, and the Lisus, and many other tribes by the head waters of the Irrawaddy, who dwell in the No-Man's Land of Burma, Tibet, and China, and whose names and whose dialects seem to change every few miles. And these have lived in their hills and valleys since the dawn of history. And on the borders of the Eastern Shan States there are many other tribes, Palaungs, and the Wild Was still head-hunters, all Animists, propitiating their demons, nats, and evil spirits. These are all the peoples of whom geographical Burma is the homeland, but there are yet many others.

In the big seaports, in the Delta, and at centres scattered over the whole country there are colonies of Indians and Chinese, and mixtures sprung from the marriage of Burmese women with Chinese and Indians, and Danes and Portuguese and French and Germans. There are Anglo-Indians and Anglo-Burmans, as well as Armenians and Jews of Baghdad, and there are great missions, French, Italian, and American, besides those of British origin.

The Indians in Burma have been derived from three sources—first the Indian traders of adventurous trading classes, Hindus and Mahommedans, who came to the seaports to ply their commerce; second, the Indians who were brought away in whole masses from Manipur and Assam when the more powerful Burmese kings raided Manipur and Ahom and brought back whole populations as captives to their sword. Amongst these the Brahmins became Burmanised Brahmins, and prepared horoscopes and calendars for the Burmese kings, and the artificers plied such crafts as they might, and all the humbler captives became pagoda slaves. The remnants of these colonies have flourished under British rule, under the name of Ponnas, and these are now asking for separate representation under the reforms. Third came the Indians who followed the British flag into Burma. They include all sorts and conditions of men from every part of India, officials and clerks who came over to man the departments and offices when the Burmans were not forthcoming to do the work. There also came for the military police, Sikhs, Punjabis, Gurkhas, and Hindustanis, and these and other Indians are also found among the civil police in Rangoon. And the traders and moneylenders came from Madras, Guzerat, and Marwaris from Rajputana. In Rangoon and the Delta you may find the Chettis who lend money, and the Madrasi Brahmins, and the Naidus and Pillais who man the offices, and there are many butchers from Madras in Rangoon, and turbulent Pathans from Peshawar, and all the milk-sellers of Burma are Indians who keep herds of milch cattle near the largest towns and penetrate the interior right into the Shan States. And among the Indians in Rangoon will be found Indian intelligentsia, commercial and professional, journalists, and a few politicians and lawyers, who before Mr. Montagu came were more interested in their professions and their amusements than in the political future of Burma.

And last, but not least, we must mention the British, with their trading corporations, their teak, their great mining enterprises, their oil industry and their rice milling, and by their capital and their industry they altered the face of the country. And besides all those in the Army and the Services there are the lawyers and doctors, and the bankers and the business men.

And all these together make the Burma of to-day.

(ii) HOW DYARCHY CAME TO BURMA

The first stirrings of political life in Burma followed the first echoes of the proposals to make India a self-governing country; for to Burma the idea of subjection to an Indian democracy was *anathema maranatha*. A deputation went across to Calcutta to explain their fears to Mr. Montagu and Lord Chelmsford, with the result that the Montford Report left the question of reforms in Burma to be settled in whatever way was found suitable to the genius of Burma and her peoples. For Burma was forty years behind India in her political growth, and distinct in her origins, her races, her religion, her habits, her languages, and her sentiments. The author took over the reins of the Lieut.-Governorship of Burma just about the time of that deputation to Calcutta.

It was after the midsummer of 1918 that the Montford Report was published, and the Lieut.-Governor was directed to prepare a scheme. The scheme devised after the fullest consultation with all the interests concerned was not dyarchy but was designed to give Burmans the best opportunity for training in the exercise of responsible functions. No sooner had the scheme been promulgated for criticism than, largely at Indian instigation, the Burmans of the Young Party, now just nascent, with difficulty raised some £2000 and despatched three representatives to London. The scheme submitted by the Burma Government was forwarded to Simla in the spring of 1919, but the Government of India were too pre-occupied with their own troubles in the Punjab and Afghanistan, and with hurrying through their own Indian reforms, to be able to spare much time for the affairs of Burma, and the scheme submitted remained in a state of suspended animation for nearly one year. In the meantime the ardour of the young Burmans began to increase in strength, and when the Indian reforms were before the Joint Select Committee of Parliament they induced that body to hear one of their number. During this interval the Secretary of State had begun, knowingly or unknowingly, to queer the pitch for the Burma scheme. I have no official cognisance of what Mr. Montagu said to these three Burmans, but I know what the Burmans cabled and wrote concerning the statements alleged to have been made to them by Mr. Montagu. These statements were such as to encourage the agitation and induce them to demand a scheme at least as advanced as that given to India. The Joint Select Committee heard one Burman, a junior member of the Rangoon Bar, and also one Karen, whom the Karens had hastily despatched to England to see that the Burman delegates did not steal a march on them. On the strength of these witnesses the Select Committee included in their Report the following sentence: "After hearing evidence the Committee have not advised that Burma should be included in the scheme. *They do not doubt but that the Burmese have deserved and should receive a constitution analogous to that provided in this Bill for their Indian fellow subjects.* But Burma is only by accident part of the responsibility of the Governor-General in Council. The Burmese are as distinct from the Indians in race and language as they are from the British."

I yield to no one in respect for the members of a Select Committee of Parliament, but even Solomon had his off moments. If the Select Committee had omitted that sentence which I have put in italics they would have said all that the occasion required, for they were not dealing with Burma at all. They took no cognisance of the fact that the Burma Government had been ordered to prepare special proposals, or the fact that the Government of India's recommendations, which were indeed not formulated until seven months later, had not been received, and on the meagre evidence of two inexperienced individuals they committed themselves to a consolation prize for Burma and uttered that *obiter dictum* which finally queered the pitch.

Dyarchy itself was so unique and strange a bird that to find a constitution that was not dyarchy but analogous to it certainly passed the wit either of the Burma Government or of the Government of India. It was not until many months later that the latter sent home their own modified scheme, but when the parcel was opened the bird inside was dead. For in all this long interval the Burmans had raised funds for a second visit of the deputation, and the agitation had gone to a pitch when acceptance of the original scheme, at one time so probable, had passed out of the range of practical politics. Committees were formed in London, the first of which had upon it no single man with any knowledge of Burma; and, at a later stage, when two Burma administrators were brought into consultation, little attention was paid to their opinions. That famous abracadabra "responsible government" had an easy walk over.

The Burmese deputation returned back to Burma in triumph, having won for Burma the same reforms as for India, and expected to be crowned with laurels as victors at a public meeting convened to welcome them. But alas for their hopes! They were looked coldly upon, for the demand had now risen for something much better than despised India had been given, in fact for complete Home Rule. At the meeting this motion was carried with amazing enthusiasm by a hall packed with women, monks, students, and schoolboys, to 95 per cent. of whom the terms "Dyarchy" and "Home Rule" might just as well have been Hebrew words. "Ho' Ru" became a Burmese word and was passed round the villages, with their mushroom associations, so that at the first elections under the new reforms a voter wanted to record his vote for "Maung Ho' Ru," for the intelligent fellow thought that the man to vote for at the election was Mr. Ho' Ru, and that his ticket was a cheap passage to a millennium. There was nothing further for the Government to do than to make the best of a bad business, and go through all the processes for the new constitution. Sir Frederick Whyte and his Committee performed the functions of the Southborough Committees in India, and in due course the spadework was over and the new reforms in all their beauty arose from the foam.

That is how dyarchy came to Burma.

(iii) THE WORKING OF THE REFORMS AND THEIR RESULTS

During the interval between the despatch of these deputations and the introduction of the reforms, Gandhi's Non-Co-operation movement was being freely imitated in Burma. One of his lieutenants came over there, and his speeches and private instructions were potent in fanning the flames. The Indians flattered Burmese vanity, and the Burmese claimed the movement as their original idea, labelling it "Non-Participation." The Burmans have a genius for organising associations (Athins), which spring up like mushrooms in the night. While the toy is new the funds flow in, but when they tire of the toy the funds dry up. But for a while their boycotts catch on rapidly and penetrate into many villages. The Buddhist Church itself gave no approval, but its authority over numbers of the yellow robe has lost its power. Under that robe there shelter criminals and coiners and other bad characters who scandalously violate the vows of their order, and to these have now been added seditious agitators. In olden days the Buddhist archbishop could call in the aid of the secular power to enforce its discipline and its penances, but the British Government can no longer employ the methods of Burmese kings and order a holocaust of pestilent priests. Some of these men, mostly young, but a few old renegades of the order led them, vigorously backed up the boycott campaign, and their religious exhortations were full of sham politics, and their religious texts garnished with vulgar obscenity. Yet are there left, however, many of the old order who follow humbly the ordinances of the Lord Buddha and live their lives of piety and renunciation. The ostracisms of the boycotters became so merciless and persistent that the Burma Government enacted an Anti-Boycott Act which made criminal intimidation an offence cognisable by the police and rendered penal the incitement to a political boycott. This stayed the menace, and has been employed at a later date to combat the no-tax agitations which followed the introduction of the reforms. The stress of the boycott faded away. Even before that Act the boycotted university had emerged triumphant, and the attempted boycott of H.R.H. The Prince of Wales was a complete fiasco, for as soon as the intimidators were suitably dealt with, all people welcomed the Prince with whole-hearted enthusiasm.

With the institution of the reforms the new Minister for Education, formerly one of the leaders of the boycott, as a gesture of conciliation ordered the recognition of all the new national schools—good, bad, and indifferent. That it would have been necessary to recognise the best of these had all along been foreseen, but this wholesale reception of all these unrepentant prodigal sons was a measure which lacked those sound principles which had hitherto always characterised our administration.

Among the older generation of Burmans, the Elders as they are called, there are many endowed with shrewdness and strong commonsense, but in the last few years the young political bloods have thrust out all their authority, and the positions of the Elders and the young men have been wholly reversed. The British in Burma have always been a little kind to the virtues of the Burmans and a little blind to their weaknesses. Before the reforms the staunchest supporters of Burman merits were the British members of the higher Civil Services and the leaders of European commerce. There is no place where racial feelings were less noticeable than in Burma. The people were so attractive that the Europeans loved them in spite of their faults, and minimised their deficiencies. For, indeed, Burmans have always been the spoilt children of the East. But with serious responsibilities committed to their irresponsible hands they have failed to make good. At the Bar, in the professions, and in higher commerce they have never been able to compete successfully with other races, and good-natured efforts to bolster them up have merely resulted in offering a premium on inefficiency.

The Burma Government's Report on the working of the reforms is the most lenient of all, and its "constitutional" charity has covered up a multitude of sins, including some of its own misadventures. No inkling is given of the dry rot that is going on below the surface and of the corruption and embezzlement that distinguishes the sphere of local self-government in the Boards and Municipalities. These latter are in this Report passed over in silence, but it is a silence that can be felt. The Government has only functioned with the aid of the nominated officials, the other nominated members, and European and Indian supporters, but for whom its state would have been parlous indeed. The real question of Burmese fitness for self-government and for any sort of responsibility is wholly obscured, for it is only the foreigners on the Legislative Council that have saved the Legislature and the Government from a serious breakdown. One of the two Ministers is a Chinaman, and the Burmese member of the Executive Council is a Burmese Christian who has spent many years out of the country. The methods by which the " Golden Valley Party " of a few Burman supporters of the Ministry were kept together are not disclosed, and the Chinese Croesus that led that party, so warmly commended by the Burma Government in its Report, of him it can only be said that his affairs are *sub judice.* Even the Burma Report has to refer to cases of obstruction, walks out, attacks on the police and the forests, but it piloted itself through these difficulties with the aid of committees, of which half the members were nominated, supplemented in many cases by experts from outside. It is necessary to go outside the Government Report, to other sources of information, to find a real picture of the working of the reforms. From some notes of an experienced observer I learn that "in Rangoon Municipal elections are a farce; in the European and Chinese communities there is genuine choice; among the Burmans personalities alone count, and the candidates usually arrange among themselves such withdrawals as are necessary to avoid a contest. The Hindu community is dominated by the coolie vote; the leading labour contractors can always get themselves or their nominees elected. The first thing to be done is to stuff the register of electors with names like Yenkaya, etc. Telugus seem to have few names to go round, and no one but a Telugu can distinguish one from another. The next item in the programme is to ensure that on the polling day a vote is cast for every name on the register. Coolies are brought up to the booth by motor lorry loads, and are furnished by the agents of the contractors with a ticket giving their name, their numbers on the register, and their addresses. They are then carefully coached in these names and addresses and sent in to vote. The only hitch in this procedure that sometimes occurs is that they often don't know—their preceptors have forgotten to instruct them—the name of the candidate they are supposed to vote for."

He shows that two men can return any candidate in any election for the Hindus. Much the same occurs in the case of the Mahommedans. One man can direct the vote of the lower class Chittagonians. Shopkeepers, traders, landowners, etc., are dominated by an important market and land-owning company. The observer goes on to say: "So far as one can see, short as has been the experience of elections, it has been enough to teach the Burmans thoroughly all such vices as bribery, intimidation, and personation. The last is rife and it is impossible to stop. In the districts at the last Legislative Council Election intimidation was rampant. The Pongyis were the principal offenders, but every party that had the power to intimidate opponents used it freely." He goes on to cite some notorious instances of bribery. Even on the Rangoon Corporation only the presence of an I.C.S. commissioner, a strong contingent of European and nominated members and the failure of Indian and Burman cliques to combine, enabled the business to be carried on. Burmese and Indian Councillors belong to the same grade as the subordinates on the staff. Intrigue is rife and discipline hard to maintain. Appointments which are made by the Corporation give rise to the most acrid exhibitions of communal and racial feeling. In the opinion of this observer the Secretariat is top-heavy, and is constantly being reinforced by new appointments, permanent and temporary, which draw all the best men from the districts. The districts are starved and are going from bad to worse. The advertised decrease in crime is partly the result of "fresh classification." Cases wander about the Secretariat from secretary to secretary, and between members and ministers, while orders tarry.

This observer sums up by the following: " The root of the evil is that no minister or member will ever tackle any question of difficulty, or pass any final orders, if he can possibly shirk doing so. If the Governor remains 'constitutional,' what can this system end in? I say little of the communal and party pull, which is always active, but the nominal rulers will not rule, they will only temporise and delay, or hold up the papers until a crisis develops; then the orders issued are those issued under the influence of panic." Of the Rural District Boards he writes: " It was impossible to get Burmans to serve on these until it was found that they would have money to dispose of. Then school managers and teachers came forward, and now run most of the Boards. The outlay is called 'expenditure on education.' "

I cannot say whether this picture is too sombre or no, but it accords with the news that comes over from many different sources.

There is another document, which has been issued in public, the Memorandum placed before the Statutory Commission by a recently-formed "Association of Professional and Business Men in Burma." This Association, with members of all races, determined to show the Statutory Commission that some people besides professional politicians had a case to be heard, for the Burma Chamber of Commerce was necessarily only concerned with commercial interests. They quote from the Burma Government's own previous Reviews of the work of Municipalities and District Councils, passages which show gross abuses, corrupt practices, and embezzlements. As an example, "the acceptance of high tenders for public works from untried contractors on the ground that they were Burmans." Of elections they tell the same tale of malpractices as those described by the observer whose remarks I have quoted. They cite a specific instance of gross incompetence and dishonesty on the part of the officials concerned in the Rangoon Co-operative Dairy Society, which though liberally subsidised by Government and the Corporation, was bankrupt within a year. They add that the

Municipalities outside Rangoon are equally bad. As to the Legislative Council, they find them at the mercy of small party cliques whose supporters control certain unintelligent sections of the community, while the village voters follow the instigation of political monks. The class of member that seeks seats on the Council "is often composed of junior Advocates or Pleaders in poor practice, or of men who have made no particular mark in some other walk in life." They add that "experience shows that in practice it is from the ranks of such men that ministerial appointments have to be made." The Association then proceeds to comment on the "notorious" reputation of Burma "as the most criminal province in the Empire." In 1926 the total number of criminal cases was 134,109, equal to one person in every 100 in Burma. There are over 800 murders in a year, and the Tharawaddy District, with under half a million population, can show more than half the number of cases reported in England and Scotland. Attacks on Europeans have increased, and the Association gives instances of desperate criminals at large, and shows the serious weakness in the administration of law and justice. In its opinion this deterioration is due to five causes: (1) Reluctance on the part of courts to convict on capital charges; (2) reluctance on the part of witnesses to come forward and give evidence; (3) provisions in the Code of Criminal Procedure amended by the Indian Legislature hampering the work of the police; (4) the haphazard appointment of Government prosecutors with less regard to their ability than to their nationality and race; (5) the prevalence of corruption amongst the subordinate officers of the Police, the Judicial Service, and the Magistracy.

The Association then proceeds to cite instances of the irregularities and waste and frauds in the administration of the finances of the local bodies, and they extract their evidence from the Reports of the Audit Officers of Government. They draw attention to a loss of public funds entailed by subservience to resolutions of the Legislative

Council. In compliance with the resolution of that body the Local Government against expert advice endeavoured to bolster up a Spinning and Weaving Company with Burmese capital and management by granting it a loan of Rs. 15 lakhs at 6 per cent. interest. The loan was guaranteed to the extent of Rs. 7½ lakhs by the Directors of the Company. At the time of the loan the Company's accounts showed that the business was being run at a loss, and the whole of the 15 lakhs was required to pay off an existing mortgage on the Company's assets. The business continued to be run at a loss, and the proceedings of the Legislative Council of the 14th February, 1927, disclose that the Company was no longer able to carry on or meet the interest on Government's loan. The proposal was made and carried that Government should take over the Company's properties in full satisfaction of the 16½ lakhs then due for principal and interest, and that (despite the objections of the Accountant-General that the proposal offended against elementary canons of financial propriety) the guarantors should be relieved of all personal liability. The Audit Reports do not disclose the further losses incurred, but eventually Government had to sell the Company's assets, suffering a heavy loss in doing so.

On the assumption that this Association did not put up its representation without solid grounds, it can only be said that the Reforms have provided a sure method of teaching the Burmans how to regard their mistakes as successes. It is surely evident that the reforms have failed; that they were given to a people immature and unfit, and that the benevolent *obiter dictum* of the Parliamentary Committee has proved to be a curse rather than a blessing.

Burma had been governed first by Chief Commissioners and then by Lieut.-Governors on standards which tried to secure honest administration. With the grant of the reforms and the introduction of a "constitutional" element into the Government these standards could no longer be maintained, and the miasma of corruption is rising upwards from the ground.

The task of the present Governor of Burma is a hard and thankless one, if the evils that have arisen are to be combated aright. The people who have had control under this sort of "responsible" government have been the kind of people who make profit for themselves, and if the poor and ignorant should become dimly conscious of suffering they will only blame the Government for putting them under such a system.

(iv) THE QUESTION OF SEPARATION FROM INDIA

It is a political accident that Burma has come under the Government of India. As a race they are distinct in every way. There were always some Indians in Burma, for the Buddhist religion had come from India via Ceylon, and in very early days had triumphed over an effete Brahminism. Burma had been a bad neighbour, so far as the land boundaries permitted, and by the depredations in Chittagong, Manipur, and Assam, of the different kings, by their refusal to abide by any international comity, arrogant refusals to give compensation, and ill-treatment of British subjects, they brought upon themselves each step of annexation that fell to their lot. At each stage British administrators were brought in to administer the newly-conquered country, and Indian subordinates were required to fill the offices until such time as Burmans could be qualified in their place. The Indian Government had borne the cost of these wars, and had to continue its subventions through several years of guerilla strife, as well as to supply the bare necessities of communications and buildings. It was, therefore, only natural that the Government of India should administer Burma. But the Government made the mistake of supposing that Burma was just one of several Indian Provinces. She was a provincial child, but she soon became a step-child. When she was poor she was treated with a certain liberality, but as she began to grow rich her contributions to the step-mother became fatter and fatter, while she herself, in spite of her increasing resources, remained thin and ill-nourished. The Government of India did not perceive any injustice, because on paper they treated her on the same lines as her Indian sisters, but they did not realise either the extent of her contributions or the fact that what was left to her did not suffice for her needs. For example, a contract figure of 80 lakhs a year allowed in her budget for public works seemed to compare favourably with the contract figure of other provinces, but if that sum be translated into miles of road and cubic feet of building its miserable inadequacy is at once made manifest. The great size of the province, the nature of the Delta, which contains no good stone, the thinness of the population, and the necessity for importing labour from a thousand miles away by land and sea, imposed conditions which made statistical comparisons wholly unreliable. The Meston Award was not ungenerous to Burma, and her finances were thereby vastly improved, but that improvement was almost entirely swallowed up by the huge expense of increasing the pay of all establishments that the high post-war cost of living in Burma rendered essential. As a maritime province, Burma is self-contained and her Customs relate to her own consumption. With no caste prejudices and social restraints she imports foreign commodities in much larger bulk. She contributes on rice and petroleum sums out of all proportion to her population. She resents imposts justified by Indian conditions which do not apply to her. She is not interested in paying high tariff rates for assisting Indian industries which do her no good. The result of this is that while she contributes so largely to Central revenues the Central expenditure within her borders is by comparison small. The large expenditure on the defence of the North-West Frontier of India does not vitally interest a different country more than 2000 miles away. This surplus derived from the Central revenues in Burma is required to make good deficits in the Central revenues derived from other provinces. She may be forgiven if she thinks that 307 million people in India should bear their own expenditure and not take from her 13 million inhabitants, a larger sum than is fair to her interests in the Central Government.

Her few representatives on the Legislative Assembly, though their support may be useful to Swarajist wreckers, are of little benefit to her in securing her own needs. Just as Indians in Burma fear subjection to a government by Burmans, so do the Burmans in Burma fear subjection to a government under Indian control. European commerce is drawn two ways.

As long as the Central Government in India is controlled by the British, and if financial relations are reasonably adjusted, it is better for Burma to remain under India's wing. But the Burmese could not, would not, and should not consent to become a vassal state of a Nehru's commonwealth.

But if Burma was separated from India she could not become a self-governing Burmese State. Her military forces, her military police are not Burmans, her prison warders, her clerks, her post-offices, her labour force are largely manned by the Indian races. In her capital, Rangoon, there are 190,000 Indians, or nearly 60 per cent. Her captains of industry and her richest men are almost entirely non-Burmese; her women mate freely with men of other races, her men hardly at all with foreign women. She could neither defend herself from foes without nor maintain order within. These 9 million Burman Buddhists with 4 millions of other races, by no means friendly to them, would have 300 million Indians on the one side and 400 million Chinese on the other, as well as her hereditary enemy, Siam, whose ancient capital, Ayuthia, Burma raided and besieged time after time and finally sacked and burnt. Under the British Raj penetration by all her neighbours is yet peaceful; but outside it she would fall to the invaders around her whom with her racial pride she would rashly provoke. Her men have fighting qualities for guerilla warfare, and enlisted well during the latter part of the War; but in peace time they cannot bear the discipline and routine and desert; and the Burman has virtually disappeared from the Army, for the solitary Burma Regiment is composed of Karens, Kachins and Chins, and one company of Sappers and Miners is the sole contribution of 9 million Burmans to the Indian Army.

The Burmese proper have a strong national feeling. There is no country with less marked extremes of poverty and wealth. The poorest can rise to the highest positions. There is no hereditary aristocracy. Birth is of little account. Surely here was ideal ground for democracy; and yet Burma, beautiful Burma, with all her cheerful people, so radiant in gaiety, so feckless in purpose, taking no thought for the future, must be born again before she can enter even the Dominion of Home Rule. The explanation lies in the want of moral fibre, and Acts of Parliament are powerless to supply it. It must be a plant of local growth.

PART II

POLITICAL DEVELOPMENT IN INDIA UP TO THE WAR, DURING THE WAR, AND AFTER THE WAR

CHAPTER XII

LOCAL SELF-GOVERNMENT IN INDIA

Observations based on the Author's own Experience—Confirmed by Latest Reports of the Local Governments—Absence of a Civic Spirit after Long Trial—Grave Deterioration that has resulted from Control by Politicians

THE co-operation of the people in the administration of municipal affairs had been invited for many years before Lord Ripon's day, but it was during Lord Ripon's Viceroyalty that the principle was seriously extended to rural areas. It has met with some varying degrees of success and many glaring instances of failure. In the municipalities limited powers of taxation were given; in the rural areas such powers have even to this day been very sparingly conceded, and, if conceded, reluctantly used. Nomination played an important part in the early beginnings of these new institutions, but election was continuously extended, and the powers and duties of the local bodies were from time to time amplified by new legislation and by increased rule-making power under the various Acts. Naturally no single man can have first-hand experience of the progress of urban or rural self-government except in those parts of India where he has been in personal contact with local bodies. In my own province (the Central Provinces) I was for many years in close touch with these bodies, and, having studied many reports and reviews of other local governments, and compared notes with administrators from other provinces, I have formed certain general conclusions which are, I believe, not unfair deductions from the knowledge so gained. There was one advantage in the Central Provinces (backward as they were reputed to be), namely, that from the first the practice prevailed in the larger municipalities and the more advanced District Councils for the local body to elect its own office-bearers, though the local government retained the power to appoint a nominated official or non-official chairman if election had been working very badly. In this respect the Central Provinces were more liberal than many of the older and larger ones where the District Officer (Collector or Deputy Commissioner) was generally *ex officio* chairman.

I must make it clear, however, that the conclusions that I have formed do not directly relate to the large corporations of the Presidency towns and Rangoon, where conditions more closely resemble those of European cities, where there are large contingents of European (and in Bombay, Parsee) commerce, and the Indian population includes a good many modern business men. In these also proper rating systems can be put into force, and there is a better informed public opinion in civic affairs. There are also at such places Chambers of Commerce, Port Commissioners, and Improvement Trusts which exert an influence that is almost entirely lacking in all but a few inland towns. Further, there is the concentration of wealth in these cities which has enabled the corporations concerned to pay for more highly-qualified executive officers and professional and expert services, as well as better-trained inspecting officers. Lastly, there is in these cities a more powerful European Press to bring public opinion into the realm of action. Even so, there are many complaints in these cities of excessive talking and too little effective administration. Most authorities would probably give the palm for businesslike work to Bombay, while Calcutta is reputed to excel in excessive deliberation. Having had no personal contact with the working of the corporations of the Presidency towns I do not venture an opinion.

It is, however, common knowledge that even these bodies have not been able to dispense with the services of a selected Municipal Commissioner, generally a member of the Indian Civil Service, to be the chief executive officer of the corporation.

However this may be, the success or failure of local self-governing institutions over the length and breadth of India cannot be deduced from any results obtained in the Presidency Corporations; their conditions are altogether special.

To return first to municipalities. The revenues of municipal towns have been generally insufficient for any high standard of administration, and Municipal Committees have always hankered after grants from Provincial Revenues for schools, hospitals, and water works. They dislike all kinds of direct taxation, and much prefer octroi and terminal taxes, as well as market and bazaar dues. Besides disliking direct taxation they hate taxes which rise above a very low maximum, and their graded taxes are generally fairly stiff on the poor and inadequate on the rich. I have had, in various capacities, many struggles with municipal bodies in efforts to induce them to adopt a more equitable scale and system.

Not so long ago one could find a town of over 100,000 people with a total municipal revenue of not more than £30,000, a sum which does not go very far. In the smaller municipal towns resources only suffice for the employment of low-paid and not infrequently corrupt executives and clerks. These municipalities varied very greatly in efficiency, but in my observation the whole machinery depended on the personality of particular men. One of the most efficient presidents I knew was a Hindu landowner, who knew no English, but was a thoroughly shrewd and commonsense man, greatly respected by all. On his death the presidentship passed to a well-educated pleader, of advanced political views, and the efficiency of the municipal administration rapidly declined. In another case it was a shock to find that in a district supposed to be specially advanced in education and politics the municipality had become almost bankrupt; the roads were quagmires; the public latrines tumbling down; taxes in large arrears; and members of the Municipal Committee among the greatest defaulters. One among these had not paid the ground rent due to the municipality for ten years. There is undoubtedly in some towns more civic spirit than was formerly the case, but it is a plant of very slow growth. Parties are divided not as Progressives or Reformers and so on, but by castes, or races, or, as often as not, as adherents some of a Montague and some of a Capulet. Persons count much more than policies, and the electors will go on time after time electing the same men, however useless and negligent they may be. Since political reforms have been granted, political shibboleths have more and more intruded into municipal matters for the purpose of election, to the great detriment of efficiency. Sometimes, however, extreme politicians have steadied down and done well. I was talking to a number of townspeople one day who were complaining of the bad condition of the town and of the manner in which municipal members were furthering their own instead of municipal interests. I said to them: "The remedy is with you. Why not elect better men next time?" They said: "Sir, there are no better men. Anybody we elected would act just in the same way as these." I said: "Well, you people always ask for government by elected representatives." They replied: "We never asked for them, it is you who put us under these men." These were days when communal representation had not even been thought of. To-day it is the constant cry.

I come next to rural local self-government as conducted by District and Local Boards. Here the trouble has been that the pleaders and townsmen, who were the leading men in the District Board, were very chary of delegating powers and allotting funds to the Rural Boards, and as most of these people on the District Board seldom or never went out into the district the touch of local knowledge was often lacking. Some of the members of the Local Boards showed a great deal of interest in their circles, but their responsibilities were very limited and their recommendations frequently ignored by the District Board. My constant endeavours in the case of rural areas was to obtain a greater degree of independence for these local men, who had a much clearer understanding of what was required in their areas than the pleaders at the headquarters of the district, who had little time to spare from their professions to devote to the interior of the district. The District Boards had at that time no powers of taxation, and their revenues (apart from the land cesses which they neither assessed nor collected) were comparatively small. Consequently they were largely engaged in asking for and spending extra grants given them by local governments. These men were generally very keen on education, especially on Anglo-vernacular schools, or English classes in vernacular schools, but they neglected communications, and it was seldom possible to entrust them with any but unimportant roads. It is true that these local bodies were in most districts struggling with insufficient resources, but in the districts where their resources were much larger they had a tendency to accumulate balances instead of spending them on development. On the other hand, local self-government has had no lack of help and encouragement from District Officers and Commissioners. These authorities have always tried to help these bodies out of difficulties, to stimulate and applaud every real effort and every success obtained, and to be as lenient as possible to defects. The reviews of the various local governments have been similarly indulgent, and if ever unfavourable comments on account of apathy or neglect have been absolutely necessary, great emphasis has been laid on such good points as could be discovered. Such expressions as " Signs are not wanting, however, of a greater interest or an improved public spirit," are generally to be found in these reviews, and this remark is followed by some individual case of merit specially singled out for commendation. I used to read these expressions of hope forty years ago, and I still find them appearing in the latest reviews that

I have seen. Latterly District Boards have been given, in most provinces, a limited power of taxation, of which they are not at all keen to avail themselves.

In the last ten years these local bodies have been given greater independence, and in the Non-Co-operation period many of them spurned aid and resented any advice; as to interference, it was not attempted. I do not think that any impartial person could say that these experiments in local self-government have been an unqualified success, either in themselves or as a training ground for higher responsibilities. It was sometimes a great pleasure to observe real keenness here and there, but proportionately disappointing to find that with the death or retirement of a particular man interest flagged and apathy returned. Often the man who did try his best made enemies of those whose ill-gotten gains he checked, until at last he gave up the struggle.

In these matters it is very difficult to strike the happy mean between leaving people of this kind entirely to their own devices and propping them up too much with outside control and initiative. It was one of the chief tasks of our administration to find that mean, and it was a most interesting study in men and in measures. The great trouble has always been that one cannot find that sense of public spirit, either in the men who elect or in the men who are elected, for which we are for ever looking. There are always exceptions to every rule, and both municipal and district fund administration have had some shining lights, but the lights shone because of the men and not because of the system. The best men have not been the most highly educated, and not many of those in the front of the higher political fray won their spurs in the more humble but perhaps more fruitful field of local self-government, and many who have taken the worthiest part in this humbler sphere, especially in the practical work of it, will find no place of honour among the politicians of to-day. The recent access of the communal spirit is doing no good to these institutions and is further retarding the growth of the civic mind. Until we can find more members rendering service on these local bodies for the sake of what they can give and not for what they can get, improvement tarries.

In case it may be thought that my own touch with this subject is out of date I suggest a perusal of the latest reports of the various local governments in India dealing with local self-government under the reforms. They bear date 1927, and were prepared with an eye to the investigations of the Simon Commission. The Madras Government, which is obviously seeking to make the best of unsatisfactory material, can only bestow the faintest praise. The Bombay Government emphasises that communalism has neutralised all progress. "Wealth," they say, "is of minor importance. The tendency of those who have the biggest stake in the country to stand aloof from local politics is in some places a regrettable sign of the times. Hitherto the increase in the electorate has not led to any marked change in the constitution of the local bodies, the members of which consist mainly of the predominating castes of lawyers and fluent politicians." According to them the general cry is: "No increase in taxation." Only in Sind and in some districts outside Guzerat have these bodies agreed to some increase in taxation for the expansion of primary education. They add: "It may be taken as a rule that in local self-government the influence of one man for good or bad in the local Councils is the deciding factor between good and bad administration." There are, as usual, some brighter spots which the report mentions, and there is the usual comment that "there are some signs of growing interest."

The Bengal Report, which has also the approval of the Ministers, contains a most scathing condemnation of the Calcutta Corporation, under Swarajist management, and caustically remarks: "Until the administration is conducted in the interests of the inhabitants of Calcutta and not of a political party the chances of an improved administration are small." Of outside municipalities it wrote: "Generally speaking, it is correct to say that neither the standards nor the principles of municipal administration were affected by the working of the Reform Constitution." It adds that "Their transfer to the control of a Minister has made some of them less inclined than before to attend to the advice and instructions of Local Inspecting Officers."

The Government of the United Provinces opens with the statement that: "The general progress of both self-governing bodies in the sphere of local administration is not as satisfactory as should be expected. It would be easy indeed to cite instances of serious retrogression." It also notes with satisfaction some brighter spots, but is obliged to point out some very dismal ones. On the whole it tries to discern some improvement. It is the old story of the personality of the chairman rather than the interest of electors.

In the Punjab, District Boards still retained their official chairman. In the case of Municipal Committees, the withdrawal of control from within, which formerly prevailed, has been prejudicial to the administration. The intrusion of communalism has had a bad effect, and ministers in charge of local bodies have been divided between the policy of strengthening control from without and the policy of giving further independence, with the consequences that ensue.

The Government of Behar and Orissa are most emphatic in their condemnation of the effect of the reforms upon the local bodies. There is not in this case a redeeming feature. The only hope they express is that with the gradual replacement of Swarajist influence things might improve, but they wind up this part of their report on the reforms with the words: "But the most experienced officers of the province are not sanguine about the likelihood of improvement. The electors are too apathetic to combine, and their votes are generally secured by appeals to pecuniary, religious, and other motives. Meantime the misappropriation of public funds is generally regarded more as a subject for mirth or envy than reprobation, and it remains to be seen whether the successors of the existing Boards will be able to resist the temptations of the spoils of office."

The report from the Central Provinces is obviously trying to make its geese into swans, and to put a thin layer of whitewash on the darker colours. It has to admit, however, that: " The system of assessment and collection of taxes leaves much to be desired." It has to admit that: " The state of accounts of local bodies has, generally speaking, deteriorated." It discloses that: " The affairs of the local bodies are in a state of confusion." But in spite of all these things it is hopeful: " That when things have adjusted themselves to the changed conditions, a higher sense of public responsibilities will begin to assert itself." It is just lip optimism.

The Assam Government is also anxious to be as indulgent as possible to failings. It likewise deals in hopes rather than facts, though it too feels obliged to say: "A regrettable feature of the present administration of some local bodies is the laxity of supervision in account matters and the reluctance to take adequate action in cases of fraud or culpable negligence on the part of subordinates."

In Burma things are so bad that the Government of Burma is afraid to describe them and evades the issue. It will not wash its dirty linen in public. (See Chapter XI.)

The net result of all experience is that, after fifty years' trial, in the field of local self-government, though there has been some success due to the ability of particular personalities at particular times, there is an almost complete lack of the civic spirit. The men in office or power mostly use these powers for their own benefit, the men not in office expect nothing else but wait their turn. It is just what the citizens said to me in the case that I have quoted: " Sir, there are no others." The people understand private property well enough, but they do not understand public property, or that by injuring it they injure themselves. If they suffer under mismanagement they blame neither the people who mismanage nor themselves for electing them—they blame the Government, and the people who mismanage take good care to encourage that belief. The Government of

Behar and Orissa when they say that "misappropriation of public funds is a subject rather for mirth or envy than reprobation" have in a phrase explained the kind of spirit which has been vitiating all efforts to make local self-government in India a reality and a success. There is no public conscience. Public conscience is defective even amongst the most developed peoples—how can it be expected among the masses in India? And yet without a strong degree of public conscience responsible self-government becomes a mere farce.

The table below, attached to the Bombay Government's Report, tells its own story of what happened after Mr. Montagu began to disturb contentment. It is progressive deterioration shown statistically.

Year	Cases of Embezzlement of Municipal and Local Funds	Arrears of Revenue in Municipal Towns	Number of Municipalities with a bad record of collection
1916-17	3	296,555	7
1917-18	5	430,000	6
1918-19	15	406,000	7
1919-20	19	373,000	16
1920-21	30	504,741	19
1921-22	16	872,575	34
1922-23	38	1089,825	36
1923-24	40	1058,068	37
1924-25	51	1137,500	64

These figures relate to a total of 155 municipalities; and the first three years were pre-reform.

For the last two years only further information has been extracted, to the effect that in 1923-24 there were 10 municipalities in which Councillors refused to pay taxes or evaded payment. In 1924-25 the number of such municipalities had risen to 27. This is in the Province which prides itself upon being the most enlightened in India!

CHAPTER XIII

POLITICAL ADVANCE IN INDIA BEFORE THE WAR

Early Development of Constitutional Politics leading to the Morley-Minto Reforms—Mr. Gladstone's Caution—The Merits of the Morley-Minto Constitution—Movements outside the Constitution—The Development of the National Congress—The Growth of Revolutionary Movements—Their Origin and Consequences up to the Outbreak of the Great War

THIS book does not purport to be a history, and in this part of it I am merely sketching the course of political progress, and do not delve into the early history of legislation from the beginning of the East India Company to the assumption of the direct authority by the Crown in 1858. Chapter III of the Montagu-Chelmsford Report contains all this information for those who wish to study it. In 1861 Legislative Councils were created as Legislative Committees, to which non-officials, including some Indian members, were admitted, but except for the particular Bill put before them the Councils had no part or lot in the government of the country. It was not until 1892 that a fresh move was made, and the Montford Report (para. 66) describes accurately the change in attitude. Whereas in 1861 men said: "We'd better hear what a few Indians of our own choosing have to say about our laws." They said in 1889: "Our laws have positively benefited by Indian advice and criticism; let us have more of it, and if possible let the people choose the men they send to advise us." The first steps towards election on a very small scale were taken by the Act of 1892, the form being one of recommendations by local bodies and associations. In effect the Councils instituted in 1892 were advisory, but local bodies recommended some of the advisers instead of Government selecting the whole.

The next advance was initiated in 1906 and carried into effect in 1910 by Lords Minto and Morley. It is the fashion now to talk disparagingly of the Morley-Minto Reforms, but so Radical a statesman as Lord Morley considered them to be a very liberal advance. They gave non-official majorities in the Provincial Councils and left only a small official majority in the Imperial Legislative Council, but the method of representation was by classes and interests and not by territorial units. It was made plain by the authors of these reforms that they had no idea of introducing any democratic or British Parliamentary system into India. The whole idea was to give educated representatives of the country more voice and influence in shaping the policy of the Government than they had ever enjoyed before:

(*a*) By means of the right of interpellation, including supplementary questions by the interpellator.

(*b*) By full discussion of the budget.

(*c*) By moving resolutions.

I think that most thinking men agreed with the policy of those reforms. Although it is impossible to satisfy extreme demands, yet there were probably a larger proportion of politically-minded Indians at that time welcoming these reforms than was the case with the Montagu-Chelmsford scheme at the time that it took shape. Mr. Gokhale, for example, readily admitted that Government must have a majority on the Legislative Councils, both Provincial and Imperial, and after non-official majorities had been granted in the case of the Provincial Councils, speaking in 1913, not very long before his death, he pronounced that the next advance to be made was that the small non-official majority upon those Councils should consist of elected members instead of partly elected and partly nominated. Lord Morley had also taken a step which had not figured in the proposals sent round for discussion, preparatory to the Morley-Minto Reform Scheme, by admitting an Indian to each of the Executive Councils in India, and placing two Indians on his own Council in London. This step was very welcome to advanced Indian opinion, which had not expected it.

The despatch with which the Government of India submitted the proposals of Lord Minto's Government in October 1908 quoted remarks made by British statesmen in 1892, including those by Mr. Gladstone, who drew attention to "the danger of having persons who represent particular cliques, or classes, or interests, and who may claim the honour of representing the people of India." That despatch also cited the then recent utterance of His Highness the Aga Khan: " In India no such union as is essential to the creation of a strong, independent, homogeneous State is possible without centuries of consolidation. Even if we assume that the forces tending to unification are quickened by the machinery of modern civilisation, generations must pass before India is a nation."

Lord Morley in reply approved the principle of representation of classes and interests as necessary in India, and advocated the device of electoral colleges to provide for all minorities, and for linking up the more general electorate with a system of local self-government. These reforms were summed up in Lord Morley's own words as follows: " While repudiating the intention or desire to attempt the transplantation of any European form of representative government, what is sought by your Excellency in Council is to improve existing machinery, or to find new, for recognising the natural aspirations of educated men to share in the government of their country. I need not say that in this design you have the cordial concurrence of His Majesty's Government." Afterwards, in sanctioning the Constitution of the Imperial Legislative Council, Lord Morley laid it down that the Governor-General's Council "in its Legislative as well as its Executive character should continue to be so constituted as to ensure its constant and uninterrupted power to fulfil the constitutional obligations that it owes *and must always owe* (the italics are mine) to His Majesty's Government and the Imperial Parliament." (Montford Report. para. 76.)

The author was for five and a quarter years a member of the Imperial Legislative Council, by virtue of the office that he held as Home Member in the Governor-General's Executive Council. I took up that office in the last session of the first Councils elected under the Morley-Minto scheme, and I laid it down after the first session of the third and last Council under that scheme. I deny emphatically that it was a failure. It exactly secured the objects laid down by Lord Minto's Government and confirmed by His Majesty's Government for "recognising the natural aspirations of educated men to share in the government of their country." They had no right to claim more than this, and we had no right to give them more. They could not truthfully claim to represent any more than their own class, and we had no right to put the masses under their heel against their will and without their consent, or while they were nothing but minors quite unable to judge for themselves. Although the non-official members could not carry a vote against Government, they could and did exercise a most valuable influence upon the action and policy of the Government. It was a point of honour with Government to secure as many non-official votes as they could in support of Government measures, and to meet in a spirit of compromise every non-official resolution which had substantial non-official support. The Morley-Minto Reforms would have continued to hold the stage for twenty years or more but for the War and the appearance into power of Mr. Montagu, who brought to his task doubtless the highest intentions but founded his schemes not upon the solid rock of facts but upon a quicksand of mingled fallacies and dreams. I will endeavour to prove this statement in a later chapter, but in the meantime must include in this one some remarks upon the doings of politically-minded Indians outside constitutional bodies.

It was not until 1885 that the Indian National Congress was founded partly, if not mainly, on European inspiration. It was quite true that there was no public means except through the Indian-owned Press in which the more highly-educated men could give vocal expression to their rising aspirations. For a long time the Congress was merely an annual conference at which, for three or four days, subjects of public interest were discussed and resolutions passed, and then nothing more happened until the next Congress. In those days the Congresswala was rather a man apart. Most of the topics discussed were ideal rather than practical, and it can scarcely be said that they have lost these characteristics even now. The attitude of the Government was one of indifference. In its earlier years the sentiments of the Congress were not disloyal, and it afforded a useful outlet for the expression of opinions. Many of the most prominent figures in the early history of the Congress were men of moderate sentiments. As time went on, its organisation was improved, and it began to assume permanent instead of periodical activity, the Congress itself being supplemented by subsidiary provincial conferences. But the difficulty always has been that it simply adopted Western ideas and called for their immediate introduction in India regardless of their suitability or unsuitability to local conditions. Thus universal trial by jury, the complete repeal of the Arms Act, the complete separation of executive and judicial functions, the rapid Indianisation of the Services, were all counsels of perfection in the social, communal, and educational conditions of India. They sounded very fine as enunciations of high policy, but it was more sound than substance. We could move in some of these directions by cautious steps, perhaps, with pauses for rest, but the seven-league boots policy, for which they clamoured, was only fit for Utopia. The Congress was always calling for large reduction in taxation to be accompanied by huge increases of expenditure on their own pet objects. It may have been wise or unwise on its part, but it is scarcely a source of wonder that the Government of India never took the National Congress at its face value. As time went on the proceedings of the Congress began to take a stronger anti-British line. At first, like the more moderate Press, it had always been careful to emphasise its loyalty to the British connexion, though criticising in strong language the policy of the acts and omissions of the various governments or of particular British officials. The violent agitations that sprang up from time to time in various parts of India over particular issues speedily had their effects in the Congress, and its Left Wing, which included the most prominent seditious agitators, gradually strove for mastery in its deliberations. In 1907 a split occurred at Surat, and the Congress broke up in confusion. For eight years the extremist section remained outside, but from 1916 and onwards the extremists obtained re-admission and with it complete supremacy, and ever since then the Congress agitation has been simply seething with sedition, which the great concessions given from time to time have entirely failed to appease. The reason for this is simple. Each position conceded by Government is made the starting point for fresh and more extreme demands. The British public have no conception of the nature of these agitations. They wake up for a minute or two at the news of some special outrage, but speedily go to sleep again.

Of these agitations over particular issues the Ilbert Bill controversy was one of the earliest. Then followed the excitement over raising the age of consent from ten to twelve. Later on there were several anti-cow killing agitations, and the establishment in Poona of the Siwaji cult in which the leading spirit was the late Mr. B. G. Tilak. In 1897 an orgy of violent writing broke out in Bombay over the vigorous attempts made by the Government to stamp out the plague in Poona. This agitation culminated in the disfigurement of Queen Victoria's statue in Bombay and the murder of two British officers in Poona. Firm action was taken by the Bombay Government and the agitation subsided. The great efforts of the Local Governments and the Government of India to relieve the famines of 1897 and 1900 brought about a reaction in favour of Government, and the death of Queen Victoria in 1901 produced a genuine regret which was felt all over India at the passing of a sovereign whose long reign had been most auspicious, and whose constant interest in the welfare of her Indian subjects had been so often manifested. The sorrowful event had a striking effect upon peoples with whom reverence for great hereditary rulers is almost a religion. Her fidelity to the memory of her consort, which continued until her death so many years after, struck a particular chord of sympathy in the hearts of Hindus.

The better times that followed the famines in the new century were inimical to political agitation, just as bad seasons were wont to have the contrary effect. With the Partition of Bengal, however, began a new era of anti-British conspiracies which, starting in Bengal, presently spread their ramifications all over India, the Mahrattas of Poona being the most prominent in joining up their activities with the Bengalis. The effects extended both to Central and Northern India on the one side and to Madras on the other. This agitation over the Partition ushered in the Swadeshi and boycott movement, and with these came the first inclusion in the Congress programme of the term " Swaraj." For public consumption and for use in time of need in the Law Courts, Swaraj was interpreted as "self-government on the Colonial system." But the term was well understood in extremist circles to denote absolute independence, which in fact the word itself means. The Swadeshi movement, if it had been confined to an objective such as is denoted by the slogan " Buy British Goods" to which we are accustomed in England, would have been a proper and legitimate movement, but it was conceived and carried out in hatred, not merely of foreign goods, but of foreigners themselves, as was emphasised in many speeches and articles in which the Mahratta leaders were prominent. It was accompanied also by a boycott and by foolish destruction of imported cloth, sugar, and salt, without any corresponding effort to ensure an increase in the production of the indigenous articles. The only result of destroying these articles was that more goods of the same kind were bought to replace them, and in spite of the movement the sea-borne imports largely increased. The only people who suffered loss were the people whose property, which had been paid for, was destroyed. Violence of the Indian Press at this time resolved itself into the most dangerous incitements and introduced anarchist conspirators and the cult of the bomb and the revolver. The Swadeshi and boycott movements of that day were, as economic measures, a complete failure, but the anarchical conspiracies to which they gave rise have continued to this day.

Some partition of Bengal was an administrative necessity, but the particular redistribution adopted was unfortunate. The Hindus of Eastern Bengal took very short views of their own welfare, while the Mahommedans were in favour of the partition, partly because, in the new Province of Eastern Bengal and Assam they were in a marked majority, and partly because the Hindus disliked it. The real focus of the agitation was Calcutta, where the lawyers scented loss to themselves in the present and further loss in the future when the new capital of Dacca should develop and demand its own University and its own High Court. Western Bengal had not hitherto shown much affection for the people of Eastern Bengal before this issue was raised, but the Bengali is particularly sentimental among the Indian races, and the sentiment that the Bengali race was being cut in two had even a stronger effect than the losses and inconveniences anticipated. The redistribution remained in force for about six years, during which the agitation had almost died down, and Eastern Bengal was becoming accustomed to its new capital at Dacca, which had profited greatly by its rise in status. The second Partition, when it came, gave as great a shock to the Mahommedans as the first had to the Hindus, for they felt they had been left in the lurch in favour of the agitator. During the whole of the agitation the Mahommedans had supported the Government and had borne persecution and loss in doing so. A bitter jest "No bombs no boons" was passed round among Mahommedans at Delhi when His Majesty the King-Emperor announced the reversal of the Partition at the great Coronation Durbar in 1911.

The first Partition added fuel to the anti-British movement in Bengal and caused it to burst out into flames, but it did not originate it, and the appeasement of the Bengali Hindu by the reversal was evanescent, while the resentment of Mahommedans had effects of a far-reaching and lasting description. Over the rest of India the Partition agitation was purely factitious and fictitious, but it suited disgruntled seditionaries to take up the cry in sympathy with Bengal until they could think of some good local issue upon which to base an agitation in their own provinces. In the Punjab the Canal Colonies Bill afforded a pretext, and this agitation flamed out in an outburst of sedition accompanied by serious rioting. The arrest and internment of the late Lala Lajpat Rai and Ajit Singh at the instance of Sir Denzil Ibbetson calmed down the excitement in the Punjab and had a great effect over the whole of India. Had similar action been taken in Bengal at an earlier date the conspiracies there might have been nipped in the bud. In Eastern Bengal Sir Bampfylde Fuller took the agitation seriously and dealt with it firmly, but he was not supported, nor was similar action on those lines permitted in Bengal proper, with the consequence that the agitation there spread and gathered force until its suppression became a matter of great difficulty. It is surely significant enough that Lord Morley and the Government of India were compelled by the force of circumstances to approve, less than a year later, action far stronger than any that Sir Bampfylde Fuller had taken or proposed to take. The Lieut.-Governor of Eastern Bengal and Assam had done nothing that went beyond the enforcement of the ordinary law, and in the light of subsequent events it seems almost incredible that a head of a province should have been so impeded and restrained for doing what was nothing but his plain duty. He was told that he was wrong to move his Gurkha military police to centres of disaffection; he was told that he was wrong to withdraw Government advertisements from a paper that had circulated malicious falsehoods against public servants and refused to withdraw them; he was told that he was wrong to sanction mild disciplinary measures against unruly and turbulent students. Law-breakers do not usually like the law to be put in motion against them, and the Press began to shout condemnation and to put it about that the people were really most loyal, and that the whole trouble was merely due to the arbitrary actions of a tactless "Jack in Office." Some of those in contact with Lord Minto, himself the soul of courage and chivalry, induced him to accept these suggestions of the Press as being founded on truth, and the same view of the case found favour with Lord Morley. The indiscipline among certain private schools and colleges, recognised by or affiliated to the Calcutta University, was having its effect in criminal assaults upon Europeans without any redress being procurable from the authorities of these institutions. So Sir B. Fuller's Government approached the Syndicate of the University, suggesting the withdrawal of recognition and affiliation if the managers of these institutions continued to be obdurate. The reference to the Syndicate was considered to be unwise, and the Lieut.-Governor was requested to withdraw his letter. To this course Sir B. Fuller naturally demurred, and upon this the step was taken by Lord Morley of virtually recalling Sir B. Fuller by accepting a resignation which had been mooted rather than proffered. This action revived an agitation in Eastern Bengal which had been on the point of collapse. Such a veritable triumph for the seditious Press in Calcutta had its inevitable result. Before many months were out the Government of India had itself to instruct local governments to take the very same action in similar circumstances for taking which Sir B. Fuller had been held so unwise, and within the short space of a year the Government of India found it necessary to sanction stern action in the Punjab, and to pass measure after measure to deal with the surge of lawlessness among the seditious youth of Bengal. If the vigorous action taken in Eastern Bengal, and afterwards in the Punjab, when the cause arose had been taken from the first in Bengal itself, not only might the innocent victims of many outrages have been spared, but many foolish, and some even brilliant, youths, possessed with a distorted idea of patriotism and self-sacrifice, might have been saved a miserable death on the scaffold or the embitterment of long years of imprisonment or transportation. The same Government which recalled a Lieut.-Governor for using the whips of the ordinary law found itself obliged very soon after to resort to the scorpions of special repressive legislation. Men's memories are short. They forget these things. But they are true. If the law does not overawe the lawbreakers the lawbreakers will soon overawe the law. From 1906 to 1910 these conspiracies and their manifestations, sometimes bombs, sometimes pistols, and sometimes what are called political dacoities, followed one another in melancholy sequence. After that they began to yield somewhat to the stronger measures taken, and the Press Act and the prosecution of writings invoking hatred or inciting to violence produced greater restraint. The conviction and imprisonment of the Poona leader, the late B. G. Tilak, against whom action was taken by the Bombay Government in 1908, completely quieted Western sedition. The whole anarchical movement, had, however, been confined to a limited Left Wing of the educated section and made a special appeal to excitable students. The great masses of the people, including also the best elements of the intelligentsia, had no sympathy with it. The visit of Their Majesties as Prince and Princess of Wales in 1905-6 had a short calming effect, and all sections welcomed the royal visitors as being outside and entirely separate from the political controversies that were then raging. Again, the Morley-Minto Reforms, though a few extremists held aloof, were accepted by the great bulk of moderate opinion as a liberal step forward. These, with the announcement of the royal visit to the Coronation Durbar at Delhi in 1911, brought in much happier feelings, and a considerable lull in seditious activities occurred during the years 1911-12. Their Majesties' visit, the great Durbar, and all the celebrations connected therewith in the principal towns of India, produced a feeling of enthusiasm for the Crown, of which the effect was by no means evanescent among the best elements of the whole country and the masses alike. The reversal of the Partition gave the more moderate politicians the occasion for exerting some restraint, albeit for a short time only, over the violent section. The removal of the capital to Delhi, announced by His Majesty at the Durbar, was a coup which was received with mixed feelings. Welcomed by some, disliked by others, it created a diversion from current controversy. Whether this step was wise or not cannot even yet be determined with certainty, and only a more distant future will supply the answer. It isolated the Central Government far away from the too dominant influence of Bengal, but also far away from the centre of European commerce and the true European capital of India. It set in motion ideas of increasing autonomy in the provinces, meaning the greater independence of the local governments from interference by the Government of India, but the politicians interpreted it to mean popular self-government. The terms of the despatch which dealt with the change of capital were somewhat ambiguous, for the words "self-government" and "self-governing" were used as synonyms for "autonomy" and "autonomous." The Under-Secretary of State for India, Mr. Montagu, interpreted the despatch in one way to his constituents at Cambridge; his chief, Lord Crewe, in the House of Lords, interpreted it in another. By the politicians in India it was regarded as a promise of popular self-government. In fact it merely intended to convey the idea of a gradually diminishing interference by the Government of India with local governments "until at last" they became autonomous administrations in local affairs. How these local governments should be composed the signatories of that despatch neither did, nor could possibly at that stage, attempt to declare. If there had been any such declaration intended as the politicians thought to extract from the despatch it would obviously have been reserved for the King-Emperor himself to announce at Delhi.

Within a few months of the royal visit the anarchist conspiracies began once more to raise their heads, and the bomb outrage upon Lord Hardinge upon his first public entry into the new capital on December 23rd, 1912, was the most formidable manifestation of their revival. Along with this came, as a new feature, the Mahommedan discontent. Disgruntled by the reversal of the Partition they became easy prey for Pan-Islamic agitation over the Balkan War, and incidents, such as that of the Cawnpur Mosque, which at other times would never have aroused attention, were eagerly seized upon by people of the Ali brothers stamp and made the subject of inflammatory writing. Thus to the movements in Bengal, which were frankly treasonable, and included propaganda for the complete expulsion of the British from India, supported by invocations to the Goddess Kali, and by many bloodthirsty leaflets and several outrages, was now added the Mahommedan Pan-Islamic movement. The two movements were entirely unconnected and mutually antagonistic in their aims. Nevertheless, the extreme leaders on either side were later on to join hands occasionally against the common enemy, the British.

By this time also a third movement had developed among the Sikhs on the Pacific Coast of America, which was fostered by anarchists, Indian and foreign, in many parts of the world. The Ghadr[1] Sikhs, as they called themselves, sought to raise a second mutiny in India, with themselves as the central figures.

Not one of these movements had any clear and long-sighted aims in front of them. They were mischievous, destructive, and murderous. Beyond these short objectives their ideas were vague and chaotic, and there was not a man among them capable of leading more than an undisciplined rabble. They were a source of danger, rather for the mischief they could do among ignorant and fanatical men than for any final results they sought to achieve. The Indian mind turns upon anniversaries. The year 1907, the fiftieth

[1] "Mutiny"

anniversary of the Mutiny, had proved a fiasco. They fixed upon 1917 as the sixtieth anniversary as the next most auspicious time for the culmination of their mad schemes.

All this time the moderate and loyal Indian held his own, and the great masses of the people were entirely untouched. The extreme section of politicians was still outside the regular Congress fold. The Government also, though it had been in the beginning late in grappling with the forces of disorder in Bengal, had now at any rate left no doubt in the land that it was determined to deal sternly with anarchy and violent sedition, and in these aims it had been well supported by the local governments. The Report of Lord Islington's Commission on the Public Services was awaited, and there was no definite movement for any further instalment of constitutional reforms; in fact some of the more advanced politicians, who had held aloof from the first Councils under the Morley-Minto constitution, were now participating. There were, of course, all the troublesome agitations that I have described, and there were numbers of newspapers on the look-out for all pretexts which could become the focus of fresh agitation, such as the treatment of Indians in South Africa and other parts of the Empire. Sedition in India advances in waves with troughs of comparative quiet in between. We were just beginning to rise up from the last trough when the Great War broke out.

CHAPTER XIV

INDIA DURING THE WAR

The Lull in Agitation, and the Outburst of Loyalty—The Revolutionary Movements: Sikh, Pan-Islamic, and Anarchist—Their Futility in Execution—Mrs. Besant's Home Rule Agitation—The Profound Effect of Mr. Montagu's Appointment as Secretary of State—British Gratitude exploited to reward the People who had deserved least

The days of extreme tension and suspense during the interval between Austria's ultimatum to Servia and the fateful decision of the 4th August, 1914, were not fully comprehended either by the Indian Press or by the politically-minded classes. They did not realise either the imminence or the magnitude of the coming struggle, or the issues involved. But once Great Britain declared war on Germany, Simla, the ports and the cantonments began to buzz with activity, the censorship over telegrams was established, the internment of enemy aliens began and war ordinances were issued. The politicians, moderate and extreme alike, were for the time being half stunned, and a hush fell over political agitation. The princes and chiefs, the great land-owners and the commercial magnates vied together with offers of service and loyal demonstration. This outburst of loyalty was the greatest tribute to the belief in the impartial justice and stability of British rule. The temper of the Indian Army was admirable. The question of Turkey had not then arisen to excite Mahommedan sentiments, and, with the absence of political agitation, there was nothing to disturb the atmosphere except the feeling of some common danger vaguely understood. For the time being the masses were but dimly conscious of what was going on, though rumours flew about of the wildest description. Planets were mistaken for aeroplanes carrying lights, German warships were reported to have been seen up the Jumna. The Marwari traders in the great sea-ports fled back to their houses in Rajputana, and the Lascars for a time, but only for a short time, deserted the sea. The raids of the *Emden* in the Bay of Bengal, coupled with the brief bombardment of Madras, excited much alarm, but when that danger disappeared the excitement began to subside. Outside the ports the large cantonments, the railway centres, the war hospitals, and the immediate recruiting areas, the phrase "Business as usual" was not a mere slogan to keep up courage, it was an actual fact. The consequences of the war were to be felt at a much later stage. Among constitutional politicians on the Imperial Legislative Council Lord Hardinge called for a truce on both sides from all legislation or resolutions of a kind calculated to excite controversy, legislation necessary for the conduct of the war alone being excepted. For some time the spirit of the truce was admirably observed by legislative bodies, and on the Government side it was rigidly kept throughout. It was indeed eight months before the British "D.O.R.A." had its Indian complement in the Defence of India Act, but when this was enacted it was already overdue, for events had begun to happen which portended grave dangers if not held in check. Although in India itself the outbreak of the war for the time being hushed the intemperance of political agitation, among the various groups of anarchists and seditionaries in different parts of the world the war was at once regarded as the great opportunity for doing the maximum of mischief. India House, the seat of Indian sedition in London, had already been broken up, and its activities transferred to Paris, whence it had sent out its incitements, but with the landing of Indian troops in France the French authorities recognised the necessity of dispersing a focus of conspiracy inimical to the Allied cause. Geneva was the next shelter, and then Berlin. In British Columbia immigration laws had long been exciting the Sikhs, and the refusal to allow the "Komagata Maru" to land her Sikh passengers at Vancouver afforded a special pretext for inflaming the Sikh Ghadr (Mutiny) Movement. The original day fixed for rebellion in 1917 was put forward, successive ship-loads of seditious Sikhs returned to India, establishing or attempting to establish small nuclei of sedition in all the intermediate ports, such as Hong Kong, Singapore, Rangoon, as well as in foreign territory in Japan, Java, and Siam, wherever any disgruntled Indians were to be found. It was intended to repatriate these returning Sikhs quietly and free of cost to their homes in the Punjab, but their own turbulence and violence rendered force necessary. Some of them settled down peacefully in their villages, but a great many thought to raise the standard of rebellion. Strenuous efforts were made to seduce troops and to rouse the masses. Their successes with troops were confined to very few men, and with the masses they only got hold of a few wild spirits to participate in dacoities. They committed several murders, some bomb outrages, and planned captures of an arsenal and some police posts. The situation was met with great firmness by the Punjab Government under Sir Michael O'Dwyer, and the passing of the Defence of India Act enabled these rebels to be effectively dealt with. These men were exceedingly dangerous at such an inflammable and critical time, but their leaders were divided and jealous of one another, their plans constantly miscarried, their plots were given away, and they were so careless that they missed *coups* by missing trains. A good many were rounded up and interned in their villages, some shot in encounters with police, others arrested, tried, and convicted. The trouble would have greatly increased if they had brought off any of their projected *coups*, but they all failed, and the movement was rapidly discredited.

Serious attempts were also made in Burma by entry from Siam to corrupt the military police there, but excellent police work and the loyalty of the military police completely frustrated these plans, the ringleaders being tried and convicted.

The coming into the war of Turkey stimulated the Pan-Islamic Movement, which was the forerunner of the Khilafat movement, and attempts were made to use the Arab revolt against the Turks in the Hejaz as a further cause for Mahommedan agitation. The Turks have never lifted a finger to help Indian Mohammedans; they never subscribed a penny to Indian famine funds, and very few Indian Mahommedans had ever seen Turks. I have never believed that there was any genuine feeling over the fortunes or misfortunes of Turkey, but cries of "Islam," or of the holy places in danger, or relating to the sovereignty of infidels over what are called "the Islands of Arabia," were freely used to excite emotion among congregations of the faithful collected for prayer. Various intrigues, conspiracies, plots and incitements to Jehad (a religious war) were devised or attempted in bases outside India, notably at Kabul, where the plotters were most coldly received by the Amir Habibulla. His services to the Allied cause, by keeping his country from intervention on the side of the Germans and Turks, were of the utmost value. Various foolish people, including some college students as well as some older men, were inveigled into complicity in these conspiracies. The importance of being a secret conspirator in a grandiose plot appeals to the vanity of a good many fools, for only fools would have been impressed by the Mahommedan agitator, Obeidulla, with his so-called Provisional Government of India in Kabul and by his famous "Army of God," in which the chief firebrands of Mahommedan agitation in India were nominated for commissions. The army was to have its headquarters at Medina, with secondary headquarters at Constantinople, Teheran, and Kabul. The tables of these nominees for commissions showed three patrons, twelve field-marshals, two generals, thirty lieut.-generals, sixteen major-generals, twenty-four colonels, ten lieut.-colonels, five majors, two captains, and one lieutenant. These grand schemes have their ludicrous side, but the general plan of the union of all the Islamic nations against India, backed by a Mahommedan rebellion in India itself, would have been welcome enough to Germany and Turkey, who were easily led to believe in the tales of intended

Mahommedan risings in India at the right time. These schemes were potentially very dangerous, but they remained schemes because of the admirable work done—not only within India itself, but at the many foci of sedition in various parts of the world by the C.I.D. under the late Sir Charles Cleveland—and by many devoted and daring Indian police officers, Hindu, Sikh, and Mahommedan. Practically all these conspiracies were detected before they had any chance of gaining hold, but, without the special powers with which authority was invested under war legislation, it would have been impossible to checkmate them.

Both the Sikh and Mahommedan conspiracies were mainly concerned with Northern India, but the anarchists and seditionaries in America and the Far East had another string to their bow, viz. to obtain arms by German help and land them on the coast. The idea was to set free all the convicts on the Andaman Islands and land them in Burma, and then trust to a rising of the population. The same thing was to happen when arms were landed in Bengal. These schemes also fizzled out, owing to the efforts of our Secret Service, and the watchfulness exercised by British representatives in the various countries concerned. The Bengal anarchists, of whom a few of the leading spirits were in touch with these outside conspiracies, very soon after war was declared started a regular outburst of activity and showed an increasing truculence. They had one successful stroke in the seizure of fifty Mauser pistols and 46,000 cartridges by a conspirator who was a clerk in a British gunsmith's firm and managed to purloin them when clearing a consignment of the firm's goods from the Customs. Thereafter outrages increased in number, and early in 1915 the anarchists had begun to establish almost a reign of terror. Prominent Indian politicians received threatening letters and mysterious messages, and when, with the passing of the Defence of India Act, it was possible to take effective measures against the anarchists, these politicians were greatly relieved, although for form's sake they did not like to say so in public. In the course of a year or two the action taken to intern or confine to residence in selected villages the men and youths implicated in these plots broke up the gangs and their activities.

All these conspiracies, whether of Sikhs, Pan-Islamic plotters, or Bengali anarchists supported by German spies in America or the Far East, were based on the belief that, if once a beginning was made, the country would rise up in revolt against the Government, and Turks and Germans alike were easily duped by these fatuous assurances of mere braggadocios. There was never any sign of sympathy with the plotters, and, when the occasion arose, villagers readily helped to round up dacoits or anarchists. Naturally, in Bengal evidence was difficult to obtain in prosecutions because so many informers and witnesses had been shot. It was fear and not sympathy that accounted for this reluctance to give evidence, for harmless shopkeepers and villagers were the chief victims of these political crimes.

Lord Chelmsford succeeded Lord Hardinge in 1916. Lord Hardinge had always been sympathetic to all legitimate aspirations of educated Indians, and had been fearlessly outspoken in championing the Indian cause in respect to the South African trouble. At the same time he was firm in dealing with all law-breakers once he was satisfied that milder measures would not suffice. Lord Chelmsford continued the same policy, and an Indian Press deputation, which at that very inopportune time asked for the removal of all restrictions in regard to the Press, received no encouragement from him.

During all this period the moderate politicians of the country had maintained the correct attitude, but the extreme section grew steadily bolder in their demands. As the war proceeded and the claims of the Dominions for an equal voice in Imperial counsels became the subject of many articles in the Press, and as President Wilson's famous "Self-Determination" was passed round the newspapers of the world, political India began to ask itself whether the time had not come for advancing political claims and pitching them high. Just as European inspiration had taken a large share in the establishment of the Indian National Congress, so it was an Englishwoman, Mrs. Besant, who really started the cry for Home Rule, not Home Rule as a distant goal but Home Rule in less than no time after the war. The campaign which she conducted in her newspaper, *New India*, did not at first win much support, for even advanced Indian politicians regarded it as premature, but she persisted in her propaganda until the time came later when she found herself outstripped by her followers. She is one of those people who can convince themselves of anything. Her writing took on so violent a complexion that in 1917 the Madras Government found it necessary to restrict her liberty and restrain a pen which apparently the writer, in spite of warning, could not control. This action, which had the support of the Government of India, was absolutely necessary unless the British Government, at this very critical period of the war, was to surrender to a campaign of unbridled insolence. The extremists had returned and captured the National Congress, from which they had been for eight years excluded. The Moslem League had formulated its demand for "suitable" self-government, and Congress and League had joined forces to prepare a Congress-League Joint Scheme.

Mrs. Besant's internment, which was of a very mild description, naturally produced an outcry, which, if the Government had remained firm (and it was no use to intern Mrs. Besant unless it did intend to remain firm), must have died down as soon as the agitators realised that any bluff that they put up would be useless. No part of the Empire, then fighting for its life and liberty, could possibly tolerate violent schism within its own borders. The terms which Lord Hardinge had impressed on his own Government for temporarily damping down controversy had been shamelessly violated by this lady, with the self-inspired conviction that she was designed by Providence to lead these millions to a state of bliss, and that her own countrymen must be always and in all circumstances wrong. That is the most charitable view to take of her state of mind.

It was at this juncture that there occurred an event which altered the whole current and course of the constitutional history of India, and of which the ultimate consequences cannot yet be foreseen, viz., the appointment of the late Mr. Edwin Montagu to be Secretary of State for India, followed by his announcement in Parliament of August 1917, and of his approaching visit to India. The author, on the eve of his departure to take up the Lieut.-Governorship of Burma, had the privilege of a farewell interview with Lord Curzon, and mentioned to him his misgivings that Mr. Montagu's visit might be fraught with unfortunate consequences to India. Lord Curzon replied that any action taken would be the action of the Cabinet and not of Mr. Montagu, and that there was therefore no cause for alarm that any visionary scheme would be accepted. Lord Curzon said that in regard to the Morley-Minto reforms some people had prophesied various consequences but that no harm seemed to have resulted. I replied that those reforms had granted *influence* and not *power*, and that there was thus all the difference between them and the developments foreshadowed by the announcement in Parliament. Lord Curzon repeated that it would be the Cabinet and not Mr. Montagu who would have the last word. Being acquainted with Mr. Montagu's lines of thought when he was Under-Secretary of State for India, and visited that country in the cold weather of 1912-13, I am afraid that I was not entirely consoled by Lord Curzon's assurances. I was not to know then the share that Lord Curzon had taken in the form of words in which the announcement had been couched.

Mr. Montagu, as well as being an adroit Parliamentarian, was, without doubt, actuated by a strong desire to do what was right by Indian aspirations, but he was impulsive and he dreamed dreams. He fancied that he was one of the few people who held the key to the solution of Indian political problems. He was impatient of all who disagreed with him. The arguments of the "Round Table" Study Circle (largely based on analogies from the Dominions) seemed to carry more weight with him than the advice of those with a life-long experience of Indian conditions. He assumed that actions which produce certain reactions in Western minds would produce precisely the same reactions in Eastern. He failed to perceive the difference between daughter nations anxious to be free from their mother's apron-strings, but still recognising her as their mother, and the Oriental ambition, confined to a particular class, to be free from alien control. He did not appreciate that what between mother and daughters would be understood as a trustful relaxation of control no longer necessary would in the East be interpreted as a mark of fear rather than confidence, and as proof that further clamour would produce more and more concession until there was nothing left to concede. Before he went to India on this memorable mission of constitution-making he desired to create what is so often miscalled "a calm atmosphere," and he therefore compassed the release of Annie Besant and of a certain number of interned people. This action, regarded as a surrender to bitter agitation, entirely threw over Lord Pentland in Madras (who would certainly have resigned but for the critical conditions of the war), and would have done the same by the Viceroy also if Lord Chelmsford, with his usual chivalry, had not accepted the responsibility for the release. The so-called "calm atmosphere" thereby created was an atmosphere of exultancy among the enemies of British rule and of consternation among its loyal friends. "We are all extremists now," was the phrase that went round many moderate circles. Many times have I heard loyal friends of the Government in India say: "We do not approve of these things, but if Government gives them we have to keep quiet. How can we be more loyal than the Government?"

The terms of the announcement of August 1917 and the Montagu-Chelmsford Report are discussed in later Chapters, but the whole atmosphere in which the announcement was made requires description before the policy can be fully understood.

England was profoundly grateful for the wonderful loyalty which India displayed, and was anxious to recognise it in a spirit of ungrudging generosity, but both the British public and the British Parliament were far too engrossed in the tremendous task of winning the war to have time or inclination to appreciate by whom exactly the services were rendered, to whom the reward was due, and what kind of reward would be most acceptable to those who had rendered the service. The martial races gave their men; the princes their men and their money; the land-holders and the trading classes subscribed generously to numerous patriotic and relief funds. Among the intelligentsia the loyal ones also contributed to these funds, but the element that clamoured for the reward did none of these things, neither did their sons go to the war, nor did they contribute towards it. The vote of £100,000,000 as India's contribution was opposed by some of their chief representatives in the Imperial Legislative Council. They and their Press, after a very short lull at the outset, did nothing but carp and agitate, and, so far as they dared go, encouraged sedition. There were doubtless a few honourable exceptions, but they were few. The most that this intelligentsia can claim, and some of them claimed it, was that they might have done much more harm to the Government cause than they actually did, but they did all they dared, for it was a time when Government could not be too easy with overt sedition. As to the people at large, they scarcely noticed that there was a war, until the time when the shrinkage of shipping, the severe contraction of British manufactures, the shortage of silver currency, the scarcity of imported commodities, and the sharp rises in prices brought it home to them that the war was beginning to affect their own lives. The recruiting campaigns at the crisis in 1918 drained the resources in men of the Punjab, but the response elsewhere was by contrast meagre, and in many places practically *nil*. The supply of men for Labour

Corps was obtained with some difficulty by the offer of wages unheard of before to Indian labouring men, but the Government were nevertheless obliged to draw on the jails for Jail Corps for Mesopotamia.

The people of England, where men and women worked and suffered as never before, knew what was meant by war, but away from the recruiting grounds of the fighting men the people of India did not. It did not affect their lives or their thoughts, or their imaginations, and, not until towards the latter part, their comforts and conveniences. The princes and the landed nobility and gentry, and loyal Indians who gave liberally of their generosity, deserved all the praise that the British people could give. In so far as honours and grants of land could go, and liberal pensions to the families of the fallen and to the maimed and helpless, these men were rewarded from the State's own resources in India, but the crowning reward of all by the British people to the people of India, the grant of political concessions, was reserved for those who had deserved least or who had rendered only disservice. Providence sends its rain upon the just and upon the unjust, and the rain benefits both equally, but this rain of political concession fulfilled the desire of the unjust and left the just "afraid with much amazement."

CHAPTER XV

INDIA DURING THE WAR
THE ANNOUNCEMENT IN PARLIAMENT

Views of Eminent Viceroys Disregarded—Lord Chelmsford's Conversion—Drafting of the Formula—Its Defects—"Responsible Government"—A "Term of Art," and in Indian Conditions a Farce.

LORD HARDINGE, shortly before he vacated office, had been considering informally the policy to be followed after the war in recognition of India's great services to the Empire, but, as is evident from a farewell speech that he made in March 1916 to the Imperial Legislative Council at Delhi, he did not contemplate any drastic advance in the direction of constitutional development. This is an extract from the speech he made:

"During the past few months I have seen mention made in speeches made at meetings in the country, and in the Press, of self-government, colonial self-government, and home rule for India. I have often wondered whether these speakers and writers fully realise the conditions prevailing in Dominions, such as Canada or Australia, which render self-government possible. I wish that some of them could visit the Dominions and see for themselves. A study of the history of these Dominions would show that the development of their present self-governing institutions had been achieved not by any sudden stroke of statesmanship, but by a process of steady and patient evolution which has gradually united and raised all classes of the community to the level of their enhanced responsibilities. I do not for a moment wish to discountenance self-government for India as a national ideal; it is a perfectly natural aspiration and has the warm sympathy of all moderate men. But in the present position of

India it is not idealism that is needed but practical politics, and practical solutions to questions arising out of all the social and political conditions of this country. We should look facts squarely in the face and do our utmost to grapple with realities. To lightly raise extravagant hopes and to encourage unrealisable demands can only tend to delay and not to accelerate political progress. I know that this is the sentiment of many wise and thoughtful Indians. In speaking thus frankly it is far from my intention to create a feeling of discouragement, for nobody is more anxious than I am to see the early realisation of the just and legitimate aspirations of India, but I am equally desirous of avoiding all danger of reaction from the birth of institutions which experience might prove to be premature."

It is a great pity that the Joint Parliamentary Committee could not have studied that speech of Lord Hardinge's made at the end of over five years' tenure of the Viceroyalty, by a man of wide experience who entertained the most friendly feeling towards Indian progress, and had not been deterred one hair's breadth from the path he had set before him by the dastardly attempt on his life which was so nearly successful.

Lord Chelmsford, upon assuming office, took up the question at once of the goal before India, and it was only about eight months later that the proposals of his Government were laid before the Secretary of State. No one could tell at that time when the war would end, but it was generally expected that any important announcement of a political nature would take the form of a Royal Proclamation upon the termination of the war. Politicians in a hurry might be pressing for an immediate declaration, it was their rôle to do so when they thought that the iron might be hot. But it is quite certain that if it had been announced in Parliament that the question of the policy to be followed in India was too great and serious an one to be handled successfully at a moment when the whole Empire was fighting for its very existence and amidst pre-occupations so grave, all reasonable opinion in India would have been satisfied, and unreasoning politicians would have had to possess their souls in patience. The despatch of Lord Chelmsford's Government was never published, nor was any detailed reply ever given to it. Its receipt was acknowledged and it was filed *sine die.* When Parliament was faced with the famous announcement of August 20th, 1917, it was presented with a *res judicata* which committed it to the abdication of its own authority by progressive stages without its having had any opportunity at all for discussion. Thereafter any criticism of schemes of advance put forward was liable to be put out of court at once as conflicting with this or that promise contained in the announcement. Parliament has always the right to ratify or refuse to ratify a treaty, and the Government of India Bill in 1919 could have been modified in regard to details, but the Preamble to that Act was a declaration having the binding force of a treaty which it could not alter by a single syllable. Nothing has ever yet been published to show that Lord Chelmsford's Government examined and considered with due deliberation the wording of the announcement in its final shape and all the implications involved by it, or that any lesser authority in India was ever consulted at all upon so vital a subject as the scope, objective, or the precise language of so momentous a document. Ever since the question that has puzzled the brains of Great Britain and India alike is not whether the promise was wise or unwise, but simply how, in the name of heaven, it could be honoured. The announcement may have been magnificent, but it was not peace, nor did it lead to peace. The actual words of the announcement are of such importance that they must be reproduced:

"The policy of His Majesty's Government, with which the Government of India are in complete accord, is that of the increasing association of Indians in every branch of the administration and the *gradual* development of self-governing institutions with a view to the *progressive* realisation of responsible government in India *as an integral part of the*

British Empire, and that substantial steps be taken in that direction.

"Progress in this policy can only be achieved by successive stages. The British Government and the Government of India, on whom the responsibility lies for the welfare and advancement of the Indian peoples, must be the judges of the time and measures of each advance, and they must be guided *by the co-operation received* from those on whom new opportunities of service will thus be conferred, and by the extent to which it is found that *confidence can be reposed in their sense of responsibility*."

The Earl of Ronaldshay has thrown a light upon the manner in which the words "responsible government" crept into the form of promise.[1]

To anyone who knew Lord Curzon's views—and they are fully proved not only by his whole career but also by his subsequent attitude of dislike to the Montagu-Chelmsford Report and the Act of 1919—the insertion of these words by him is explicable only as an extraordinary temporary lapse of a brilliant brain.

Lord Ripon never planned out anything so remarkable. Lord Dufferin and Lord Lansdowne, Lord Curzon himself, Lord Minto, Lord Morley, Lord Hardinge and Lord Chelmsford had expressly deprecated the introduction of any Parliamentary system in India. Even Mr. Montagu himself did not venture to suggest a complete departure from established conviction which threw all caution to the winds. Lord Ronaldshay tells us that Mr. Montagu's formula did not go beyond "the gradual development of free institutions in India with a view to ultimate self-government within the Empire." When Mr. Montagu had obtained Lord Curzon's formula, as he afterwards informed an authoritative person, he, to use his own words, "threw up his hat."

It may be that Lord Curzon thought that his formula so emphasised what is now called the inevitability of gradualness that something more definite and sonorous as the goal

[1] Earl Ronaldshay's *Life of Curzon*, vol. iii.

before India would be so distant as to carry with it no untoward consequences. It may be that his lapse was to forget the significance attaching to the word "responsible" in the phrase "responsible government." The older term employed as a synonym for Parliamentary Government was "Representative Government." This latter term was used by both Lords Morley and Minto in dealing with the Morley-Minto Reforms, and Lord Minto's disclaimer that his Government were in any sense advocates of "Representative Government" for India, as they called it, "in the Western sense of the term," was endorsed by Lord Morley.

All political formulae are open to serious defects, because it is almost impossible that they will not be interpreted differently according to the interests or supposed interests of different parties interpreting them. Constitutionalists may be able to say when the term "responsible government" was first introduced into their vocabulary as a synonym for "Parliamentary government" on the British model. It is possible that it first emerged out of discussions forming the constitutional literature of the Dominion. But wherever it came from it is a very faulty and equivocal word. What is the opposite of "responsible government"? Is it "irresponsible government"? Is not every government responsible to the people governed? Do we not talk about a responsible Press, although the proprietors and editors of newspapers are not elected by the public? Do we not talk about a man with no sense of responsibility? In this very announcement August 1917 we read further on—"The British Government and the Government of India, upon whom the *responsibility* lies for the welfare and advancement of the Indian peoples"—and again the last four words in the announcement are—"their sense of *responsibility*." If "responsible government" is a term of art, as lawyers would say, it is not a very happy one. To whom is the "responsible government" responsible? Is it to the whole nation, or only to those who have the franchise, or only those who by their votes put it in power? Or can it be that "responsible government" is merely a synonym for democracy? If it is, then why talk about "responsible government," why not talk about democracy? All political India is engaged now talking about democracy, but democracy was not mentioned in the announcement. Did we mean oligarchy when we said "responsible government," and is it contended that the meaning of this "term of art" is satisfied if peoples, however numerous, have a government elected by individuals, however few, as long as the members of the government and the legislature are elected by somebody, however ignorant? Surely commonsense cannot be strained in this way by the devotees of a form of speech, or of a narrow technicality. Is there or is there not such a thing as a responsible electorate, and, if there is, does it or does it not mean an electorate of which the majority consists of individuals who have "a sense of responsibility"? Until, therefore, there is a nation (or a group of nations competent to govern themselves and each other jointly) having a majority of its citizens with a sense of responsibility, and capable of exercising a considered choice in respect to the mandate that it gives to its elected representatives, it is idle to talk of "responsible government." It may have a technical meaning, it may be "a blessed word," but as a method of governing, in the absence of that essential condition just described, it is a complete fraud and sham.

The Coalition Government entrusted the decision as to the wording of the announcement to Lord Curzon and Mr. Montagu, thinking that the knowledge of the former would correct the idealism of the latter, and that anything upon which they both agreed would be safe. But neither Lord Curzon nor Mr. Montagu realised that they were in effect seeking to conciliate not the moderate aspirations of loyal subjects of the Crown but the truculent ambitions of avowed enemies of British rule. Apart from the rash inclusion by Lord Curzon of the words "responsible government," the form of announcement was also in other ways very defective. It promised substantial steps in the desired direction in advance of the inquiry which Mr. Montagu, with the aid of Lord Chelmsford, was about to hold in order to see whether any substantial steps at all were possible in the immediate future. While it clothed the promise with every conceivable limitation of gradual development instead of stating what the limitations were and emphasizing their solid character, it left them liable to be treated as a flimsy wrapper to be torn off at will, a mere concession to appearances of which no serious account need be taken. It failed even to notice that the princes and chiefs, whom it did not mention at all, could not be a party to any such scheme. It omitted to state that wide diffusion of education and the complete dying down of all racial and religious animosities must be the absolute conditions precedent to any serious political advance. Mr. Montagu announced the verdict first, and commenced to hold the inquest afterwards. He began to build a tower before he had counted the cost. He may have been the dupe of his own ambitions; his ambitions were doubtless worthy, but whether he deceived himself, or whatever his ambitions were, could make no difference to the fact—the tower that he began building is proving to be a second Tower of Babel. Perhaps the substitution of one word in Virgil's lines may sum up the whole proceeding:

> Quo non mortalia pectora cogis
> Laudis sacra fames?

CHAPTER XVI

THE MONTAGU-CHELMSFORD REPORT AND THE PASSING OF THE GOVERNMENT OF INDIA ACT

Mistaken descent into arena of controversy by Viceroy and Secretary of State—Effect to Stifle Criticism—Most able Report but based on delusion that Minute Dose of "Responsibility" Would Solve All Problems—Tragedy of Disturbing "Pathetic Contentment" among Millions of Men in a War-torn World—Misplaced Trust of Parliament as Shown by Events.

WHEN Mr. Montagu arrived in India on his memorable mission he came with a brief, not with an open mind. The brief had been prepared mainly by himself. How he had obtained Lord Chelmsford's acquiescence to that brief which ran counter to that Viceroy's own views, expressed only a short time previously, has not been revealed. Possibly the fact that the draft announcement was actually framed by Lord Curzon may have influenced Lord Chelmsford and his colleagues to change their minds. In any case Lord Chelmsford became a hearty coadjutor to Mr. Montagu, and the word "responsible," whether applied to a minister or to a system of government, became a veritable shibboleth. Unless a man was prepared to pronounce the word "responsible" *ore rotundo* his ideas were of no account. It was no longer a question of "what to do," but simply of "how to do" something that was already decided upon. The touring of the country and the descent into the arena of controversy *coram populo* by authorities so highly placed as the Viceroy and the Secretary of State was in itself unwise. The result of this personal investigation of the problem was announced to the world. How could lesser authorities argue effectively against professions of faith expressed with such fervour by the King-Emperor's representative in India and the mouthpiece to India of the British Parliament?

The Montagu-Chelmsford Report was a wonderful piece of work. Its severest critics would not deny this. As one who dissented from the scheme of dyarchy I cannot too warmly praise the fairness with which it marshalled "The Material," as the first part of the Report is entitled. With great skill and persuasiveness it went on to unfold its proposals in the second part, until many a dissentient would put down the Report and say: "Almost thou persuadest me to be a dyarchist." But on the second and third reading it became manifest that the first part of the Report provided the strongest possible reasons for negativing the proposals of the second part. No attempt was made to minimise the problems, but no attempt was made to solve them. All that was repeated and reaffirmed was that the magic of "responsibility" would solve them all, and that the famous system of dyarchy was the first step that counted. It was the only way. Every other route was a blind alley. It was the only road to Rome. Yet it was all based on the assumption that a tiny novitiate of electors out of the vast masses of illiterate India, bristling with its racial feuds, its religious antagonisms, its castes, its social exclusions, its babel of tongues, its fierce communal controversies, would start functioning in response to a system absolutely alien to them in the same way that the experienced electors of educated England to-day respond to a system which the people have gradually developed for themselves in the course of many centuries.

The four principles on which the Report defined the scope of the proposals were:

(1) There would be as far as possible complete popular control in local bodies and the largest possible independence for them of outside control. (*Report*, para. 188.)

(2) The Provinces are the domain in which the earlier steps towards the progressive realisation of responsible government should be taken, and our aim is

to give complete responsibility as soon as conditions permit. This involves at once giving the Provinces the largest measure of independence, legislative, administrative, and financial of the Government of India, which is compatible with the due discharge by the latter of its own responsibilities. (*Report*, para. 189.)

(3) The Government of India must remain wholly responsible to Parliament, and, saving such responsibility, its authority in essential matters must remain indisputable pending experience of the changes now to be introduced in the Provinces. In the meantime the Indian Legislative Council should be enlarged and made more representative, and its opportunities of influencing Government increased. (*Report*, para. 190.)

(4) In proportion as the foregoing changes take effect the control of Parliament and the Secretary of State over the Government of India and Provincial Governments must be relaxed. (*Report*, para. 191.)

These four enunciations of policy read admirably in the abstract. It is the application of them to the actual facts in the concrete that is the real crux. So far as the first is concerned it may be interpreted into vulgar language as an injuction that local bodies should, as far as possible, be allowed to "stew in their own juice." In the first Chapter of Part II I summarised the opinions of local governments up to 1927. The framers of the Report paid little attention to the fact that there had been abundant experiment for over thirty years in the establishment of the required actions and reactions between the electors and the elected in this sphere. During that period official guidance had been constant and unremitting to help, advise, and most conscientiously to stimulate the civic sense. It had encouraged good work by high praise and passed over indulgently the shortcomings. The electors remained apathetic, or, if they were aroused, it was over the bickerings of faction or the demands of caste or creed. Good work was a question of personality, not of pressure by electorates honestly indignant at failure. It can truly be said that, except where good personalities have taken control, the juice in which local bodies have been stewing has been polluted by corruption.

As to the second proposition, it merely repeats in effect the announcement in Parliament, and advocates "Provincial autonomy," which had been advocated long before, the chief protagonist having been Bombay.

The third proposition enunciated was admirable, but the machinery created to carry it out was better calculated to frustrate it than to give it effect, and it has frustrated it.

The fourth proposition was the obvious concomitant of the scheme so far as the provinces were concerned, but it was not a necessary complement of the third. The first, the third, and the fourth propositions could have been given effect by mere process of devolution and decentralisation if there had been no reforms at all.

The second proposition was the crux of the whole changes, and it was to effect this that dyarchy was invented, after the rejection of possible alternatives. Briefly, it divided the local government into two parts controlling "reserved" and "transferred" subjects. The "reserved" half of government remained as before, viz., managed by the Governor in Council. The "transferred" half was to be in the charge of ministers selected from the elected members of the Legislative Council. Special stress should be laid on the statement made at the end of paragraph 218: "*As we have said they* (*the Ministers*) *will not hold office at the will of the Legislature but at that of their constituents.*" The Legislative Councils soon made mincemeat of that pious aspiration. The whole of these paragraphs, 218-223, are full of pious aspirations which took insufficient account of facts. The Report proposed to leave the actual constitution of the Legislative Councils, the determination of the franchise, and the distribution of departments between "reserved" and "transferred" to two special committees to be appointed for this purpose. The Report condemned communal electorates, but proposed an exception in favour of Mahommedans generally and of Sikhs in the Punjab. Other interests were to be provided for by nomination. The question of communal electorates is still with us. The framers of the Report were conscious of some of the many difficulties which would arise and proposed several props and safeguards, some of which were removed by the Joint Parliamentary Committee at a later date. But so full were they of the wonderful effect that the ballot box would have on all sorts and conditions of men that they begged many questions and made many assumptions in formulating and supporting their proposals. They assumed first that one man could serve two masters. "It is our intention that the decisions of the Government should be loyally defended by the entire Government, but that the Ministers should feel responsibility for conforming to the wishes of their constituents." They added, it is true, that these two forces may pull different ways, but said that even in England a member of a Government might have to choose between loyalty to the Government and to his own constituents. This was no true analogy, as they admitted, for the Minister in England would have constituents of whom the majority would be of the same party as the Government, whereas in India the position might be similar to that of a Labour Minister in a Conservative Government.

There is a notable passage of the *Report*, para. 144, giving the justification of an advance as the authors saw it, in which they disclaim any idea that their proposals have been evoked at the bidding of 5 per cent. of the population. They would have proposed the same policy, they say, whether the proportion of the population asking for free institutions had been 20 per cent. or only one-half per cent. Their reasons were "the faith that was in them." They measure the growth of impulses towards self-government "not by the crowds at political meetings or the multiplication of newspapers, but by the infallible signs that indicate the growth of character." They believe that: "The sheltered existence given to India by British rule cannot be prolonged without damage to her national life." And they end by the passage: "We have a richer gift for her people than we have yet bestowed on them, that nationhood within the Empire represents something better than India has hitherto attained, that the placid, pathetic contentment of the masses is not the soil in which such Indian nationhood will grow, and that in deliberately disturbing it we are working for her highest good." This is a very fine and nobly-intentioned statement in which the authors have allowed their hearts to run away with their heads. One cannot but feel that that "richer gift" is rather like the "rare and refreshing fruits" which Mr. Lloyd George made famous. The authors were here refuting any suspicion that they may have been actuated by a desire to sacrifice the interests of the masses to the demands of a group of politicians. But the disclaimer is too thin. Everybody knows that the whole affair was pursued in this red-hot haste, not because of the urgent necessity of making a start with a richer life for the ryot, even amid the throes of the great world-conflict, but because of the growing pressure and importunity of agitators pressing for a premature Home Rule. The attempt to stir millions of ignorant men out of their contentment, however pathetic that might appear to the authors, was surely, at such a time, not the height of statesmanship, but the most reckless and dangerous policy that it is possible to conceive. When you make peaceful and plodding, but wholly ignorant, men thoroughly discontented with something, what do they do? Gradually learn the secret of the ballot box, or break out into riot and revolution? The contentment of the ryot was too placid to be disturbed by a paragraph in a Report which he could not read and could not have understood even if it had been read to him, but the hint was not lost on the agitators, and from that time forward they have devoted their money and their energies to tampering with the loyalty and contentment of the masses. We have often heard of divine discontent, the kind of discontent no doubt that the authors had in view when they wrote their famous passage, but when is discontent divine? When it is discontent with your own shortcomings. If it is discontent with other people's better success it is sure to degenerate into envy, hatred, and malice. When a man is burning with discontent at some gross injustice to himself the exercise of a vote is a very dilatory remedy. What the ryot requires is liberty to enjoy the fruits of his own toil, with education to enable him to use that toil to better advantage. That liberty can only be enjoyed by full protection from every form of oppression. As he already had the benefits of a twentieth-century government, instead of a twelfth-century government, which was all that he had to enjoy before British rule began, it is not quite clear what his discontent, which was so desired, should concentrate upon. Seemingly that he should be governed by Vakils instead of by British. The agitators took that hint also, and became busy suggesting to him that the British Government was " Satanic," and that if he supported the Vakils he would soon witness a millenium of cheapness free of taxation. It was only on this soil of discontent that Indian nationhood could be built up, urged the Report, ignoring entirely that their proposals would be letting loose racial and religious animosities, and that among these heterogeneous crowds the old disputation would begin as to who should be greatest in the kingdom of Swaraj. It is really pathetic that men of such high intentions, striving to make India an ideal Dominion, should have penned a document which, however ably drafted, was full of such dangerous fallacies.

The Report was duly published for criticism in the summer of 1918. The local governments agreed in disliking dyarchy; the Heads of the local governments were called to Delhi for a conference early in 1919. Two of them—Lord Pentland from Madras and Sir George Lloyd (now Lord Lloyd) from Bombay—did not attend, Lord Pentland because he disapproved of these political schemes altogether; Sir George Lloyd, who had recently assumed charge of the Bombay

Governorship, because strikes of mill hands required his presence in Bombay. Of the seven heads of provinces who were present at Delhi, two assented to a trial of dyarchy because they considered that a scheme publicly approved by the Viceroy and Secretary of State had raised such expectations that they could not be disappointed; five dissented and submitted an alternative scheme which they had to prepare with only such consultation as was possible in two or three days. The scheme they submitted was something like the plan discussed in para. 217 of the Report. The five Governors' minute dwelt on the difficulties inherent in a government divided in two, pointed out that there would be no genuine responsibility in it to an ignorant electorate, and laid stress on the fact that it went further than the terms of the announcement required, since many substantial steps could be taken in the desired direction without this precipitate departure from all precedents, ancient or modern. But all these objections put forward by administrators of long experience, who had seen service between them in all provinces except Madras, having also served in the Government of India, were of no avail. By this time Mr. Montagu had elevated "responsibility" of this particular brand from a pious opinion to an article of faith, and none but true believers in his creed could secure a hearing. Mr. Montagu has himself passed over, and it would ill become a critic of his policy, however hostile to it, to impugn his motives, but it is not unfair to say that having become a bigoted believer in his own doctrine he used all his political skill and adroitness to win the approval of the Press and to pilot his measures through Parliament, while he naturally had a dominating influence upon the Joint Parliamentary Committee on the Government of India Bill, which became law in October 1919.

In the meantime Lord Southborough's Committees had rushed through India and had written their reports on the franchise and on the division of functions, while the Government of India had submitted a series of despatches upon the various difficulties, and they were many, which arose for discussion on this vast subject. Thus the work, compressed into the short space of two years, carried out at break-neck speed, partly during the distractions of the war itself and partly amidst the aftermath of troubles which became more intense immediately after the armistice, committed the British people and the British Empire, in India, and throughout the world, to a policy and to precedents of which the ultimate consequences are but yet dimly recognised, while the developments so far manifested bear but little relation to the high hopes of sober and gradual fructification of a generous ideal.

The Report of the Joint Parliamentary Committee is, as emanating from such a body, a weighty document, restrained and dignified in its language. It emphasises the importance of the change that the Bill would make in the political structure and life of India. " It marks," they said, "a great step in the path of self-government, and it is a proof of the confidence reposed by His Majesty's Government in the loyalty, wisdom, and capacity of our Indian fellow-subjects." The Committee's decision to embody the announcement of August 1917 in the Preamble to the Bill was a decision of much wisdom, but a great many cautions of the Montagu-Chelmsford Report were incautiously dispensed with. The spirit in which these changes were made were all in the direction of that "confidence" expressed in the passage just quoted. But did the honourable gentlemen envisage when they adopted these words that the " loyal, wise, and capable men" to be found in their thousands in India would have no influence on the deliberations of the comparative handful of politicians to whom they were committing all this power? Did they foresee that before the short space of a year from this expression of their generous confidence India would pass through three years of seditious non-co-operation with the " Satanic" Government so warmly commended by the Joint Select Committee in paragraph 15 of their Report, and did they expect that before ten years were out these same politicians would be flouting the authority of Parliament itself, and subjecting its chosen delegates to scorn and insult?

"Trust begets trust" has been a phrase in the mouth of the Indian journalists and orators ever since I can remember reading articles and reported speeches in the Indian Press. It is a phrase which is pre-eminently British both in its sentiments and its application. There are many people in India to whom it applies, but you must have some idea of the character of your man before you apply it. The trust of the fly, when it accepted the courteous invitation of the spider to walk into his parlour, inspired no corresponding confidence in the spider, except his confidence in the simplicity of flies.

CHAPTER XVII

INDIA AT THE END OF THE WAR AND FOLLOWING YEARS

Disastrous Effect of Reform Proposals on Moderate and Loyal Indians—Intensification of Hostility to Government in Political Circles—The Rowlatt Agitation and Outbreak in the Punjab—Mistaken Amnesty and Its Results.

A few months after the publication of the Montagu-Chelmsford Report came the armistice. During the last year of the war two things had been happening. In political circles hostility towards the Government had become more acute. Having been astounded by the extraordinary generosity of the Montford proposals, the politicians, after Indian fashion, began to belittle them, and Mrs. Besant[1] at first took the line that it was an insult to offer such small concessions to India, a line in which she was followed by the extremist Press. What really astonished the politicians, though they took care to conceal their astonishment, was that for the first time there was a real move in contemplation which would put British officers under the orders of Indian non-officials. They had blustered a great deal before, but they had never in their hearts expected that any such transposition of power would materialise so rapidly. And all the talk in the Montford Report about British officers declining in status from the men who issued orders to the men who merely tendered advice which need not be taken stimulated their palates and produced an appetite for even greater power. On the other hand, genuine old moderates,

[1] When, later on, she for a time became more reasonable on the subject, her following made themselves so objectionable as to wring from her the cry "My young Tamil brethren, why do you hate me so bitterly?" That hatred was only assuaged by her electing to follow her followers.

no less patriotic in their hearts than these extremists, were full of anxiety. They had always loyally assisted British officers and used their influence on behalf of the Government, and they now found themselves likely to be superseded by men of a lesser status and having less stake in the country, who had consistently and indeed virulently abused British rule. I met such an one, an old moderate friend, who had been in a prominent position for some twenty-five years, early in 1919, and found him in a state of complete depression. I said to him: " What do you think will come of all this?" He said one word: " Chaos." I had a letter from another old Indian friend, as accomplished a lawyer as any to be found in India, a man of the highest character, absolutely straight, but of a retiring disposition, whose honours had come to him solely on his outstanding merits as an honest, able, and far-seeing man. He was completely sincere in his desire for the advancement of the Indian peoples, but he knew very well their limitations, and there was a note almost of despair in one of the sentences he wrote: " Oh that my fellow-countrymen would be wise enough to profit by the unprecedented opportunities offered them." These men, staunch supporters as they were of Indian progress, knew well the politicians who would now have the upper hand, and feared the worst.

The second thing that was happening affected the masses, and this was the growing strain of the war. The recruiting areas, where the martial races were to be found, had been tapped as never before, and the demand for men for Labour Corps, for service in France and Mesopotamia, albeit attracting the men themselves by high wages, had begun to touch the rural areas, previously completely sheltered from war's alarms, while the rising prices were causing murmurs and dismay. With the armistice an immediate fall of prices was expected, but instead of this prices kept mounting higher. In the midst of all this trouble came the fell epidemic of influenza which swept over the whole country, penetrating the nooks and crannies and the hills and the forests. Many villages were decimated, some lost 25 per cent. of their population; hundreds of thousands of people were debilitated and enfeebled for work; all the various authorities did what they could, but it was very little that they could do over vast rural areas where doctors are few and nurses non-existent. And along with all these troubles the year 1918-19 brought crop failure and scarcity and still higher prices of food. Rumours were diligently spread around that the British were going to withdraw, and that the scarcity of silver was due to their packing up all the silver in the country to carry off with them. It was a splendid time for calumniating the Government, and the ill-wishers of British rule were not slow to seize their opportunity. The crowds in the large towns, with their large contingents of bad characters, were ripe for mischief, and political agitators were looking for pretexts. They soon found one in the Rowlatt Bills, which were introduced in the Imperial Legislative Council at Delhi. These Bills were designed so as to give power to the Government to deal with anarchical crime and with anarchist criminals. The history of anarchical conspiracies in Bengal (and there had been repercussions and imitations throughout India, though never on the Bengal scale) had proved over and over again that anarchical crime of this kind could not be dealt with by the ordinary law unaided. (This has again been proved since in Bengal in 1924.) There were large numbers of anarchists interned or restricted in their movements on the hands of Government, and everyone knew that with the termination of the Defence of India Act this dangerous form of crime was bound to recrudesce. No one could then foretell that the peace negotiations with Turkey would drag on for so long, and thus keep the war legislation alive for a considerable period. The Bills were drafted on the strong recommendation of a Committee which comprised Indian members and was presided over by one of the English High Court Judges, not the kind of man who could be persuaded without very good cause to put his name to what the politicians described as "a lawless law." The Bill that was passed was a stringent one in regard to anarchists, but many safeguards were introduced. The passage of the Bill afforded an opportunity for impassioned orations about the liberty of the subject (a conception entirely alien to the Oriental mind had it not been for British rule), and all sorts of fanciful pictures were drawn of the oppression that would arise. There has always been the same cry every time that Government has found it necessary to strengthen its armoury against outrages and murderous incitements. The concessions that Government made in the shape of amendments, and in giving the Bill only temporary force, were simply thrown away. There were Indians in the Council who would have supported the Bill, and in private highly approved of it, but were too timid to vote in its favour under the pressure exerted by the professional politicians and the Press. I know this because I have heard it from some of them. In the circumstances, however, the Bill was passed only by the use of the official majority. The opposition inside the Legislative Council confined itself to the fanciful effects of the messure, but the agitation outside was nothing but pure mendacity of the most shameless description. We are accustomed in the West to fantastic twisting of measures as election cries, but this agitation went far beyond these. It attributed to the Bill such ridiculous provisions as the arrest of more than two people seen talking together, and their indefinite imprisonment without trial. Funeral and wedding processions, they said, would no longer be possible. The first principles of religious liberty would be violated, and property freely confiscated. Copies of the Act, with full explanations, were distributed broadcast; they were torn up or treated as lies. When lies are started in the West it is difficult to catch them up; in the East it is impossible. The agitation spread in the U.P., through Delhi into the Punjab, where, with the turbulent city populations, it culminated in outbreaks of riot, murder, incendiarism, and rebellion directed against British authority in general, and against everybody with a white skin, however innocent, in particular. It is useless arguing about riots, rebellions, and revolutions, and the precise point at which one merges into the other. I would prefer to term the Amritsar affair a conflagration. There is inflammable material in every place, and the sparks from one area will kindle another, while the agitator goes about with his incendiary language lighting fresh fires wherever he can find fresh material to set alight. A crowd in England can be rough and violent at times, but seldom calls for more than a baton charge by the police to check its wildness, but a crowd in India may suddenly be transformed into a host of murderers and incendiaries, sparing neither age nor sex, nor innocence, nor sanctity; it will behave, as the Indians say, "like a *must* elephant," and it may be several days before this hot fit leaves it. But its foul deeds are generally done when it is ten to one, twenty to one, or fifty to one. When it is in this mood nothing but superior force will curb its passion. That is what had happened in Amritsar, had started to happen in other places, and would have gone on to happen everywhere if General Dyer's stern action had not quelled it. That action excited controversy at a later date. It was many months before it was investigated by the Hunter Committee, and at a still later date evidence and arguments regarding it were further investigated by a British judge and jury in the detached atmosphere of a British Court in the well-known case of O'Dwyer *versus* Nair. It was a British judge who held that General Dyer's action had been justified. The Government of India, though firm at the outset in support of Sir Michael O'Dwyer, began slowly to weaken in their attitude. That there were foolish acts done by individuals concerned in the administration of martial law cannot be denied; there were a few punishments inflicted that were stupid and humiliating, for none of which the Punjab Government could be held responsible, since the administration of martial law was not under their control. The shooting at Amritsar of the crowd collected in defiance of orders, and capable at any moment of being worked up to fresh deeds of horror, was not the real cause of indignation to the Indian intelligentsia. Even to those who regarded it as a mere reprisal it was an act of wild justice, as Bacon has described revenge, to which Indian sentiment has been for centuries accustomed; but the humiliation inflicted by certain orders touched Indian pride, and was repeated about with every embellishment of exaggeration that ill-will could supply. None of these punishments, however ill-advised, were cruel in their nature. In the atmosphere that prevailed they may have deserved censure, but not punishment. The conflagration that had been recklessly lighted by those seeking to subvert British rule itself, by means of a campaign of mendacity, incitement and hatred, could not be put out by thimblefuls of cold water, and thousands of law-abiding Indians in Lahore and Amritsar were devoutly thankful that strong measures had been taken to extinguish the flames, for if General Dyer had not quenched the fire the conflagration must have spread not only over the Punjab but to any city where bands of bad characters and turbulent men can be gathered together. These things spread as if by the virus of an epidemic, of which the symptoms are sabotage and indiscriminate murder. What greater proof is there of this than the assurances given to the new Amir of Afghanistan that the Punjab would receive him with open arms. It was these assurances that induced him to take the fatuous steps that he took of mobilising his army and invading British territory in force. As soon as he found out his mistake he repented, but succeeded in making terms which he was able to claim as a victory. The vigorous attitude taken against the forces of disorder, the trial and conviction of the murderers of the bank managers at Amritsar, and of many of the chief instigators of these outbreaks, coupled with the complete repulse of the Amir's invading forces, restored belief in the firmness and strength of British rule. But, once more, what had not been conceded to overt violence was given away to the insidious craft of the political agitator and the incurable optimism of the Secretary of State. Mr.

Montagu had to pilot his scheme of reforms through Parliament, and he trembled lest the Punjab outbreak should disturb the even tenor of their way. The lull that vigorous action had inspired carried him and them through, and he once more thought to clinch the success of his endeavours by one of those gestures of conciliation at the wrong moment to which he was so inordinately addicted. The National Congress was actually allowed to select Amritsar for its meeting-place, and an amnesty was announced which permitted most of the interned firebrands to attend it. These men, flushed with success and reading the amnesty as a thin disguise of fear, went there and bellowed for the recall of Lord Chelmsford, by whose goodwill they had been set free. In a moment the tables were turned; the loyal were crushed into silence and the turbulent elevated in triumph. The Hunter Committee, tardily appointed to investigate the outbreaks in the Punjab, at Delhi, and at Ahmedabad, and the rioting in Bombay (the last two had taken place merely on the rumour that Gandhi had been arrested), found themselves in a position in which the accused had become the accusers and the real criminals were now not the men who had instigated the crimes but the men who had restored order. And all this arose because the authorities responsible seemed to imagine that violent hatred was a mere lovers' quarrel to be dissolved in tears and kisses. With the Reform Scheme in process of induction, and a Royal visit in the offing for their inauguration, the policy of shaking hands all round was the constant aim of the Government of India, but the Congress put their hands behind their backs and acclaimed Gandhi's movement of non-co-operation.

CHAPTER XVIII

THE INAUGURATION OF THE REFORMS AND THE NON-CO-OPERATION MOVEMENT

Non-Co-operation Programme Outwardly Futile—In Reality Undisguised Rebellion—Campaign of Sedition, Intimidation, and Violence—The Passive Attitude of Government—Glaring Instances—A Profound Mistake in Psychology.

"NON-VIOLENT non-co-operation," as expounded by its apostle Gandhi, is a long-winded periphrasis for a general strike, but it differs essentially from a general strike in a self-governing country which is intended to force its own elected government of the day to yield to its demands, or give way to another elected government. Or it may be a class revolution, but it cannot be called a national movement. In India it is designed to bring foreign rule to an end; *vis-à-vis* the foreign government concerned, it is a rebellion; *vis-à-vis* its own indigeneous population, it claims to be a national movement. The hypothesis that underlies it is that the foreign government, finding it impossible to govern, abdicates. If this movement had been a genuine national movement, in which the whole of the 319,000,000 people participated as one man, it would certainly have paralysed the Government, always supposing that the Government had remained passive. "Mahatma" Gandhi hoped to work a miracle and achieve this wonderful result by sheer soul power, but he indicated to his following various practical stages in the plan, and he reserved "civil disobedience," as he called it, for the last stage, in fact this paralysis that was to overcome the Government was to be a creeping paralysis. Some of the intermediate stages appeared to be more disadvantageous to the people who followed his principles than to the

Government that was to be intimidated. Thus all who had received honours from the King-Emperor or the Viceroy had to abjure them and return the insignia. A mere sprinkling complied with this. Then all pleaders and barristers were to abjure the courts and give up their practices, while litigants and complainants were to refer their complaints to self-constituted tribunals created *ad hoc*, and to boycott the ordinary authorities empowered by law to meet these necessities. So far as these lawyers were concerned the loss to them was far greater than to the Government, and, in the matter of litigants, the self-constituted tribunals might give decisions but there was no certainty that they would be obeyed; while persons who took it upon themselves to impose penalties for offences against one another, if they executed these sentences became themselves liable to the criminal law.

All schoolboys and students were to cease their attendance at public schools and colleges. As private institutions, or improvised national schools, were quite incapable of undertaking the education of all the boys who deserted the Government schools this injunction was purely suicidal in its effects. There were a few legal practitioners who deserted the courts, but these few consisted mainly of persons who, having made their pile, could afford to retire, or briefless young men who could seek compensation as paid agitators. There were also some students who ceased attendance, boycotted, and tried to make their fellows boycott, the public examinations, again to their own hurt. Another great feature in the campaign was to make bonfires of foreign clothes, and the faithful were obliged to make a practice of wearing homespun and home-woven clothing, and don the Gandhi cap, a singularly unaesthetic head-dress. Then it became everybody's duty to spin a fixed quantity of yarn, whatever his normal occupation or station in life might be. This was not only tedious, but if everybody had carried out the injunction the spinning and weaving castes would have starved, and the mills would have shut down for want of labour. Efforts were also made by the non-co-operators, and by their temporary allies, the Khilafatists (for it was by feigning the utmost concern for the sorrows of the Turks and the future of Islam that the Hindus hoped to keep Mahommedans in the movement), to seduce troops and police from their allegiance and to induce other Government servants to resign their appointments. The Mahommedans had a little more success than the Hindus because they could make a direct appeal to religion, while the Hindus could not urge more than that as the Government were trying to destroy Islam, Hinduism would be the next victim of their destructive designs. The success attained was insignificant, for Government servants with pay and pensions assured were not going to sacrifice these prospects until they could be sure that similar security would be conferred on them in their place. This was, of course, impossible. Apart, however, from this motive, the vast majority of Government servants were perfectly loyal and regarded this movement as ridiculous. Except for a few seceders, who were hypnotised sufficiently to yield to the seditionists, this movement also failed. Most of this wonderful programme was tacitly dropped or died down as time wore on, but the faithful continued to wear the Swadeshi raiment and the Gandhi cap, while the Mahommedans revelled in the Turkish fez, little dreaming that before long it would be contemptuously rejected in favour of a foreign hat by the Turkish Dictator himself.

The Government of India were faced with two alternatives in dealing with this movement. The first was to ignore it, in the hope that it would die of its own inherent folly, dealing, of course, with any actual resort to violence which might occur. The second was to declare the leaders of the movement to be revolutionaries and take action accordingly. They chose the first alternative. If India had been quite a different and well-educated country, and Gandhi had merely been the originator of a new cult, of which the tenets were for men to turn their backs on modern materialism and return to a physical and moral Arcadia by means of successive acts of self-denial, this negative attitude on the part of the Government of India would have been the correct one, for to make martyrs of a saint and his foolish following might have merely directed sympathy to a harmless and impracticable reformer whose creed was pacific, though his measures were quixotic, and thus obtain for him some adherents whom he would not otherwise have gained. But the country was inhabited by ignorant and credulous people; the objective was to subvert the Government of the King-Emperor, and the only possible method of obtaining converts to carry out the programme was to represent the Government as so evil, and indeed "Satanic," trampling on liberty, impoverishing the country, a Government in fact which no well-disposed or patriotic man should co-operate with, unless he was a traitor to his country's good. Gandhi, in fact, could make no progress with his programme unless he excited hatred and disaffection in respect to the Government established by law in British India. The Government actually promulgated its intention not to use repressive measures against non-co-operators, but to deal with any violence that might occur, trusting in the meantime that the good sense of loyal and moderate men would suffice to subdue the whole agitation. This policy of masterly contempt let loose a flood of unpunished sedition all over the country. It is true that the Government prosecuted persons actually guilty of criminal violence, but the effect was to punish a few dupes and allow the instigators a free hand to go on instigating. The hands of the local governments were tied; they were permitted to arrest the small fry, but were on no account to deal with Gandhi's lieutenants and principal agitators without a previous reference to the Government of India. That the prestige of the Government was steadily ebbing was manifest to anyone who studied the Press or the periodical reports of the various local governments. In their perpetual search for that elusive calmer atmosphere, and in order to emphasise that the reforms were a surrender of power, the Government went out of its way to further the repeal of several[1] enactments which had enabled it to deal with emergent conditions, and the residuum of arms left in its legal armoury became painfully inadequate. The rebellion in Malabar, which was due to the incitement of unchecked firebrands, required fresh ordinances to be issued to meet the situation. Later on, again, the Government of Bengal had to certify a special law to deal with the revival of anarchy in that province. The time lost before these measures could be sanctioned was a mere gift to the enemy. The result of all this inertia proved to be the cause of much suffering and loss of life. The Mopla rebellion resulted in deeds of unmentionable barbarity from which the unfortunate Hindus of Malabar were the main sufferers, and troops had to be employed on a considerable scale before the Mopla rebels were suppressed. There were other minor revolts, including one among the aboriginals of the Upper Godavary Valley, in Madras. At one time a Civil Disobedience Committee was allowed to tour about the country unmolested. Local bodies even presented it with addresses of welcome. Even the peaceful villagers of the most loyal districts of the Central Provinces were churned up into a state of complete insubordination. It is scarcely surprising that some local governments were unnerved and others rendered very restive by this negation of firm government forced on them by the Government of India. When His Royal Highness the Duke of Connaught came to Delhi to inaugurate the new Councils the princes and the councillors paid him honour, but the populace held entirely aloof. Gandhi arranged to visit Delhi on the same day, and was escorted by a triumphant crowd of 80,000 people. A distinguished official, serving with the Government of India, described his feelings on that day by the phrase: "I'd never in my life eaten so much mud."

The agitation was also distinguished by the most fatuous folly that men with good education could possibly have committed; indeed, in no country except India could it

[1] The Press Act and the Rowlett Act were among the Acts repealed.

have been committed at all. The Ali brothers and their Khilafatist admirers were actually able to persuade thousands of simple Mahommedans to sell their lands and houses for a song and migrate into tribal areas or into Afghanistan or beyond, on the ground that India under British rule had become a country unfit for devout Mahommedans to live in. It was a new Exodus of the Children of Israel from Egypt, but there was a difference, as in this case Moses and Aaron sent out their co-religionists perhaps to starve in the wilderness while they themselves stayed behind "among the flesh-pots of Egypt." Even after this disastrous fiasco, for most of the survivors came straggling back in a miserable condition, the authors of the folly still dared to go about holding up their heads as leaders of men. What a bitter commentary upon the optimism of the British constitution-maker who expected "responsible government" to find Indian soil congenial!

The workers in the tea-gardens of Assam were in their turn victims of this insane policy of non-cooperation. From being peaceful labourers, who had bettered themselves and had been given plots of land to cultivate, they were seduced and deluded into abandoning a comfortable employment and making their way back hundreds of miles to the distant districts from which they had originally come. The ordinary transport did not suffice for the numbers seeking to return, and disorderly crowds accumulated on the route. Epidemic disease broke out, many died, and those who eventually returned to their original homes found themselves destitute, and unwelcome guests, at a time of high prices and scarcity, for famine conditions had again followed the drought of 1920-1921.

Gandhi had an unlimited capacity for persuading himself that evil is good and good evil, and an unlimited belief in his own influence. He thought, or affected to think, that after working up an audience into a paroxysm of indignation he could simultaneously calm them by repeating some of his texts; when violence and truculence inevitably followed he thought that a self-imposed penance would atone for everything. How far he has all along deceived himself or deliberately deceived others it is impossible to say, but it is certainly true that megalomania in the scanty attire of a Hindu ascetic, while it cannot for long impose upon the intelligent, exerts a most dangerous influence upon ignorant and superstitious men. Lord Chelmsford's Government devised its policy as if all the people of India belonged to the intelligent class. Because the councils debated, the courts functioned, and the revenue was collected, it tried to persuade itself that all was well, and that its non-intervention was really a masterpiece of policy. All over the country thousands of incidents were occurring, each not of much importance but collectively indicating that the authority of the British Government was being sedulously and disastrously undermined. The Government was, in fact, losing caste. From being a super-Brahmin, respected by all, it was being defied by a Vaisya as one who could be insulted with impunity. Such was the state of affairs when Lord Reading came out in April 1921 to succeed Lord Chelmsford.

Lord Reading brought out with him the decision that His Royal Highness the Prince of Wales would visit India in the following November. Lord Reading's position was one of much difficulty. He could hardly be expected to revise his predecessor's policy from the moment that he took charge of his high office, and if he waited to learn the position by independent enquiry the process must needs take time. Once again the situation was rendered more difficult by the approach of the Royal Visit. That perpetual necessity for creating a "calm atmosphere" for the Prince's visit again became prominent. With this situation before him Lord Reading before very long took two steps—he communicated with the leader of the Khilafat party, and he also sent for Gandhi, with whom he had many hours' discussion. In some countries this course might have been wise, but in the then conditions of India it did no good. The impression that India received was that the Viceroy considered these opponents of loyalty so influential that even he found it necessary to treat with them. The Khilafat leaders would give no promises of amendment, and members of that party had so flagrantly broken the law by attempts to tamper with the loyalty of the troops that they had to be prosecuted and were convicted and sentenced. But Gandhi remained at large, free to encourage his following to enter upon a general boycott of receptions in honour of the Prince of Wales. By the time that the Prince arrived in India, *Hartals*, the constant weapon of these agitators, by which reluctant shopkeepers were ordered to close their shops and all trade and traffic was suspended as a sign of sham mourning, were organised throughout the country. The disgraceful rioting that occurred in Bombay on the day of the Prince's arrival, and the paralysis of business in Calcutta which the agitators enforced, will long remain in the memory of those who were at those places. The Government of India were at last moved out of their passivity and renounced their embargo upon the enforcement of emergency laws. The great masses of the people were most anxious to give the Prince a really royal welcome, but they had been cajoled and intimidated for months before. The first signs of firmness on the part of the authorities gave them the necessary encouragement, and the Prince's wonderful personality did the rest. But so much time had been lost, that, almost everywhere, except in the Indian States and in Burma, abstentions and ugly attempts to mar the cordiality of his reception were unfortunately in evidence. The Prince was never in any danger of personal insult, except it might be from some stray fanatic or an anarchist, but the non-cooperators were still sufficiently venomous in their resolve to be able to intimidate a great many people who were only too willing to join in the celebrations. The people who are now seeking Home Rule are the same people who tried their utmost to secure that the King-Emperor's son and heir should make a royal progress through deserted streets, a slight to the Crown which, in a country like India, is most hurtful to the prestige of the ruler. Fortunately, even where the *Hartal* was evident on the day of his arrival, the enthusiasm of the crowds broke through all these seditious attempts before the Prince had been long in each centre that he visited.

It was not until after the Prince of Wales' visit had terminated that the Government of India decided at long last to take action against the prime mover, Gandhi. He was found guilty of sedition and sentenced to six years' imprisonment. From that moment this senseless agitation began to wane, and since that time Gandhi's influence has greatly diminished, for the people, tormented for months by these perpetual instructions to close their shops and pretend to be mourning when they wanted to rejoice, at last had the sign given to them for which they had been so long looking, that the Government was stronger than Gandhi. With the subsidence of this agitation the old relations of confidence between the masses of the people and British officers were gradually restored in all the rural areas. Since that time, however, and during the last four years, the peace of the large towns has again and again been disturbed by violent Hindu-Moslem riots of a most bloodthirsty and determined description. Fresh forms of disorder have also developed under Communist inspiration, in regard to the urban factory hands and railway workshop men, which are now proving a most serious menace not only to the peace of these cities but to all industrial and commercial progress. If, in spite of all these, India has continued to progress in many directions with the aid of improved financial resources, the result has been due to a fortunate sequence of better harvests and to the able management of her finances by the Finance Member of the Governor-General's Council, a third reason being the subsidence of the non-cooperation movement which caused much loss of revenue and considerable extra expenditure. One thing is certain, that the reforms cannot claim any part of the credit for these improvements. During the last two years the earnestness and high character of the Viceroy, Lord Irwin, his sincere desire to come into closer contact with the feelings and troubles of the ryot have greatly impressed all classes, but his noble appeal for the abandonment of senseless communal strife has been unheeded, and his efforts to conciliate the irreconcilable in the matter of the Simon Commission have been unavailing.

PART III

THE PRESENT IMPASSE

CHAPTER XIX

THE RESULTS OF THE REFORMS IN THE PROVINCES

Reforms have not brought Peace as was intended—Reports of Local Governments of 1927—Behar and Orissa the only Local Government that is outspoken—The General Effect is to damn with Faint Praise—Growing Deterioration

This chapter falls into this part because it is on the results of the reforms that the next step must be based, and the next step seems to lead to an impasse. There is one proposition about them which not a single man, British or Indian, moderate or extremist, constitution-maker or administrator, illiterate ryot, or polished English-speaking politician, mill-owner or factory hand, can or will deny: *The reforms have not brought peace to India.* Yet for this cause, to allay unrest, to reconcile differences, to instil self-respect, to create only divine discontent (for the authors did not contemplate a devilish discontent), to produce a leap forward in education and health, to uplift, to create a sense of responsibility, to inaugurate the first steps to democracy assumed to be the last word in government whether the country concerned contains 40 million educated people speaking one language, or 300 million illiterate people, speaking many scores of tongues, for all these objects the reforms were carried triumphantly through both Houses of Parliament. That poor devil, the British bureaucrat, who, with all his faults, had been doing his best for the country for over a hundred years, was to be cast out, slowly but surely cast out, with his foolish ideas of efficiency and his stupid insistence upon clean and honest administration. But can it be that seven other devils are now taking his place? and that the last state of this great sub-continent will prove to be seven times worse than the first? *Similia similibus curantur.* That was the assumption of those who persuaded Parliament to pass the Government of India Act, but what if the little prefix "dis" had to be placed in front of the first word of the maxim? Did it make any difference? The reformers thought not, or they would not stop to listen. The "dis" was drowned in the prevalent enthusiasm for the *similibus.* Anyone who mentioned it was liable to be dubbed a blind reactionary. Some people may say: "Unrest in India has no connection with the reforms—world causes have been at work." True, they have; they have greatly helped the agitator, for the unrest is fomented not merely by the speech of a pundit or by a leading article in an Indian newspaper, which very few can read, but by hordes of petty emissaries, ignorant and irresponsible, who spread calumnies among the credulous. The people who employ these emissaries and devise cunning tales which they, in their turn, repeat with every embellishment that an Oriental can add in transmission, are the politicians to whom the reforms have given a prominence which they could not in any other way have achieved. It was in the belief that they would placate men like these, and so produce peace, that the British Parliament unwittingly risked the security and happiness of the great masses of the people loyal to the British Government and ready to follow a lead on its behalf, if any lead were forthcoming. But any lead that came was only from these politicians seeking to stir up unrest.

And now that the time has come to hold an inquisition into the working of the reforms, the true results are in danger of being neglected, while attention is concentrated upon the superficial aspect of how the Councils functioned as deliberative bodies. In other words, the roof of the structure will be surveyed, while there will be little chance of anyone really examining the beams and the girders, and the state of the walls and the foundation of the building upon which that roof is supposed to rest.

The lawyers, journalists, and schoolmasters who supply so many of the leaders in the Councils, are men of considerable legal or literary attainments, the lawyers especially having the gift of forensic eloquence which stands them in good stead in debate. They know by heart all the catchwords of Western political thought, just as they know the maxims and manners of the British law courts. They are easily capable of assimilating and using parliamentary conventions, and of assuming all the verbal phylacteries of the politician and parliamentarian. They are seldom guilty of any serious breach of decorum, and in all of these outward appearances they have earned commendation from critics who do not probe below the surface. The Council of State has been the most successful of all the legislative bodies created, for it has largely consisted of men of the older generation who in their youth were brought up to feel respect for the British Government. They are returned by a very select body of electors, but even in regard to the Council of State there can be no security that it will not be invaded later on by less responsible men. The first Legislative Assembly, which was completely boycotted by the extreme section, also contained a good few of the old moderate class, but even that assembly upon many occasions proved utterly irrational in its proceedings. In the cases of non-contentious legislation, where no racial or communal interest is involved, these men can bring to bear reason and experience, but if a racial issue is in any way raised their attitude changes, and especially if any suspicion of a conflict of British and Indian interests can be even faintly scented in the proposals of the Government. Further remarks regarding the Legislative Assembly are reserved for a later chapter, and we can pass now to a consideration of the reforms in the provinces.

The various local governments, in their published reports

at all events, are inevitably circumscribed in their comments. There are Indian members on all the Executive Councils, and ministers have seen, and been consulted, as was proper, upon the replies of the local governments. In some instances the ministers have recorded separate opinions. It was therefore inevitable that Government should follow the same rule as they did in the case of district boards and municipalities, namely, to stress the good points and deal gently with the bad ones. Indians of all classes are naturally sensitive about criticisms which might appear to reflect severely on the capacity of Indians generally or their ulterior motives, and their British colleagues are also anxious, as far as possible, to soften criticism. The real difficulty about these councils is that the Governments have no regular supporters outside the few official and European members. In the first councils, which the extremists boycotted, they could manage to carry on with some difficulty, but since the Swarajists have gained the upper hand every non-official member, with only a few exceptions, is a Swarajist of sorts, though he may call himself by some other name, according as he is prepared to co-operate fitfully in working the reforms or is committed to a degree of partial or complete obstruction at the dictation of the particular group of politicians which calls the tune that he must dance to. In Bengal and the Central Provinces the wreckers have more than once gained complete ascendancy. In relation to the public interests they have been useless and worse than useless; in relation to their own aims they have carried out their destructive programme, though not without much inconsistency and sometimes inefficiency. The net result has been, however, that while the ultra-Swarajists are blatantly anti-British, there are many men of the other parties who would like to support the Government but are on many occasions afraid to do so through fear of being pilloried in the Press as traitors, or, at least, very lukewarm patriots. Occasionally there have been splits on communal lines inside these groups, and Government has thus secured a majority on the whole

Council, but it is obvious that the position of the Government is wholly precarious. Writing of the parties in Madras, where the division of Brahmin and non-Brahmin has made things seem to work better than in some of the provinces, the Madras Government is careful to explain that the term "parties" has reference only to the educated, and particularly the English-educated, section of the community. "Until education is on a far wider basis," it adds, "political parties will represent, in the true sense, only the upper layers of the population." To the outside observer, reading the Madras Report, it would appear that the cleavage between Brahmins and non-Brahmins, which marked the first council, under the respective heads of co-operation and obstruction, has lost its force temporarily. For as soon as the Brahmins recovered from the surprise of finding themselves in a minority, they set about organisation so effectively that many non-Brahmins contesting non-Brahmin seats had to turn Swarajist or not be elected at all by electorates which the Brahmin Swarajist organisation could manipulate to their will. The non-Brahmins are no match for the Brahmins in a battle of wits or organisation, and would certainly come off worse under Home Rule.

Of all the other provinces the more virile Punjab has for the present developed parties of urban and rural division, but here also communal questions between Hindus and Mahommedans or Sikhs may at any time bring about re-arrangements. The Punjab, however, seems to be the only province in which the non-cooperation party consistently failed to secure that ascendancy which has been so destructive a feature in the other provinces.

In Bombay the second council saw the complete rout of the more moderate men by Swarajists, who were pledged not to take office themselves, so ministers had to be selected from smaller groups. Some of the Mahommedans were generally ready to support the Government, but non-Brahmin support was very precarious, largely depending on whether they were temporarily assisting or at loggerheads with the Swarajists. The Bombay Government in its conclusions gives as much credit as it can to the Legislative Council by stating that: "On the whole it has not been unreasonable." Its praise is very faint.

The Bengal Government remarks laconically that: "Recognition of responsibility to electors is absent." For considerable periods dyarchy could not be worked at all, and several Bills and Budget grants were passed only because the Swarajists walked out altogether. The report makes it clear that, public opinion being negligible, members took practically no trouble to maintain relations with their constituencies. This Council also attempted to reduce grants for European education. The Bengal Government states that the parties found in the Council "followed communal lines, or a division of established government versus obstruction." It is made clear that nothing that the Council did or omitted had any effect on the electors, for 62 per cent. of the Mahommedan electors and 42 per cent. of the non-Mahommedan were totally illiterate.

The Government of the United Provinces has had many embarrassments. The Swarajist party, at first the only recognised party, has been followed by Nationalists, who formerly called themselves Liberals, practically all Hindus. The Nationalist Party has no formal alliance with the Swarajists, but there is no real difference between their aims and policy. Both parties find it easy to combine in rancorous criticism of the reserved side of the Government. Towards ministers the attitude of the Nationalists is mainly determined by personal considerations. The urban electors are taking an increased interest in the doings of the Legislative Council, but the peasant still knows nothing of what goes on there, and is indifferent to most of the issues there debated. "The gap between the legislators and the people remains a profound one." It is also pointed out that the increase of communal feeling and the lack of foresight and cohesion of the landlord party prevents it from holding its own against Nationalists and Swarajists. Lastly, "there is an apparent lack of goodwill on the part of the Nationalists and Swarajists to any form of administration in which the British element has an effective voice." The Government is therefore insecure.

The Report of the Government of Behar and Orissa is the most outspoken of all the reports, and I reproduce several passages from it:

" The ingrained determination of the Legislative Council not merely to control policy but to meddle in details of the executive administration is directly responsible for the feeling that Government officers are now required to serve two masters. Even more serious is the feeling of insecurity in the case of Services working directly under the transferred departments; their very existence depends upon the annual vote of the Council, and though in the last resort the Governor might interfere to save a Service, it is felt that neither the Governor nor the minister might avail to save individual appointments. There is solid ground for the fear in the past action of the Council, and the inevitable result is the tendency of members of these Services to regard individual members of the Council in some degree as masters of their fate, an attitude leading to demoralisation and fatal to good work.

" The position of the District Officer has definitely changed for the worse; it is true that the poison gas let loose by the non-cooperation movement has passed, and in many districts the personality of the District Officer has reasserted itself; but the new system has inevitably diminished his efficiency. In the pre-reform days the District Officer was actuated by the guiding principle of improving the district of which he was in charge, and he had power in his manifold capacities to give effect to his ideas. But this idealism cannot survive the complete transfer of his responsibilities in the sphere of self-government, and has to some extent been replaced by an attitude of half-cynical criticism. The prophecy of Mr. Montagu that the District Officer would find a worthy substitute for his past position in the training of men who can relieve him of much of his burden is far from realisation. The modern politicians, as elected to the District Boards and Municipalities, have no desire to be trained. They resent interference, and it is not possible for the District Officer to continue making futile attempts to improve matters. This is where the reforms touch him most nearly, and as he sees the structure built up by his predecessors in the District Boards and Municipalities travelling down the easy descent to chaos and bankruptcy he has strong doubts of the wisdom of the policy that the people should learn by their mistakes. The people who pay the cost of these mistakes have not the remotest conception that they have even had the opportunity of making mistakes, and pathetically reproach Government and its officers for allowing these things to be."

The Report goes on to describe the grave deterioration on the transferred side, which is the consequence of the dishonest standards now exemplified in the demoralisation of local self-government. It adds:

" There is nothing comparable to this landslide in other Departments. To deal first with the Reserved Departments. The insistent demand for funds for the "nation building" departments has undoubtedly led Government to curtail expenditure on the Reserved Departments to the minimum consistent with maintaining the previous standard of efficiency. The standard may be maintained but there is no progress, and stagnation may lead to deterioration. For example, the expenditure in the Police Budget is every year vigorously attacked. To avoid swelling the total, funds for necessary reforms have been obtained by reducing existing expenditure rather than by asking the Council to vote new money, and it is to be noted that though the number of police is lower in proportion to the population than in any Province in India, the total Force has been reduced since 1921 by nearly 800 officers and men, in order to provide a living wage for the remainder. The institution of a Detective School and the employment of a detective staff, measures which are really necessary to cope with organised crime, have been held up. The housing of the police in suitable barracks and stations is still an urgent matter, but the amount of money assigned for the purpose annually is insufficient.

" Matters of land revenue administration and administration of justice are at present stationary. The policy which finds favour with the Council is to abolish all supervising officers on the executive side, such as Commissioners, Deputy Inspectors-General, and Superintending Engineers. The Council apparently are blind to the wholesale fall in the standard of administration which would inevitably result. A marked feature of the Council is the inability to come to any final decision on any debatable matter. The Bengal Tenancy Act needs amendment in certain points, not of major importance; with an assured majority Government would have passed an Act which would have been fair to both sides. In the present Council Government have been forced to wait till the outstanding points of difference have been settled by the parties themselves, and the experience of the last six years shows that there is little hope of such settlement."

In fact the Government is unable to protect the ryot.

One of the most interesting points in the Report is the effect of the reforms on the Transferred Departments. In regard to this, the report states:

" Considerable advances are claimed in the Transferred Departments as a result of the Reforms, but it is not easy to estimate how much is really due to them. The Ministers claim that the efficiency of the administration has been increased, and cite in support of this the fact that large grants have been made for the development of primary education, the extension of medical relief, and for secondary and university education, and that medical, engineering, and veterinary colleges have been opened or started. There is no doubt that reforms have given an impetus to education and public health administration, and development in these Departments, which would have been of slower growth under the old régime, has been quickened. The Ministers are entitled to the credit of this expansion. They have pressed vigorously for funds, and have obtained (albeit at the expense of other branches of the administration) from Government and the Council the lion's share of any funds available. But the very Reforms that made this possible have hampered them in the administration of these funds. They cannot use the pre-reform machinery. They have to work with the local bodies as their agents and carry with them the Council at all stages and in almost every detail. Unfortunately, therefore, the increase in efficiency is not measured by the increase in expenditure."

Speaking of the interest of the public in the work of the Council, the Local Government repeats as still correct its opinion of four years before that "the work of the Council excited interest among the town people, who read the newspapers and follow the course of politics, and in educated circles generally, but some 95 per cent. of the electors neither know nor desire to know what is going on." The Report further describes what is by courtesy called party organisation in the constituencies, and explains how the Swarajist organisation, which alone had any funds, were able to swamp their opponents and capture the local bodies, with the result that at the Council election of 1926 the following description reflects what happened:

"This party (the Swarajist) in many districts, by converting the District Board staff and the village gurus (village schoolmasters) into an electoral organisation, secured a far larger number of seats than in the previous elections. Even the Swaraj party can hardly be said to have any permanent organisation. Agents and canvassers, whether employees of the local bodies or others, are only appointed shortly before the election, and no candidate has yet been known to nurse a constituency. Ordinarily, when candidates have been selected and agents appointed, appeals are made to the voters; in particular to their communal and caste prejudices; or even to their predatory instincts; in one division the cry of ' Down with the Zamindars,' with its logical inference of 'no rents,' was raised with considerable success. The voter in fact gives his vote under the stimulus of any motive rather than a consideration of the merits of a candidate or his policy."

Under the head of "General Political Atmosphere" the Local Government further describes how the general defiance of Government authority by efforts to set up national police stations, arbitration courts, and schools and colleges in opposition to Government institutions, were complete failures, as also the attempt to cripple Government financially by a fictitious temperance campaign. The Government in another part of the Report gives warm credit to one of the ministers in resisting pressure by the Council to introduce an impracticable policy of prohibition. It goes on to say:

"The anti-Government action is now more indirect. The control which the Congress Party have secured in local bodies gives them a dangerous hold on the primary schools, and propaganda is largely directed to the conversion of the coming generation. A good deal of the influence so exerted is too subtle to be dealt with directly. The primary school teachers, summoned to classes of training and instruction, are really imbued with politics to be passed on to the pupils. The cult of the *Charka* (spinning-wheel), with its political implications, has been introduced into the schools. On the other hand, some of the methods attempted have been countered by Government. The alteration of school holidays from those prescribed by Government to the birthdays of Nationalist heroes has been stopped. The attempt to get sub-inspectors of schools out of Government control and directly under the local bodies has failed. . . . A typical instance of the Congress methods may be quoted; several District Boards directed that the schools should open daily with the singing of a hymn which Government proscribed as seditious. The Boards appealed to the High Court for a reversal of the order, and were only brought to their senses by the stoppage of Government grants when they were recalcitrant. The effect of all this work in the schools was seen in the recent elections, where schoolboys paraded with Swaraj flags and hustled and hooted the non-Swaraj candidates and their supporters."

The ministers have dissented from the Behar Government in some respects, and have recorded a separate minute in which they have tried to brighten the picture. But even they are obliged to admit: "In our opinion the Swarajist party is the only party which has been formally organised, but it has no general relation with the constituencies, nor does the party secure any mandate from them."

In the Central Provinces there has been a general breakdown, and the province has been repeatedly deprived of having any ministers at all. There are men in the Central Provinces who are capable of doing good work as ministers if the Council would only let them, but their number is very limited, and the Swarajist majorities, obtained by shameless imposition upon the ignorance of simple voters, forbid all progress, except for short intervals between the resignations of ministers. The Council at one time refused all the Budget provision entirely, and all expenditure on new projects had to be abandoned. There are growing antagonisms between Hindus and Mahommedans, between non-Brahmins and Brahmins, and between the Hindi speakers in the north and the Marathi speakers in the south. In addition there is a conflict of opinion between Berar and the Central Provinces.

Under such circumstances it is only the influence of British administrators, with whom the masses are once again on friendly terms, that has enabled the Government to be carried on.

In Assam the Swarajists were ready to play their usual antics, but fortunately in that province there were too few of them to succeed in their wrecking tactics. The Assam Government report that the Council has little or no influence on any but the educated classes, and even among a large section of the latter there is little interest in the wider political issues. They also state:

"There cannot be said to be any public opinion in the political sense outside the educated classes, a very small section of the total population. The large majority of the people are interested only in their own immediate material needs; they care nothing for larger political questions, and know little about them. Members of Council, championing the cause of the poor and illiterate are ordinarily representing their own views, or the views of their party, and not the opinions of those whose cause they are upholding, except in so far as they may have succeeded in impressing their own views on them in any matter concerning their interests."

There is no doubt that the working of this Council has been assisted a good deal by the small group of members representing the tea industry, a contribution to the Council which is lacking in most of the provinces of India.

From a long experience of "reading between the lines" of Government reports, in dealing with these political questions, I have the feeling that (with the possible exception of the Punjab, in which the tale to be told differs largely in character from the story unfolded in the reports of the various governments) the Government of Behar and Orissa is the only one that really gives an accurate picture of the shades as well as of the lights. Any candid criticisms in the reports of most of the other governments are constantly qualified by indulgent attempts to minimise defects and suggest that they are possibly inevitable or incidental to all novel experiences. The real story of what is going on cannot be fully appreciated by casual readers of these reports, who have no other index to the movements below the surface.

The first Councils, which were totally boycotted by extremists, did not give a true picture of the difficulties that Government would encounter when, at later elections, the extremists entered the Councils with the avowed object of wrecking them. With the invasion of the Swarajists, who felt that they were not pulling as much weight as they wanted, the troubles began. Thereafter, in all the legislative bodies, in a greater or lesser degree, the Councils have been dominated by a majority of non-officials bent on opposing Government; of the old moderates who survive, except a few of the Mahommedans and some landholder representatives, the remnant call themselves by various names—Liberals, or Nationalists, Responsivists, or whatever other names they fancy, but they are all really part of the opposition to Government, which can only carry on precariously by the fickle support of this or that group, when for communal or other motives, often unconnected with the intrinsic merits of the case, it finds itself ephemerally on the Government side. The Councils are given credit for having passed certain measures, though scrutiny would show that but for the official and nominated vote and European non-official support, the Government would have been defeated nearly every time. A large proportion of the Bills passed have been non-contentious or purely formal. But the fact that certain more important Bills were passed does not give the whole story, for some of them have been passed only with amendments which Government conceded with great misgiving, while there must be many other legislative measures, eminently reasonable, but not introduced, simply because in the temper of the Council there was no chance of their passing. Such restraint upon a government is, of course, not unknown even in our own parliament, but if the number of such cases were numerous then the government nominally in power would be completely at the mercy of the opposition. Legislative Councils have repeatedly attempted to encroach on the executive sphere and to interfere in details. An Act, for example, to amend the District Police Act in Bombay included a provision which enables the Council to revise decisions in regard to punitive police, which means that decisions passed by lawful authorities, after enquiries made, as prescribed by law, can be modified or reversed by a vote of a body which should exercise no executive functions. It is recorded in the report of the Bombay Government that this Act was assented to by the Government of India "after very considerable hesitation and with grave misgiving." It is certainly not the function of a parliament to interfere in individual cases decided in accordance with magisterial enquiry and confirmed by a competent authority.

Ministers and Legislative Councils have been, of course, enthusiastic about making a splash over education and sanitation budgets. Did anybody expect anything else? The transferred side had at least to justify its existence, but the same Councils and ministers were very reluctant to agree to finding the money if they had to find it themselves, and it was largely found for them by stinting the reserved side. The Councils made ridiculous cuts in the Budget, and endeavoured to abolish appointments which would have the result of reducing essential posts held by members of the "All India" Services. They made special attacks on the police estimates, which, if conceded, would have paralysed law and order. Almost the only taxation to which Provincial Councils could be induced to assent dealt with stamps and court fees, and with these only temporarily. Neither ministers nor Councils could have achieved as much as they have done if the able financial administration of Sir Basil Blackett, who was fortunately aided by a series of good harvests, had not enabled him to remit provincial contributions to the Central Government. It has to be remembered also that large Budget provisions for improved education or sanitation, when funds are handed over to incompetent or corrupt local bodies, by no means connote that the money is laid out to its proper value. There have been some capable ministers in the various provinces, but there have been several without the character or ability for discharging the responsibilities assigned to them. The ministers, as they themselves cordially acknowledge, have been loyally helped by the heads of the various Departments, by their secretaries of the Civil Service who have, as has always been their tradition, done their best to make the machine work somehow, in spite of the sand which is constantly thrown into it. On the other hand, while one must condemn acts of class favouritism which are well known to have actuated some of the ministers, one must also recognise the enormous difficulties which they encounter with bodies so irresponsible and capricious as the Legislative Councils often show themselves, with a Press to satisfy with which neither hard facts nor scruples carry any weight, and with a limited public which demands that communal opportunity should be used to bestow communal favour.

Beneath all this surface of disputations there is steady deterioration going on, which has invaded the transferred sphere and is slowly sapping the standards of the reserved side also. As the older officers depart, and the ranks of many important Services are continuously depleted of their British element, the poison of corruption, which for years before had been steadily losing ground, is now as surely gaining it. Many an officer, finding that he can no longer stem that current, is learning to shrug his shoulders and turn cynic. Certain instances occur, I will not say in which province, which show what is going on. Government grants to aided schools, based on half salaries of the staff, are fraudulently increased by forcing teachers to sign receipts for perhaps double the pay they actually received, the managers of the schools pocketing the difference, while no action is taken against the persons responsible, and the evil is quietly hushed up. Embezzlements steadily increase, attempts to interfere with magisterial discretion for political objects begin to occur.

In two provinces at least the futile policy of prohibition has been accepted as the aim of the local government, though everyone must know that if it succeeded it would lead to the grievous oppression of humble working people, while if it failed, as it must fail, it would corrupt the excise officer and the police, and lead to illicit drinking of unwholesome liquor on a scale never reached under a system of control built up after years of careful experiment. Some of the people who support this policy are drinking privately foreign imported liquor, while they feign horror at the humble worker because, very often subjected to exposure and living in malarious tracts, he drinks the liquor which his forefathers have consumed from prehistoric times. As long as there are toddy palms, mohwa trees (*bassia latifolia*), molasses and rice in India, men will let their toddy juice ferment, or distil or brew their liquor in the fields and the jungles. There are, of course, sincere zealots among the men in favour of prohibition, but often only those men who are themselves total abstainers by creed or caste seek to acquire an easy reputation for enlightenment without understanding or heeding the inevitable results.

The irresponsibility of these men is nowhere more patently shown than in their attitude towards the assessment of land revenue. That they may desire to have a say in regard to general principles is not unnatural, but they are seeking to secure the direction of rent fixation, a matter which no parliament in the world could undertake. If they were successful the rise in the value of land would all go to middlemen, and most of the actual tillers of the soil would lose their protection, while the State would lose its share of the unearned increment which the present system reserves to it. Scarcely a man in the Councils has any knowledge of the difficult processes by which the fair rental value of land is determined, or of systems steadily improved and adjusted to changes by generations of trained settlement officers. The fair adjustment of the annual value of land between the State, the landlord and the cultivator has been the constant care of these officers, and the efforts of these politicians are directed to break and destroy the system, win cheap applause, and embarrass the Government.

The recent Bardoli agitation is a case in point. So far from being a triumph of peasants against the unreasonable demand of the Bombay Government, it has been a triumph of landholders of the trading class, largely middlemen, whose tenantry reap no advantage. I ask a few pertinent questions.

Why, in a tract specially selected by Gandhi for civil disobedience, where agitation was certain to be engineered by the Gujerathi Banias who exploit the peasants, was this difficult settlement entrusted to an Officer of the Provincial service without previous experience of such work?

Why did the Bombay Government not use its lawful power to offer the tenant the assessment which the landowner refused? This action would have subjected the fairness of the assessment to a crucial test, and would have brought the agitating landowners to their knees.

Why did the Bombay Government surrender to clamour and order an enquiry by non-experts which has ended in the strange conclusion that an assessment made thirty years ago, on still earlier data, could now in post-war conditions only be raised by the trivial fraction of 5.7 per cent.?

The answer to all these questions lies in the subordination of Government to the pressure of an interested clique. This thing could not have happened before the Reforms.

But the worst and most dangerous symptom among the results of the reforms is the growing contempt for authority and the weakening in the enforcement of law and order. When disturbances occur Government officers concerned are fiercely attacked for brutality if they are firm, and for weakness and inefficiency if they are gentle. In every case the blame for the disturbance is thrown not upon the disturbers but upon the Government. The National Congress increases its organisation for intimidating ignorant electorates and capturing councils, while moderate men are overawed into becoming adversaries of Government, when in their own interests they would wish to support it. If Government does not hearten its allies the allies must inevitably fall away.

We were always told that lack of power accounted for carping criticism in the Morley-Minto Councils, and that with greater powers would come more restraint. The precise contrary has proved the case. The expectation was vain. A bully will go just as far as he dares; with greater power the "daring" point is advanced. Mild acidity has become vitriol.

CHAPTER XX

THE LEGISLATIVE ASSEMBLY

Illogically Constituted—Unfit for Powers given but not Originally Intended, —Has thrown away Great Opportunities, and shown itself Irresponsible

THE Legislative Assembly, as at present constituted, is a wholly illogical institution. It was all along the cornerstone of the Montford Report that the Central Government should be so strong that it could discharge its own direct responsibilities to parliament, and could also, while leaving as much independence as possible to the Provinces, exercise its authority to support the reserved side of the local government, in case "popular control," so called, in any province should paralyse its legislative power. This object could have been better served if the old Imperial Legislative Council had been continued on the lines of the Morley-Minto scheme, with a few minor adjustments, leaving the provinces as the sole arena in which legislative bodies containing large non-official majorities should have had a chance of demonstrating their fitness or unfitness for responsible government. But in their zeal for parliamentary institutions the authors of the reforms and the British Parliament ended by creating a body which, save for the non-votable side of the Budget and the army and the foreign department, has been encouraged to consider itself to be the parliament of India, with 104 elected members (but elected by less than one million) to represent a population of 250 millions, comprised of all the heterogeneous collections of people to be found over an area of which the equivalent in Europe is divided into twenty-six self-governing nations. That in itself was an unsound proposition, but it was still more illogical in that it gave powers over the whole central field of the Indian Empire to just a few men, the top layer of educated Indian society, of a class which was not considered fit to be entrusted with control over more than a limited portion of the affairs of their own provinces. The interests of great provinces, larger than many European countries, in all the central departments of government, might thus be decided not by the few men who had some knowledge of these provinces, but by small groups of politicians who hailed from other countries and belonged to other races, but who together were more interested in defeating the proposals of the Government than in the true peace and progress of the sub-continent. The constituencies were huge, and the contact of any member with them confined to the few people of his own particular layer. These men, often supported mainly by the voices of ignorant students and their little oligarchic Press, to use Mr. Gladstone's prophetic phrase, "claimed to have the honour of representing the people of India." There were some individual members of the Assembly who had saner and more sober notions, but the abuse of this same little Press, and the contemptuous sneers of their intemperate colleagues, were a perpetual restraint upon the exercise of their saner views. The few who were equal to that test deserve all praise for their courage and firmness. Occasionally the Assembly had some lucid intervals from its mania for pure obstruction, but these were too few and rather far between. The pity of it is that these men have been the worst enemies of the political progress of India. Had the leaders of this Assembly shown themselves to be really practical men, instead of mere forensic elocutionists holding an anti-British brief prepared by themselves and their own mutual admiration society, they might have won the confidence of all the best elements in India and of the mother of parliaments in England. They were given chances in a fit of enthusiasm, and they have thrown them all away, allowing ambitions, partly high and partly sordid, but altogether premature and impracticable, to obscure all reason, sense of proportion, and recognition of fact. The judgment of these men has, alas, been perverted by envy and race hatred.

No great and righteous government, making mistakes at times, as all human governments must, but single-minded in its desire for India's progress, can be placed at the mercy of its slanderers and yet continue to function firmly and beneficently.

In a later chapter it will be seen that the memoranda of both the European bodies who have addressed the Statutory Commission insist strongly on the necessity for strengthening the Central Government *vis-à-vis* its legislature, while so unsophisticated a body as the Artisans' Association wrote their opinion upon the non-representative and self-seeking character of the intelligentsia. In the conversational ungrammatical Preamble to a draft Reform Bill which they put up they talk about "the collusion of monopolies as vested interests in the name of Intelligentsia." And again: "Whereas it is high time and a crime to allow the domination of one community, masquerading in the name of whole nation, over the other," etc.

Yet again, in the Introduction to their Bill, they speak of these cliques as "these hard task-masters and vulgar critics of Government, whose nationalism is skin deep and whose patriotism does not extend beyond their community. It is evident that these gentlemen are trying to hoodwink the people by these methods of theirs into the belief that these people are ready to support them."

In the early days of the Assembly's career it took some time before the members could feel their feet, or even realise their own powers. The first Assembly, being boycotted by the extremists, contained many elderly men of the old moderate school, and its proceedings were at first characterised by comparative moderation. Both Lord Chelmsford and Sir Fredk. Whyte, the first president of the Assembly, were in fact so astonished by this moderation that they took an early opportunity of indulging in most enthusiastic panegyrics about its wonderful dignity and reasonableness. The eulogies were so hearty that the Assembly should have blushed with pleasure, but the effect of the praise made them less and not more reasonable than they had been. For it was as early as 1921 that the Mozamdar resolution was introduced, suggesting that the Reform Scheme, just in its very infancy and so recently and enthusiastically sanctioned, should be ripped up again with a view to the early establishment of complete self-government. It is generally believed that the Mozamdar motion would have been lost on its merits as premature if the Government had not come forward with a sort of compromise resolution instead of firmly opposing it as calculated to reflect discredit on the patience and good sense of so young a legislature.

In 1922 Mr. Lloyd George's description of the Indian Civil Service as "a steel frame," and of the reforms as an "experiment," produced a resolution calling upon the Governor-General in Council to move the Prime Minister to repudiate this statement and to take the necessary steps for the early grant of full dominion self-government to India. This resolution, after a long debate, was converted into one of comparatively mild phraseology, and some of the speeches made in the debate were moderate, but in the same session the Assembly refused leave to introduce the Princes' Protection Bill, which eventually had to be certified by the Viceroy.

Thus far the Government carried on tolerably well. With the entry of the Swarajist party, however, into the Assembly, with a mission to obstruct, wreck, and occasionally make theatrical walks-out, the position of the Government became a nightmare. The whole of the Finance Bill was thrown out in the course of the Budget discussion, and the particular supply for the year which it had provided had to be certified. All sorts of necessary grants were wantonly cut down, endless speeches were made full of irrelevance and insults covert and overt. The language used may have been parliamentary in form, but it conferred dignity neither upon the speaker who used it nor upon the house that tolerated it. If a single Englishman in English public life to-day were to read all the debates in the Legislative Assembly since 1924—and it would be difficult to induce him to do so—he would find in them a compendium of prejudice, exaggeration, and animosity, interspersed occasionally with hollow protestations of friendly feeling, which could only make him wonder how men, some of them cultured and eloquent, could condescend to the banalities of debate to be found in so many of the speeches delivered.

Pundit Moti Lal Nehru sometimes excelled in these travesties of truth, as, for example, when speaking to a resolution on the Bengal Ordinance, which was designed to check murderous anarchy, he described the " British Government in India as the greatest and most powerful terrorist organisation in the country." And this Ordinance had been promulgated by the head of the terrorists, Lord Reading, a Liberal, and a former Lord Chief Justice of England! The Council refused to accept evidence about these crimes; a speaker referred flippantly to attempts upon the life of a most able British police officer faithfully doing his duty at great risk to himself, and tried to assert that there was no proof of anarchical organisations at all. This, of course, is an old story, for neither in the old Imperial Legislative Council, nor in its successor, the Assembly, was there ever more than a formal lip regret over the victims of these outrages, and all the concern and eloquence were reserved for the sorrows of conspirators (some of whom were confessed murderers, though their confessions were inadmissible in evidence) and their grievances under the most humane treatment that any government could have been expected to allow them. Government was constantly pelted with questions and resolutions concerning these conspirators, and often charged with the responsibility for creating conspirators because it had taken repressive measures to check their activities. As the years have passed the Legislative Assembly's defiance of Government has become steadily more intense, until to-day references by Swarajists to absolute independence of the British Crown are lightly made by men who have taken the oath of allegiance to the King-Emperor, and unveiled threats are uttered about paralysing the Government. If these are indulgently passed over as mere gas the Government may before long discover that the gas is more poisonous and suffocating than ever before, and that their anti-gas measures are too late to avert great injury to the whole people and to their own influence.

The Swarajist probes, pricks, and domineers, while the men who are the representatives of a Government which has given India security and progress are made the target of obloquy. The moderate recommendations of the Lee Commission in favour of British Civil servants, who were severely hit by the high cost of living and performed their duties under a most persistent rain of calumny from the politicians and their Press, would have been rejected by the Assembly if the power had rested with them, as is proved by the resolution they passed. For the Swarajists calculate that the safest way of getting rid of the British from the Services is by making their conditions of service so impossible that they would be glad to retire on any reasonable terms of pension and compensation that the Secretary of State and Parliament may confirm to them while they have still the power. The Assembly threw out the Bill to expel communists; it boycotted the Simon Commission, a direct affront to the authority of the British Parliament; it even threw out the Bill which laid the foundations for an Indian navy, of which the Nehru Report so airily talks; it threw out the Bill for the Reserve Bank; it carried by a large majority a demand for the favourite expedient of a round-table conference, at which the Swarajists hoped successfully to obtain by bargaining what they could never earn by merit. Finally, now it has upheld the Nehru Constitution! Could its folly and incapacity be more signally demonstrated?

The Legislative Assembly is an arena in which the Government is perpetually humiliated, and its spokesmen compelled to pretend that the men who indulge in these burlesques of reason are really the chosen representatives of the manifold peoples of India, voicing their feelings and giving effect to their mandates. The chivalry of the debate is all on the Government side, for the Government spokesmen ladle out most of the butter, their opponents the gall and the vinegar. Their thrusts might be amusing but for the tedium of the verbiage which surrounds them and the wearisome iteration of the stale and refuted arguments with which each speaker in turn supports his fellow. The dignity of the assembly has greatly deteriorated. Its behaviour is demoralising alike to the loyal supporters of Government and to its disloyal detractors. Among the former it creates a defeatist submission; among the latter it engenders an unbounded self-conceit. One would have expected that the Assembly would have reciprocated the goodwill of the British Parliament, so generously expressed when it passed the Government of India Act, but one speaker gleefully described the mother of parliaments as "a barren woman," a term specially spiteful on Oriental lips. These men may boast of their authority, but they would have had no authority if it had not been given them from that age-honoured institution. The remark was not original; it was borrowed from a source in which the insult was intentional. It was never thus in the old Council, where dignity and restraint were seldom transgressed. Fortunately, there are still a few moderate and loyal Indians who have not yet bowed the knee to the Swarajist Baal.

There is a pose maintained in the Assembly, and in its Press, which first incites and then applauds, that the politicians have lost all trust in the good faith of the British Government. It is untrue, designedly untrue; the very existence of the Assembly is a living testimony to the untruth. The politicians have not lost confidence; they are gaining more and more confidence that the more they abuse this meek and apologetic Government the more will its performances exceed its promises. The people who are losing confidence are its loyal friends, who find that the odium they incur in supporting it meets with scanty recompense, while its detractors receive all the rewards. The so-called great stroke of genius in selecting your adversary for special reward may cause temporary elation, but will produce you more foes than friends. Forgiveness to an honourable foe who has made his submission is one thing, but a bribe to an exultant enemy is a bribe thrown away. For one false friend that it makes it loses many friends that were true. This "no confidence" trick which the Indian politicians never cease to play is a leading feature in their political campaign. It imposes upon many well-meaning people who do not know the facts. Only in respect of the Army did we bar the door to Indian talent, and that was partly because the martial races were not educated enough and the educated men were not martial enough seriously to desire full commissioned rank. On the Civil side the door was never barred, though the avenue leading to it was not sufficiently wide. The avenue has been widened on a most generous scale.

In the case of political advances, in all countries, the time for reforms is either unripe, ripe, or over-ripe. It is in the third stage that they generally come about. In India we have been granting them in the first, or unripe, stage, while the politicians, with their excessive ambition, persistently protest that the third stage has already passed.

We have broken no promise, but the promise we have made has to depend on *their* performance. We have said this all along. Let these people perform their part of the contract before they accuse us of breaking ours.

Sir Basil Blackett, who cannot be dismissed as a prejudiced Indian civilian, after six years' experience of the Legislative Assembly, in his last speech there said: "My difficulty to-day is that I feel that at every turn this assembly is, to all appearances, trying to commit political suicide. Every opportunity that is given to it of showing that it has a responsibility and can use it, is taken to prove that it is irresponsible." I respectfully agree with Sir Basil Blackett. If the result of all the enquiries into the working of the reforms should be that the Assembly becomes a pale ghost of the departed, the verdict can only be *felo de se*.

CHAPTER XXI

THE BOYCOTT OF THE SIMON COMMISSION AND THE NEHRU CONSTITUTION

The All-British Composition of the Commission seized upon as an Excuse for Boycott—The Real Reason is the Swarajist Claim that India not Britain will decide, " India " being themselves—Utter Unreality of the Nehru Scheme

" They keep on saying Simon, Simon, but who Simon is God only knows."

This was the explanation of a barber of Calcutta who had shut his shop on order on the day that the Simon Commission landed at Bombay. His ignorance represents the outlook of about 315 million people. Even in Ahmedabad, Gandhi's own place, on the same day mill-hands not going to work explained that it had to do with seven Sahibs arriving in India. They could offer no further enlightenment as to why the arrival of these gentlemen should be connected with their staying away from their work.

The politicians had been pressing some time before for the earlier appointment of the Statutory Commission. When its appointment was expedited by nearly two years they boycotted it, and this was done not only by the extremists but by the party who called themselves Liberals. It had no doubt been anticipated that the Statutory Commission would follow the lines of the various Royal Commissions that have visited India from time to time, with a composition of, say, four Indians, four Englishmen, and an English president. They had not foreseen that Parliament might appoint a Commission of its own members to report to it on the working of the constitution which it had itself sanctioned in 1919, together with their recommendations on the nature of any changes that could properly be made.

The Statutory Commission, as composed, had some advantages and some disadvantages. As a Commission it was to be kept free from prejudice by the exclusion from its personnel of anyone British or Indian who had any acquaintance with India, and who therefore could be supposed not to have an open mind. Two classes of people were thereby excluded—the Indian politician and the experienced British administrator who had personal knowledge of the working of the reforms. As long as both were excluded neither could complain. But the difference lay in the fact that of these two classes one could raise an outcry and the other could not. As a result, both the Government and Sir John Simon proceeded to stretch conciliation to the utmost limit, in the hope of securing the co-operation of the boycotting politicians. The only result has been that the Commission have now associated with themselves a Central Committee containing some representatives from the Council of State and the Legislative Assembly (without the concurrence of the assembly as a whole) which will jointly with them hear and cross-examine all the witnesses. They will also be present at all sittings in camera. Sir John Simon is entrusted with the duty of protecting the witnesses from any tendency towards unfair cross-examination, and he can at any time exclude the Press from the sittings. Now it is well known in India that it is extremely difficult to keep confidential matters from leaking out. The members of the Central Committee would no doubt refrain from communicating confidential papers, but the general tenor of a witness's attitude is not likely to remain secret for any time. In any case, whether this is so or not, Indian witnesses especially will be timid about giving their genuine opinions lest they should presently be subjected to persecution. There were persons practising at the Bar as pleaders who gave evidence during the Punjab disorders on behalf of the Crown, but later on, when the extremists were released from internment, these pleaders lost their practices by reason of the intimidation of any clients who thought of employing them. In addition to the Central Committee, Provincial Committees of the Legislative Councils accompany the Commission as they tour through the provinces, so that a witness is faced with some twenty-three interrogators. If it is an advantage to have Indian non-officials associated with the sittings and deliberations of the Commission it must equally have been an advantage to have had some British administrators to assist the Commission in the same way. This advantage they have not had. The danger is great that the joint deliberations may tend to become an affair of politicians bargaining with each other rather than a probing investigation of the real effects and not the surface appearances of the reforms. Practically all the legislative bodies refused co-operation at the outset, and the Central Provinces Provincial Council is the only one that has not had second thoughts. The Swarajists and the Liberals, and all the various groups intermediate between them, have taken their stand upon the "insult to India," because Parliament exercised its right of sending delegates of its own members to report to itself. If Indian chagrin had been due solely to disappointment that the Commission was not a mixed body of British and Indians, and that the Indian view might suffer in consequence, one could understand and indeed sympathise, but this is not the real cause of their action. Indian politicians have refused to accept the second part of the Preamble to the Government of India Act. In Indian fashion, when a gift was offered with certain limitations, they accepted the gift but disregarded the limitations. If the limitations were irksome they should not have accepted the gift. They are estopped from refusing to recognise the whole of the Preamble, and from picking and choosing such portions of the announcement in Parliament as they like and rejecting all that they dislike. According to them it is for educated Indians alone to say "We want complete Home Rule," and for Britain thereupon to give it. This was the very standpoint taken up by the president of the Central Committee himself, Sir Sankaran Nair, in an article on the

Simon Commission which he contributed to the *Contemporary Review*. Whether he had abandoned this attitude when he accepted the presidentship of the Central Committee, which is co-operating with the Commission, can only be disclosed when the former body puts forward its own proposals. The Simon Commission have been welcomed with the cordiality and hospitality which one has learnt to expect from the true representatives of Indian courtesy and kindness, and by all those who appreciate the beneficent intentions of the British nation, and the solid advantages of British rule to India. The malcontents, full of their arrogance and folly, and pandering alike to the vanity of students and the rowdy elements in the large towns, have caused the Commission to be pestered by stupid demonstrations which could deter nobody and prove nothing except the stupidity of those who organnised the demonstrations. When the demonstrators began to indulge in rough and disorderly conduct and received a few knocks from the police they proceeded to squeal. It is not from this material or from those who depend upon it that strong or stable governments are made—sterner stuff than this is wanted.

The National Congress, stung by Lord Birkenhead's challenge that, amidst all their agitation and boycotting, carried on for some years, they had never yet put up a constructive scheme of their own, while they refused all co-operation with the delegates of the British Parliament, at last put their heads together. A so-called All Parties Conference was collected which appointed a committee to draw up a form of constitution, now known as the Nehru Constitution. The Congress have adopted this and annexed to it an ultimatum that if their demands are not granted in full by the end of 1929 there would be a non-violent non-cooperation, a passive revolution (beside which Gandhi's movement was child-play) calculated to paralyse the British Government in India and bring the British nation to its knees. A large section in the Congress, forming an important minority, is not satisfied even with this modest programme, and wildly gesticulates for absolute independence. Dr. Annie Besant, if she is correctly reported, said she could really see no difference between the two, but she voted for the Nehru scheme. Possibly this lady did not like to commit herself to a declaration of treason.

THE NEHRU CONSTITUTION

Some people might think it a waste of time to examine this Constitution at all, but Sir John Simon has himself described the Report of the Committee of the All Parties Conference as an able document. It has been drawn up by lawyers of ability, but, after all, it is only a thesis. Let there be a country of several provinces and draw up for it a model constitution on the assumption that its connection with the British Empire is limited to the single link of the Crown. That being the subject of the thesis, the Nehru Report is the answer. Not being a learned student of comparative constitutions in countries like the U.S.A. or the great dominions which form part of the British Empire, I do not feel competent to criticise the merits of the document as a thesis. It certainly represents labour, thought, and industry, as might be expected from writers of this ability dealing with a set question of this kind, but so far as India is concerned, either in respect to its past history or its present circumstances, the constitution might just as well have been drawn up for Utopia. The only attempt to deal with religious and political antagonisms is in that portion of the report which relates to the reservation of seats for Moslem minorities outside the Punjab and Bengal, and for non-Moslem minorities in the North-West Frontier Province. It is provided that this reservation of seats should continue for ten years only. These proposals have not been accepted by Mahommedans.

So far as the Indian princes and chiefs are concerned they are merely given an assurance that the treaty rights and obligations, which govern their relations with the present Government, will be recognised by the new Government, any disputes being referred for decision to a new supreme court which is to be established, in relief of the Privy Council. There is no mention of the peculiar relations between His Imperial Majesty the King-Emperor and the princes. From the report it is gathered moreover that the new Government will deprive His Majesty of the title of Emperor of India, without consulting either His Majesty himself or His Majesty's constitutional advisers in England. These proposals will not be accepted by the princes, in fact they have already made a declaration to that effect.

The problems of defence are not considered at all. The British Army in India is not even mentioned. Presumably the new Government will politely request the British nation to withdraw all British troops from India, on the easy assurance that they will themselves undertake the maintenance of law and order, and the defence of the country. They provide in their Constitution that the officers, British and Indian, of the Indian army will be given their existing salaries and allowances and pensions, or compensation for the loss of any of them, as the Governor-General in Council may consider equitable.

In the case of Civil Service officers (no mention is here made of the British officers), they can stay on or retire, but if they are not retained, or if they retire voluntarily, they will be given such pensions or compensation as they would have received if the new Commonwealth of India had not been established.

The clauses dealing with these subjects in the rough draft of the Bill that brings the Commonwealth into existence have some peculiar features. In the case of the army officers, those already retired will continue to receive the pensions they now enjoy. No similar provision, however, finds a place in respect of retired officers of the Civil Service. On the other hand, the right of retiring on a proportionate pension is not apparently to be conceded to army officers. As the clauses relating to the Civil and Army Services are in numerical sequence to one another, it seems improbable that these distinctions can have been an oversight. But, if not, why is this distinction between the Civil Services and the Army Services, which latter, it may be mentioned, include the as-yet non-existent Indian navy and an embryo air force? Possibly the idea is to induce the officers of the Civil Service to retire as soon as they like and to induce the officers of the Indian army to continue their service. It is apparently imagined that officers of the Indian army, with their King's commissions, will be only too ready to accept supplementary commissions from the new Commonwealth. If these officers stay on in service it is not quite clear how they are to be controlled. Parliament in the new draft constitution means not the British Parliament but the two new Houses to be set up in India, the Senate, strength 200, and the House of Representatives, strength 500. There is, of course, a Committee of Defence to be set up which will function as an Army Council. It is not, however, clear whether its composition will be British or Indian, or both combined.

The European is scarcely mentioned at all, and his claim to special representation disappears with the abolition of communal electorates. Very few of them are likely to have a vote at all, for though universal adult suffrage is proclaimed by the new Constitution for all citizens, the definition of "citizen" excludes anyone unless his father or himself were born in India, or had either of them become naturalised Indians. Pundit Moti Lal Nehru has since, in a supplementary note to the Press, laid stress on the point that in the Introduction to his report he referred to the willingness of his party to consider any special representations that European commerce might wish to make. This scarcely covers the question either of votes or special representation, and the pundit cannot on his own personal authority add promises to those contained in his scheme, for they would not be binding even on his co-signatories, much less on the National Congress.

The basis of the new Constitution is a declaration of rights.

It is very high-sounding and comprehensive; all adult citizens will have a vote; every citizen will have a right to keep and bear arms, in accordance with regulations made in that behalf; they also have the right to assemble peaceably and without arms, but the Sikhs are in these circumstances allowed to carry "kirpans," or swords. This was a little sop introduced at the last moment to conciliate the Sikh member of the committee and induce him to sign. Any Sikhs, therefore, that are in these peaceable crowds may always carry their swords, and thus have an advantage over all other citizens.

It is not quite clear, however, what is to deter a crowd, bent on mischief, and of which every member has lawfully arms in his possession, from arming themselves when they are bent on a so-called peaceful demonstration, merely as a precautionary measure in case the police should be so rash as to bar their progress.

The framers of the Constitution lay great stress on the fact that a clause in their declaration abolishes "untouchability." It will remain to be seen how a simple clause written at a table can abolish at a stroke of the pen caste rules and prejudices which have existed for many centuries. The declaration guarantees full freedom of combination and association, and maintenance and improvement of labour and economic conditions to everyone and for all occupations, and all agreements and measures tending to restrict or obstruct such freedom are declared illegal. It is possible that the new Government may have difficulties about its police. The Indian Parliament is to make suitable laws for the maintenance of health and fitness for work of all citizens, the securing of a living wage for every worker, the protection of motherhood, welfare of children, and the economic consequences of old age, infirmity, and unemployment, and to these obligations a subsequent addition was made by the full Conference, namely, fixity of tenure to all agricultural tenants. Every citizen is entitled to free elementary education by the State, and this right is to be enforceable by the citizen "as soon as due arrangements shall have been made by competent authority." That is to say, the clamouring citizens must not enforce their rights until the competent authority, whatever that may be, has made due arrangements. Presumably, when due arrangements have been made there will no longer be any necessity for citizens to enforce their rights.

There is to be no State religion, "nor shall the State directly or indirectly endow any religion." Apparently away will go the revenue free grants to temples, shrines, etc., made by the old Rajas and maintained by the British Government. What will the orthodox have to say about this?

To the Indian mind words are the supreme consideration. Whether facts correspond to the words is of no moment at all. Were it not so, it would be impossible that a group of intelligent men should draw up a constitution which is a counsel of perfection and has no relation to existing facts or to the ways and means by which the Commonwealth of India will furnish itself with the most modern equipment demanding the most colossal expenditure. The whole scheme is a mere castle in the air, and not even a castle of indigenous dreams, or containing a single Oriental or traditional feature. It is pure plagiarism from beginning to end, without a single original conception. The problems of poverty and ignorance are put to an end by the simple process of reciting a constitutional creed. The problems of races and languages are to be solved by splitting up provinces, although the authors must know that even the division of a district into two parts can create an uproar, and that the proposed separation of so distinct an entity as Sind calls up violent dissensions among the inhabitants of that sub-province. The problems of defence are to be solved by the Indian army, bereft of all British officers, for British officers are not likely to accept an assurance of security from pundits and Khilafatists.

There is one passage in the report relating to Sind, and giving reasons to justify its separation which is not without significance. It states (page 32) in regard to the objection that the separation of Sind involves the creation of a "Communal Province": "There is no question of creating a 'Communal Province.' We have merely to recognise facts as they are." (One wishes there was more recognition of facts as they are about the whole scheme.) "Sind happens to contain a large majority of Moslems. Whether a new Province is created or not, Sind must remain a predominantly Moslem area. And if the wishes of this large majority are not acceded to, it would not only be doing violence to the principle of self-determination, but would necessarily result in antagonising that majority population. No Indian desiring a free India, progressing peacefully and harmoniously, can view this result with equanimity. To say from the larger point of Nationalism that no Communal Province should be created is equivalent to saying, from the still wider international viewpoint, that there should be no separate nation. Both these statements have a measure of truth in them, but the staunchest Internationalist recognises that without the fullest national autonomy it is extraordinarily difficult to create an international State. So also without the fullest cultural autonomy (and communalism, in its true aspect is culture) it will be difficult to create a harmonious nation."

Pundit Moti Lal Nehru and his coadjutors have here stumbled on the truth but have evaded it. The problem is as I have stated it in the first chapter of this book. The Indian problem is not a national problem but an international one, viz. to create a single democratic nation of many States and nations, and yet keep them one. It is not only "extraordinarily difficult" but it is impossible to create an international State until the world is completely changed. For the same forces which broke up the Austrian Empire and tore off portions of Germany, Russia, and Turkey, to form new States or new combinations of territory, will cause India, thus far held together by the common bond of British rule and the Pax Britannica, to fall into many pieces. The whole of the constitutional plan formed by the learned pundit and his group of coadjutors must break up under that test.

No, Punditji, this swan song of the National Congress (for your Constitution will kill it) may sound glorious to the accompaniment of the circus performances of the last session of the Congress. Your jewel glitters, but it is not gold. We may admire your fortitude, your ingenuity, your legal skill, your fidelity to the ideal of an Indian nation—the Commonwealth of India—but we cannot admire your sense of proportion. You dispose of your aims by idealising them; your difficulties by talking round them; and the facts by ignoring them. If your dreams were a reality and your schemes founded on facts, and not the vain ambitions of a class, the British nation might accept your Constitution and rejoice at an achievement the most wonderful that the world has yet seen—the creation of a harmonious, united, self-governing democratic nation, composed out of the wrangles and the jangles of races, castes, and creeds, which together make up nearly one-fifth of the population of the world. The men that assembled round your conference table cannot command the obedience of India's millions. Punditji, you must think again.

The scheme of this committee was submitted to the All Parties Conference which had appointed it, and various messengers came along conveying the welcome but illusory message that the proposals regarding Sind were accepted by the people of Sind, and the proposals regarding reserved seats for Mahommedans were accepted by Mahommedans. The enthusiasm became almost hysterical. The president said that: "The Nehru scheme was the last hope of 300 millions of human beings suffering intolerably under the double misery of foreign domination and internal dissension." After a vote of thanks to the committee, from which one stalwart member, a Mahommedan, dissented, the second resolution was to the following effect: "Without restricting the liberty of action of those political parties whose goal is complete independence, this Conference declares, etc., viz. for full Dominion status." This resolution was proposed and seconded by two gentlemen who have sworn an oath of allegiance to the King-Emperor and have been the recipients of honours bestowed by His Majesty, and the holders of most responsible office.

Pundit Jowahir Lal Nehru then read the following statement on behalf of those who stood for complete independence, beginning: "We, the signatories of this statement, are of opinion that the Constitution of India should only be based on full independence. *We propose to carry on such activity as we consider proper and necessary in favour of complete independence.*"

The names of the signatories to this challenge are not given in the printed proceedings. The declaration amounts to a determination to deprive the King-Emperor of his sovereignty over India, and the Resolution aids and abets.

> "The mills of the gods grind slowly,
> But they grind exceeding small."

Perhaps Pundit Jowahir Lal and his co-signatories, whoever they may be, may yet find themselves disenchanted of the fair scenes of their vision splendid. Yet it may be, perhaps, that they are more honest as to their intentions than the others.

CHAPTER XXII

SOME SCHEMES BEFORE THE SIMON COMMISSION

The Proposals of the Ceylon Commission examined—Quite Impracticable for India—Fatal Defects in the Memorandum of the Associated Chambers of Commerce, and in the Opinions of the European Association—Impossibility of making Law and Order "A Transferred Subject"

In the last chapter were described the activities of the boycotters of the Simon Commission. In this one some alternative schemes which are before that body are sketched. The material, oral and written, before the Statutory Commission is vast, so vast that there is not a living soul that envies these gentlemen their task. No one who has not accompanied them can appreciate it, and nobody not in India can keep pace with it. A few items of some importance are picked out for examination in this chapter.

Among the documents of special interest is the Ceylon Report, because, though on an infinitely smaller scale, some of the problems that it deals with are of like nature to those encountered in India. My own acquaintance with Ceylon is limited; I am a distant critic, but in the light of my experience of kindred problems I have read with wonderment the scheme unfolded by the Special Commission. The island of Ceylon covers an area of 25,000 square miles and has a population of nearly 5 million. The visit of the Special Commissioners to the island was of two months and five days' duration.

The first advance towards a constitution that had been made in Ceylon was much the same as in Burma under the Morley-Minto Scheme, a Legislative Council of 21 (11 being officials and 10 non-officials—4 elected and 6 nominated). This Council was inaugurated in 1912, and a year later the

Governor reported that "It was a harmonious and efficient instrument for giving effect to the measures necessary for the good government and progress of Ceylon." I have no doubt that this reform was admirably suited to serve the best interests of the island, but the politicians are never satisfied with leaving well alone. Indian agitators visited Colombo, including the late B. G. Tilak and Mrs. Annie Besant. The people of Ceylon were stirred up to agitate and to imitate Indian politicians. Mr. Montagu's announcement in Parliament as regards India started new hares for the Ceylonese to pursue, with the result that a fresh Constitution, this time on the lines of the Montford reforms, with variations but without dyarchy, was put in force from 1921, and from that date onwards there seem to have been nothing but schemes and appeals and agitations, until in 1924 fresh changes were made. The island is about the size of a large Commissioner's division in India, and its population is much the same, but its public revenues are larger because they have not, as in India, to be divided between Central and Provincial Treasuries. The Commission, considering the work of this last Constitution, points out the illogicality of an arrangement by which the Government could carry on only by yielding, which was the natural accompaniment of placing it at the mercy of an opposition determined to make it yield. The situation which the Commissioner found was thus the same in kind, though different in extent, from the situation in India. The Government was in an impossible position and the Civil Servants liable to frequent humiliation. It became in the position of an Indian province if all subjects had been transferred, and the Governor's powers could only be exercised in matters of "paramount importance."

The Commissioners have subjected the defects of the existing Constitution to a searching analysis and find that its continuance is impossible. In considering the alternatives, the Commission examined with some sympathy a sort of Morley-Minto scheme, but decided against it, remarking it as significant that the scheme had been short-lived in India. It may have been short-lived, but the Commissioners are entirely mistaken in thinking that it was superseded because of its inherent defects. It had in no way broken down, and it was superseded because the war and the self-determination cry, and the readiness of Mr. Montagu to conciliate political agitation and his impatience to expedite a new heaven on earth in India, brought that scheme of reform to a premature end. It was ended because the rule of formulas instead of facts gained the day. Finally the Commissioners, after making it thoroughly clear that parliamentary government in Ceylon on a party system is wholly impracticable, proceed to devise a system which they themselves term as "making a virtue of necessity," but which other people might be tempted to regard as a counsel of despair. First of all there is to be a council of 63 members, to be elected by adults on a territorial basis, communal electorates being abolished as an unclean and cursed thing. There are to be three ex-officio members (who it may be remarked are to be advisory only) and twelve non-official nominated members. The council is to be called the State Council, and its functions are to be both legislative and executive. It will be sitting now in legislative session and now in executive session. The whole Council, after assembling, will divide itself by ballot into seven standing executive committees, after which each committee will by further ballot nominate a chairman, whom the Governor will ordinarily appoint to be a minister. The chairman is to receive a salary of Rs. 27,000 a year, while the members will receive only such salaries as are appointed for them as members of the State Council. There will also be certain departments under three " Officers of State," the Chief Secretary, the Treasurer, and the Attorney-General, who will be the political, financial, and legal advisers respectively of the State Council. The whole ten would form a " Board of Ministers," and the whole Council would be in permanent standing committee. Legislative work can, of course, be reserved for special sessions, with long recesses in between, but how the daily executive work is to be done, if there are long recesses and vacations, is not explained. Further, the committees, although dealing with the special departments allotted to them, can interfere with one another, since a member of one committee can always give notice of a proposal relating to the work of another committee. Presumably if one member can do this all members can do it, so that the whole sixty-six members might conceivably be intervening in the work of one of the committees in which they were specially interested. In any case, however, all decisions on major matters have to be confirmed by the whole State Council in executive session, and then ratified by the Governor, it being made clear by the Commissioners that the Governor will as a practice ratify them. After a considerable experience of council government I try to think what would have happened if, as Home member in the Government of India, I had had to explain every order of the slightest importance first to ten other people, and then perhaps to sixty-six more, before the order could be passed and action taken upon it. I also ask myself, who on earth these people may be who are to devote their time to all this public business. What time will they have to spare for their own professions or avocations? If they are to neglect these latter totally, as seems probable, they will have to be paid very highly. In fact, for a diligent, incorruptible, well-trained and well-disciplined bureaucracy, the scheme will substitute not democracy but a new political bureaucracy, greedy of power, endless in discussion, quarreling over the spoils of office for themselves and their friends, over whose dilatoriness there is no check, over whose possible dishonesty there is no control. I have had nearly forty years' experience of the administration of public affairs, but nothing would ever have induced me to accept the responsibility of office under conditions so impossible.

The Commission has proposed excellent safeguards on paper for the Services, but the Services will nevertheless be destroyed, for honourable public servants will do their best to work under honest incompetence, but not under an inefficiency that is bound to be infected with corruption. As the number of Ceylonese, clamouring for posts, increases, the pressure on the State council, the ministers and their committees, to substitute lower-paid Ceylonese for experienced Europeans, will be irresistible. It will be the first article of the creed that the Ceylonese are just as good as the British, if not better. Then why employ British, who are highly paid, in preference to Ceylonese more moderately remunerated? Ceylon has been imitating India, and is even trying to outstrip her, and the Commissioners' safeguards for the Services, effective as they may sound, may prove nugatory because there will be no Services to safeguard. For on such conditions only the rolling stones and adventurers, swimming with the tide of graft and nepotism, will dream of accepting service there, and that not for the honourable work they can do on emoluments that are honourable, but for the ill-gotten gains with which they can supplement their more modest salaries.

The franchise proposals of the Commission illustrate once again the complete sacrifice of facts to an idolatory of theories. Property qualifications, educational tests, communal representation, are swept away, in the belief that all people, however poor and ignorant, however superstitious, however irresponsible, will by virtue of this sovereign remedy, the ballot box, become enlightened, discover their stake in the country, and understand issues hitherto to them incomprehensible. The radical error is the failure to perceive that it is not the ballot box that enlightens the ignorant, it is education that enlightens the use of the ballot box. And the irony of the whole thing is that the only people who can get no value from this universal suffrage are the Europeans and the Dutch burghers, namely, the only people who are fit to put the ballot box to its proper use, whilst the Moors and the Malays, both of whom are Mahommedan, both of whom are shrewd traders, are left in the lurch. Disputations will arise between the interests of the Kandy group of the Upland Sinhalese and the Sinhalese of the coast and lowlands, of the

Ceylon Tamils and the Indian Tamils. I have first-hand information regarding these Indian labour immigrants in Burma, and they are no more fit to vote than a flock of sheep.

The Governor, reading his Instrument of Instructions, will be sorely bewildered; his lot will be most unhappy. Is he to become the target of all concentrated political venom for interfering with what will be called " the will of the people," or is he to shrug his shoulders and watch the steady deterioration of all standards of clean administration in the interests of a self-government of the island, however demoralising? Each individual mistake will not be "of paramount importance," and yet the cumulative effect of these wrongs and mistakes will be the end of all honourable government in Ceylon. The Commissioners have evidently taken their novel ideas from the methods of the League of Nations, but what possible similarity is there between the cultured delegates of the great nations of the world and the Tamils and Ceylonese, who will be the so-called representatives of several million uneducated men? If I am quite wrong I apologise to the Ceylonese and the Commissioners. Perhaps the spicy breezes which blow over the fair island of Ceylon bring with them a treble dose of virtue far above the level of a backward India, but if I am asked whether the Ceylon proposals are a good model for India, I can only say " No, emphatically no," and pray that the Simon Commission will be too wary to be deceived by the fallacious optimism upon which this admirably polished and on the surface apparently reasonable report has been based.

I have seen very few of the numerous representations to the Simon Commission, and doubt whether many of them contain solid constructive proposals. It would appear from such scraps as reach this country that they are full of a lip approval of democracy accompanied by inordinate requests for special representation on the Legislative Councils and for definite percentages of appointments in the Public Services, which are the direct antithesis of the democracy which they nominally praise but in reality totally disapprove. In this chapter I will simply notice a few of the representations of which I have seen copies, other than representations of the associations of European Government Servants, for these deal not with schemes of reform but with their own security and peace of mind when the next step is taken. On the subject of the British Services see Chapter VII.

THE MEMORANDUM OF THE ASSOCIATED CHAMBERS OF COMMERCE OF INDIA AND CEYLON

This responsible body, representing all important European commerce with interests throughout India, which claims that European capital invested in that sub-continent amounts to a thousand million sterling, has recommended complete "Provincial Autonomy" (whatever that may mean) in the Provinces, with the abolition of the Governor's Executive Council. This recommendation is made subject to the following conditions:

1. That the position of the Government of India *vis-à-vis* the Legislative Assembly should be strengthened.

2. That the Central Government is given powers of intervention in the event of a breakdown of the Government in any Province, such breakdown being certified by the Governor.

3. That Provincial Second Chambers are set up.

4. That adequate safeguards are provided for the administration of the police.

5. That a clause is inserted in the new Government of India Act forbidding discrimination against industrial and commercial interests in Central and Provincial Legislatures and in municipal by-laws and taxes.

The first of these conditions is an indispensable condition, or the Government of India will become impossible.

The second is also essential, but it will be put into effect only in very extreme cases, as, for example, when a Province is practically bankrupt or its law and order has become a complete mockery of that name. The deteriorating effect of inefficiency and corruption will have to go a long way indeed before a Governor can say that the Government has broken down. Such a declaration by a Governor cannot possibly be made on his mere *ipse dixit*, but must be supported by concrete facts and with a multiplicity of instances, of which the greater number will be individually difficult to prove.

The third condition depends upon the continuation of a supply of men qualified by character and ability to exercise a wise check, and with the necessary courage to enforce their opinions in the teeth of a campaign of vilification. The boldest man quails when ostracism is carried to the length of intimidating his wife and family, but such cases are by no means unusual. When one finds a man of so moderate a temperament as Sir Ali Iman among the signatories to the Nehru Constitution one is tempted to wonder whether the moderate and loyal citizens, numerous outside the Councils, will be found inside them in sufficient strength to control Swarajist intemperance. Moreover, if Zeppelin bombs during the war had destroyed the whole House of Commons, with all due respect to the members concerned, they could have been replaced by equally efficient and honourable men, yea unto seventy times seven, but a Zeppelin bomb destroying the legislatures in India, central or provincial, even twice over, would have wiped out the supply of men who could be held to be reasonably competent to administer the affairs of the land.

The fourth condition is in intent admirable, but in execution impossible. I do not suppose that any of these gentlemen, at least those occupied in their commercial offices, in the big cities, have any conception of the intrigue and backstairs influence which, if unchecked by a firm control, can frustrate the efforts of the members of the British Services and entirely break the heart and the courage of our district officers and police superintendents. These would soon be driven to give up the hopeless struggle and become pure cynics useless to check the evils around them, or else resign in despair. It is to these influences that ministers, however well-disposed, however personally honourably intentioned, must inevitably succumb. It must be remembered that there are powerful men all over the country who can by their wealth control gangs of men, and by intimidation and bribery, as occasion warrants, obtain the support of most influential patrons. The Central Government might be able to prevent a magistrate or a police superintendent from being himself unjustly dismissed, but having granted provincial autonomy in law and order, how can it possibly interfere with the disintegrating effects of intrigue and favouritism? Such an officer, finding himself pressed to desist in the prosecution of a particular man who had the ear of the minister, would have no remedy. How could the Government of India encourage him to make complaints against a minister under a constitution such as this? Any complaint he made would have to be addressed to the very minister whom he was accusing or suspecting of discrimination or bad faith. Finding no other course he would perforce have to comply, and thus lose all his authority in a district where a powerful criminal, or a powerful patron of criminals, could safely snap his fingers at the obnoxious interference with his activities by a magistrate or police officer. The influences brought on the minister to turn a blind eye might be those of caste, or creed, or race, which it might be well-nigh impossible for the minister to resist. There are hundreds of ways in which an official trying to do his honest duty to put down evil practices will find that those concerned in them can exert a pull with authority, by which he can be steadily harassed and pin-pricked—all sorts of false charges can be concocted against him, or he can be transferred as "lacking tact" to some remote unhealthy district, or passed over for promotion, or his leave refused on some specious ground. Already cases have been known in which influence of this kind has been brought to bear. Complaints made by subordinates are listened to behind the superior's back, and the superior's authority so set at nought that his influence for good is destroyed. There is not an Indian who does not realise much better than the Englishman what would happen if law and order became subject to a minister who could be howled down by the Press and forced to yield to save his being censured by a council and made to resign.

The Indian on the reserved side of Government has the support of his colleagues and is not at the mercy of a council vote. A minister can be squeezed until he gives in or throws up the whole business.

The memorandum suggests that all official members should be eliminated from the Legislative Councils. At first sight this may seem good as likely to encourage responsibility, but experience of many boards and committees, bereft of all official guidance, does not support the hope. Certainly the conferences and congresses organised by the politicians show neither responsibility nor sense of proportion.

The Associated Chambers wind up by saying that their recommendations for "provincial autonomy" in the provinces, including the control by ministers of law and order, are not the result of any confidence but simply of a desire, before it is decided that responsible government is a failure, to give political Indians a more complete trial than dyarchy has afforded them. This is no doubt generous in intent, but it may be more generous to the politicians than to those who would suffer from their mal-administration. The chambers do not wish to submit their own commercial interests to the slightest risk of this kind. They are quite rightly very emphatic on this subject, but it is easy to be generous with other people's security. Europeans in the busy European centres may not feel that risk, but those engaged as planters or in mining in the interior may find out the mistake when it is too late to remedy it, or at least when great mischief has been done.

THE MEMORANDUM OF THE EUROPEAN ASSOCIATION

This document will doubtless receive the most careful attention of the Statutory Commission, for it represents the views not of people who may be suspected of being biased by their official training and experience, but of Europeans living in the country who, until quite recently, were content to leave politics alone, trusting that the British nature of the Government and the British element in the administration would, generally speaking, ensure their fair treatment. They, of course, carried influence in commercial matters through their chambers and associations, but apart from these issues they took but little notice of the political affairs of the country. It is taking the European non-official community some time to realise that as British official control diminished, nothing but European non-official participation in the political business of the country could take its place. I feel grave doubts whether they have even yet realised it. In their anxiety not to seem antagonistic to the Indianisation of the Government they are prepared to go a long way in confiding powers to Indian ministers subject to safeguards of various kinds, to which it is very easy to give verbal expression but which in actual practice may be found to fail miserably. No sooner are vetoes or certifications resorted to by a Governor or the Governor-General than immediate outcries are raised, sometimes correctly raised, that this exercise of power, however necessary, absolutely militates against the sense of responsibility in those whose action, called perverse by their opponents but pronounced patriotic by themselves, has rendered such exercise necessary. The Association themselves record a spirit of hostility manifested in the legislatures against British trade and commerce, but the motive requires probing. Thus, if a council refuses to pass a vote for the police or for the office establishment of an official, whose post they would like to but cannot abolish, they may do so irresponsibly, knowing that the vote will be restored by the governor. Their action is just a pin-prick, a foolish act which they might not commit if they were fully responsible for the maintenance of law and order. But an attempt to discriminate between European interests in commerce falls into quite a different category. It is not an act of irresponsibility at all: it is merely letting the cat out of the bag, and giving a foretaste of what they would certainly do if they had the full power. European and Indian commercial men may be, and often are, the best of friends when they are doing business together for mutual advantage, but when it comes to actual rivalry and competition between the two there will not be a fair deal for European commerce if the Indian can help it. The Indian politician is certainly not responding to any mandate from the electorate when he is anxious to kill British coastal shipping, for the passengers or the merchants sending goods are not demanding that they should be carried exclusively in Indian-owned ships commanded and navigated by Indian officers; so also the politician is not responding to any mandate from the masses when he agitates for the complete Indianisation of all the Civil Services or of the army. The dislike of the Indian politicians to the success of British enterprise in any walk in which Indian private enterprise is unable to compete is easy enough to understand and indeed not unnatural, but if these parties are given a free hand they will certainly discriminate against British private enterprise. From the beginning to the end of the Nehru Report there is not a single sentence to show that those who drafted or approved it feel any sense of indebtedness either to the Pax Britannica, which had made their lives and property safe and has given them opportunities for acquiring knowledge, status, and affluence, which they might otherwise not have enjoyed, or to the benefits which India has received from British capital and British commercial enterprise. We know that there are millions of people in India who are grateful for these benefits and appreciate them, but it is not these millions who have any part or lot in the choice of policy, and the sooner that this is recognised the better. The politicians frankly consider that the British ladder by which they climbed to their present position can now safely be kicked away. That they may be mistaken about this can make no difference. Certainly any hostility to European commerce that they may feel will not be abated one jot because the European Association has recommended provincial autonomy in the provinces.

The European Association makes a somewhat different recommendation from that of the Chambers of Commerce in respect to the administration of law and order in the provinces. They suggest that this should be handed over to ministers only if local European opinion considers this safe. In those provinces where such an opinion is not held the solution proposed is that the Governor should reserve to himself the portfolio of law and order.

Action taken by the police is the target on which political attacks are concentrated, and if the governor were his own minister he would be exposed to such attacks, while he would not be able to defend his action in the councils. His office must lose dignity by his being embroiled in bitter controversy. Furthermore, a governor appointed from England, with no previous knowledge of India and no trained counsellor to help him, could not possibly administer the department with all his other duties to perform.

The European Association in 1924 prepared a statement for the Reforms Inquiry Committee, which is annexed to their present memorandum. The views which they then put forward were those formed on the experience of the first councils under the new reforms, which were not then under the domination of extremists. One would have certainly thought that the later experience of these bodies would have gone to strengthen rather than weaken the opinions then held. Their own summary of these views ran as follows:

"(*a*) We find that the Government of India Act relies for its representative form on a sort of co-operation which is either largely negative or non-existent.

(*b*) We find that the electorate which had been constituted is small, largely uneducated, so far practically devoid of political sense, and intensely liable to be swayed by irresponsible agitation. The result has been to concentrate political power in the hands of a small body of men who avowedly put forward no constructive policy and do not represent the voice of the majority. Such a system is, in our opinion, the very negation of representative government.

(*c*) We find the provisions as to the division of responsibility unsatisfactory, the Act failing to affix to the councils responsibility for those departments which it was the intention of the Act to transfer to their control, whilst they have been given power without responsibility in the reserved subjects.

(*d*) We find, finally, that the Act has neglected the development of self-government in those spheres which very closely affect the masses, and has merely accelerated a system of representation in the Central Government prior to satisfactory proof of the experiment in the provinces."

These European Associations will find out that their efforts to conciliate Swarajists will bring them nothing in return except further depression among loyal Indians.

CHAPTER XXIII

AN UNSOPHISTICATED SCHEME

A Demonstration of the Hollow Unreality of the Alleged Desire of Indians for Democracy, or for Dominion Status

I HAVE been favoured with a copy of a very interesting memorandum submitted to the Statutory Commission by a body calling itself the "All India Vishwakarman Liberal Federation," being an association of artisans and workers claiming to have branches in every part of India, and to represent classes which aggregate between 30-40 million people out of her population. The memorandum is composed in bad English, with mistakes of spelling and grammar, but it has put up a draft constitution for India "as a Free State." The document is an interesting study in Indian psychology, because it asks for a great deal of the things it denounces and is totally unaware of the inconsistency. One can exactly follow the lines of thought which have produced that document. Parliament having ordained that "responsible government" is to be the order of the day in India, this body starts on the assumption that whatever views it may hold on that point it must express some enthusiasm for some form of dominion status if it is to receive any hearing at all from the Simon Commission, merely stipulating for certain conditions, some of which preclude the introduction of such a status at all. If one were in a position to examine privately numbers of the artisan classes away from the hearing of politicians and ask them whether they wanted any constitutional reforms at all, they would have said: "No, all we want is protection from the oppression of Brahmins and other high castes." If you then said to them: "Why on earth do you put forward proposals for the machinery of a constitutional state?" they would answer: "Oh, we thought we had to do so because it was the order of the British Sirkar that we had to walk along that road." They are right in so far as a statement which wanted to go back instead of forward on the scheme of reforms would be fiercely denounced by the politicians as mere subservience to some British collector and as a further proof of the need of democracy to cure such people of "their slave mentality." That is the fate of people who are truthful. If they tell the absolute truth they are likely to lose their case. If they pretend to like something they do not like, but ask for modifications in the hope of obtaining a quarter loaf of bread, there is more chance of their being listened to.

This memorandum was put up by the President-in-Chief in a letter of July 1928 addressed to the Commission. After dwelling on Brahmin tyranny, he writes:

"The Executive Council of our Federation has resolved in favour of Dominion Status. But I cannot refrain from mentioning that a small minority, including myself, has voted against that proposal, as it considered that the direct rule of Viceroys, Governors, Collectors, and other officials which was the feature of the pre-Morley-Minto Reforms was a better system and more conducive to the welfare of the people than the 'responsible government' now in force. At present we cannot but view with fear and anxiety the decreasing power of the British element and the increasing power of a caste-bound oligarchy which, demanding justice for itself, is devoid of an innate sense of justice, law, and order for Constitutional progress and further responsibility. The entire governmental organisation should be the strongest possible. Law, police, and justice, along with land revenue, should be under the control of the Government of India. . . . In the War the Indian masses alone helped the Government, and not the so-called educated Brahmins. . . . We do not desire that the British Army, the protection of the British Navy, and Civil Service should be withdrawn from India. If they are withdrawn, not only injustice but also class war would prevail."

The writer then complains that their claim for consideration on the Councils has not been properly considered by the Government, and he goes on to cite instances in which non-Brahmins were neglected for Brahmins in nominations by the Government of Madras. He continues:

"I would next draw your attention, Sirs, to a special feature of our country to show that democracy is the most peculiarly unsuitable and even dangerous form of government for this country. India is not a united nation. It is essential that in this country of divided races, castes, and creeds, election on the basis of separate electorates should continue. Europeans, Anglo-Indians, Christians, Mahommedans, and the agricultural, labour, and industrial classes should all be accorded special privileges according to their strength and importance in the various Provinces. It is practically certain that these minority communities and oppressed classes cannot come up. As regards the Public Services, we are against the elimination of the British element in the Services, and we are of opinion that the rights of the European and Anglo-Indian members should be specially protected. . . . In conclusion, our Federation believes that the country is not sufficiently developed to maintain her own Navy, Army, and other means of self-protection without British assistance. As a member of the British Commonwealth she will have the advantage of their assistance at much less cost than that which would be involved in the maintenance of independent naval and military forces. . . . If the country is left alone, she may deviate into a state of chaos and may not be able to retain her independence. As Mr. Lloyd George declared, the Civil Service is the steel frame of the administration in India, and we submit that the British element in the Civil Services should not be further reduced. We have profound faith in British justice, but so far as the Indianisation process has gone equal representation should be provided for all communities."

The draft bill submitted with this Memorandum "to constitute the free Indian State with Dominion status and full

Provincial Responsible Government" is the quaintest possible hotch-potch of contradictory provisions, with echoes of the Nehru model accompanied by emphatic assertions of loyalty to the British connection. One of the clauses is:

" *The Government of India will have complete autonomy in all the central subjects, and the powers of the Government of India shall continue to be subject to the control of the British Parliament as at present.*"

Another clause runs:

" The Governor-General shall act on the aid and advice of an irremovable Executive Council, as in the United States, which shall consist of not less than six and not more than nine members appointed by the Governor-General subject to the approval of the King, to administer such departments of the State as the Governor-General may direct, of whom one-third number must be reserved for Europeans. Among the Indian members one seat should be reserved to Mahommedans, two for non-Brahmin Hindus, and the remaining seat may go to Christians, Anglo-Indians, Parsees, backward and depressed classes alternately."

I am afraid there is no place for the Brahmins on this council. The legislative proposals are:

Upper House - - -	The Senate
Lower House - - -	The Council of State

The franchise is to be "universal adult suffrage, excluding women, provided the electors pay a special tax according to law for each constituency." This new Council of State is to have one member for every 100,000 people. I am afraid this House will be rather large, or about 2500 in strength. The Senate will include one member for each community in each province "according to its numerical strength in the government account of castes and tribes in various provinces and census reports." But there is a safeguard for the authority of the Senate, for it is provided as follows:

" *To prevent the tyranny of members in the Lower Chamber, aristocrats of the country paying revenue of more than Rs.* 7000 *who are willing to register their names as voters may be appointed members for life by right by the Viceroy.*"

Here is a new motive for creating peers, which might be considered by our own Government in connection with House of Lords reforms!

In the provinces the executive power is to be vested in the Governor, acting on the advice of the Executive Council, which will consist of two European and three Indian members, all of them being termed ministers.

With the papers sent to the Commission is a Memorandum of the Articles of the Federation, which are all designed for improvement and welfare of artisans, and for their recognition. To these articles is attached a final one headed: "Caution," which enjoins the association not to associate itself with any person or body of persons opposed to the British Empire. The caution ends with the sentence: "No person shall be eligible for the membership of this Federation who may be actuated by any motives inimical to the continuance of British supremacy in India."

There are probably many representations on lines like these before the Simon Commission, the general purport of which is—"If we are to be given novel constitutions of this kind, do not let us be left out in the cold or at the mercy of a self-seeking and ambitious Intelligentsia controlled by the very people who have despised us for centuries and in whose protestations of sympathy and promises of protection we have no confidence."

I close this chapter with a story told me by a very experienced Revenue officer. During the non-cooperation movement he asked some peasants what they really wanted. They said: "We want Swaraj." He said: "Do you want us British officers to leave the country?" "Certainly not," they said, "we don't want you to go, how could we get on without you?" "Then, what do you want?" he said. "We want Swaraj," they said. All that they had been told was that Swaraj would be a beautiful dream condition, a millennium of cheapness and no rents and no taxes; in fact

Gandhi's dream of the simple life when railways would be abolished, the black magic of Western medicine exorcised, when everybody would live healthily in a village, growing his own food and making his own clothing, and all these blessings to be secured by refusing to obey a Satanic Government and its officers.

PART IV

THE DILEMMA: REFLECTIONS AND SUGGESTIONS

CHAPTER XXIV

OF THE APPLICATION AND MIS-APPLICATION OF PHRASES

"Self-Determination"—"Letting People learn by their Mistakes"—"Good Government is no substitute for Self-Government"—"Provincial Autonomy"—"Sitting on the Safety Valve"

HAVING reviewed in the First Part the Problems of India upon the solution of which her future political development depends; having sketched her political progress in the Second Part, and described the present impasse in the Third, I come to the dilemma with which we are confronted, not we British only but the Indians too. What then is this dilemma? What are the alternatives with which we are confronted? We must see what are the true horns before we can avoid them. That is the crucial point, but before we can approach it we must clear our vocabulary of cant phrases which obscure the issues, and must cut a path through the jungle of verbiage in which we are constantly losing our way.

"SELF-DETERMINATION"

Translated into the Concrete in the New World and in the Old—Impossibility of Application to India

No more deceptive phrase was ever invented as a political shibboleth. The proportion of people who determine their own nationality is exceedingly small. They are born as members of a particular race and they have no choice in the matter, though there are means by which they can, when adults, change their nationality. The individual who does so, does exercise his self-determination. He, so to speak, changes the club of which he was a member by birth and seeks admission to a new club in which for various private reasons he thinks that he will be better off than in his old one. He has to fulfil certain tests, or he will be black-balled on the threshold. If he can pass those tests, he has determined himself. The United States probably contain more self-determined citizens than any other national club in the world. It is a rich and comfortable club in which there has been plenty of elbow-room, and if President Wilson invented that phrase as a political concept, it is no wonder, for self-determination is the great feature of the new world, and it would be an American who would first think of the phrase.

In the old world it means something rather different. The new world invites all comers to become its nationals, though some of its countries have had to stiffen their rules of membership. The old world consists of nations who are nothing but swollen tribes, and whose self-determination was exercised by their forefathers centuries back or even in prehistoric times; except the few people who have become naturalised, their nation was determined for them and they generally speak a common language. Sometimes, however, these tribes, by choice or compulsion, coalesced with other tribes, and the self-determination now before them resolves itself into the decision whether these coalitions should continue or their component parts should separate again into single and distinct entities. Generally it will be found that when these tribes were really determined they have already shown that determination by giving effect to it. They have become facts in history rather than decisions by votes or plebiscites. France decided that it would not be governed by England; so did the Irish Free State, while Ulster would not join its fortunes with Southern Ireland and preferred the

British Parliament, which made of it a provincial government, like our provincial governments in India. Perhaps if we had thought of it earlier we might have made Southern Ireland a provincial government too, but we didn't. In the same fashion, at the end of the Great War, the Allies found themselves obliged to recognise ancient tribal divisions and turn them into nations because they spoke different languages and no longer wished to remain joint, but when, in part of the territories, the different races were inextricably mixed, the Allies had to resort to a plebiscite in which, of course, the majority exercised its self-determination but the minority were refused it. Consequently there is a bad hiatus in President Wilson's scheme, because large numbers of people are left in a club that they do not like, but of which they cannot (except a few stray individuals) resign their membership without sacrificing their homes and their property, like those Greeks and Turks who were driven out by exchange of subjects. These would have preferred to remain where they were if they had had any chance of fair treatment; their self-determination was not so much their choice as their necessity.

In India to-day, how can we apply the test of self-determination? How are we to decide it? Who is to express it? How are we to pronounce in which direction it is? Voting is impossible—the scale is too vast—we can only judge it by behaviour. If these 300 millions had been really determined against British rule, they would never have accepted it. What are we among so many? They prove it by entering our service as soldiers, policemen, officials, and clerks; they prove it by protecting us when we may have only two or three white men among half a million people; they prove it by accepting our authority when there are thousands and thousands of square miles in which there is not a single white soldier, Pundit Nehru himself proves it when he and his companions admit that they cannot expel us by force; how can he proclaim a mandate from 300 million people who have never even heard his name? To accept the self-determination of Pundit Nehru and his little company of oligarchs as the self-determination of all India would not be a blunder, it would be a crime against ignorant and defenceless humanity. This thing cannot be decided by votes. If British officers went out on a mission to catechise and cross-examine and record the opinion of every adult, male and female, in India, they would be accused, possibly rightly possibly wrongly, of undue influence. If the Swarajist champions were to be entrusted with that mission they would be accused, and, to judge by their non-cooperation campaign, rightly accused, of fraud and intimidation. The great masses of India cannot condense their whole bundle of sentiments into a single vote "Aye" or "No." If they could, there would be an overwhelming "Aye" for British rule. As they cannot, we can only judge of their opinion by their action. If my knowledge of the country, and my knowledge is the knowledge of thousands of others, British and Indians, who have watched the signs and the actions of all sorts and conditions of men, some in this province some in that, is worth anything, I would say that of the English knowing adult Intelligentsia, call them two millions if you like, 95 per cent. would at a crisis declare for the continuance of the British Government. Of the rest of the people, I will make a present to the oligarchs of a million potential dacoits and town hooligans who feel the restraints of law and order, and who would love for a while the chance of free looting of the rich, with no dispensation for lawyers and politicians. I say nothing here of the princes and their subjects, for we know what they want, but of India's vast population let us make a liberal estimate of the malcontents and give them 1 per cent. The fickle determination of 1 per cent., for even that would be fickle, is not the self-determination of India's millions. So much for self-determination in India. It will be shown by determination and not by votes.

OF THE POLICY OF "LETTING PEOPLE LEARN BY THEIR MISTAKES"

Only applies in certain defined cases where Cause and Effect are clear—In other cases a Fallacy

This is one of the suave dicta that theorists love. The fact that it is only a half-truth, or perhaps only a quarter-truth, does not deter them; they love the phrase and keep it always on their lips as a friend in need when they are confronted with the confusion that comes from bestowing matured systems of government on thoroughly immature people.

A conscientious scientist will, of course, learn from his mistakes—it is part of his profession to do so, but a great many people go on making the same mistake over and over again, and never seem to learn from it. Sometimes they never have the chance of learning as the mistake is fatal, like that of the swimmer who swims out too far in spite of warning and is drowned. Generally speaking, it may be said that a man who burns his fingers by doing something will, if he has another chance, not burn his fingers again in the same way, but then he knows how he came to burn his fingers, and it was his fingers that were burnt, and it was he who felt the pain. He will nearly always learn. But supposing it was somebody else's fingers that were burnt from his action, his sense of learning will not be so acute. Finally, if he gains something every time by his action, while the burning of somebody else's fingers is only a possible consequence of his act, or if when they are burnt he can easily throw the blame on to somebody else, and the man whose fingers were burnt does not know how it happened and cannot call anybody to account, then, although the mistake is made, there is no lesson learnt from it by anybody, while the man who gained by the action is delighted with that gain and goes on making the same "mistake." This means that you must be yourself the man who makes the mistake and the man who suffers from it, and the direct cause and effect must be manifest to you. Otherwise the magic of the maxim does not work at all. The whole theory of the maxim as applied to affairs municipal or political is that, if the electors who elected you find that they lose and do not gain through your election, they will not elect you again, and that the pain you suffer through not being elected will so distress you that you, if you have another chance, or the man who is elected in your place, seeing your fate, will take care to avoid the mistakes which unseated you. Now all these reactions depend on so many factors that the reaction often does not occur, or even if there were a chance of its occurring it is counterbalanced by some other consideration. There are many municipal electors who have had a lifetime in which to learn by this roundabout method but have never got hold of the lesson. To begin with, the candidates, one of whom you are to choose, may stand for no policy at all, or, perhaps, one is your landlord, or a moneylender in whose debt you are, or a co-religionist of yours, or a caste fellow, or a man of power and influence. You vote for him on one of these grounds because he has told you that if you don't you will incur his displeasure. This is why in so many municipal towns the electors will elect the same men every time, whether their affairs are managed badly or well. In such cases the member elected is never punished for negligence and therefore never learns to do better in future, while the electors never perceive their responsibility for the laxity of public affairs. The private advantages that they may gain by electing these men may be infinitely greater than their own small share of the public loss which they may never even realise. Furthermore, so far from the elected member feeling any discomfort from his negligence, he may profit largely by it. He sought election for the opportunity of spoils that it gave him, directly or indirectly, and from his point of view his method is not a mistake at all—it is a huge success. It is thus worth his while to cajole or intimidate or offer some small inducement to the voter, and so secure himself gain. Finally the voter, even if he may perceive that there is something wrong, will probably not vote for B. instead of A. next time because he will lose A.'s favour, and B. may not be able to offer him the same advantages. And so the maxim, in India at all events, of electors and elected learning by their mistakes ought to work, but it simply does not.

When we come to a higher political sphere, the relation between cause and effect is so much more subtle and distant that the maxim never has a chance of being established. In local affairs the inhabitants of a town may at least see some of the defects in front of their own eyes or noses, but in the case of a remote legislature they have not the vaguest notion of what is going on there, why it goes on, or how, by voting for A. instead of for B., it can make any difference in their daily lives. If such a man goes to vote at all, it is because he is dragged there by somebody whom he thinks he ought to obey in case he should incur his displeasure, or else because, like many of the people mentioned in the Behar Report, he is one among several marshalled by the village watchman to go to the poll.

In India there is one other cause which utterly prevents the proper reaction. In England an ignorant voter may blame the Government for his bad crops or his bad trade or his unemployment, and therefore thinks it a good thing to vote against the Government, but there is always somebody who speaks up for the Government and tells him what the Government has done or is going to do, and he may even succeed in persuading him to vote for the Government candidate. In India there are no parties within the voter's comprehension, and there is no Government party at all; no canvasser for the Government; no candidate for the Government; the candidates that there are are all against the Government. Their rival claims on his support may be based on no question of policy or between them the choice may depend upon who can impose upon him the most or frighten him the most, and both are agreed that if the voter is poor or down-trodden, or has to pay taxes, it is all due to the *Angrez* Sirkar. He knows that there is a white Government, and that every official, white or brown, is the servant of the white Government, and whichever way he votes there will still be the same white Government, and, as a consequence, that anything that happens that is bad, municipal or provincial, must always be due to that Government, so he votes for the Brahmin, or the non-Brahmin, or the man who lends him money, or a pleader who can talk for hours in English, and that ends his whole interest in the proceedings. Perhaps three years later he will be bothered to go and mark another piece of paper, red or yellow, or whatever the colour may be.

The townsman may understand a little better, but he, too, will be shepherded to the poll, cajoled or threatened, and vote as he is told, not for policies or parties but merely for persons. When you can get these townsmen murdering one another on a foolish kidnapping rumour, or reluctantly shutting their shops as a sign of mourning for something they had never heard of, it is surely clear that they cannot discriminate between the men for whom they vote, or see through the lies they are told, or the effect of their vote, or who gained or lost by it. How long did it take before these responsible relations were set up in England? Only after hundreds of years of parliamentary development. How apathetic even in educated England after these centuries of experience are so many voters, but here the candidates have to stand on their programmes and their parties, and there is no great government outside the parties to take all the blame and abuse. The Indian voter, when he has voted, does not notice any difference in his daily life. The changes and chances appear just the same as they always were. How can such a one learn from mistakes which he neither recognises as such nor as in any way due to him. The only remedy for all this apathy and ignorance is education, sufficient education to bring him some political knowledge. In the meantime, he cannot learn by his mistakes.

"GOOD GOVERNMENT IS NO SUBSTITUTE FOR SELF-GOVERNMENT"

When the late Sir Henry Campbell-Bannerman uttered this dictum it was of the Boer Republics that he was speaking, people steady, stubborn, and democratic, who all read their Bibles and knew what they wanted. In this case these people were going to govern themselves; they had been defeated by the British and did not like them. They could enforce law and order without British help; they could hold together without British help; they could fight to a man. The test of the Liberal Premier held good in their case, but the dictum does not apply to all races, combinations of races, and in all climes and in all circumstances. The main test is the degree of superiority of the good government by others over the self-government, and who is doing the actual governing, and who is suffering from it. The test is really measured by the security of life and property and the confidence in public justice. If the people concerned have always suffered from insecurity and injustice, they may still prefer their own because they know no other, but once they have enjoyed these advantages they will hesitate to forego them, even for governments of their own in which they have no confidence. The people in India hate changes, they are not groaning, they are prospering. Why should they wish to embark on so dangerous an experiment which may place them under the iron heel of some oppressor almost as alien as the British. There is no comparison between the Boers and the peoples of India. It is doubtful whether Sir Henry Campbell-Bannerman himself would have uttered this dictum if he had been speaking as Secretary of State for India regarding her vast population. The dictum is neither here nor there in regard to the Indian Swarajists, who do not represent any united nation, and are thinking not of governing their few selves, but of their few selves governing the rest of India. They may be rash, but that is their case. There is only one matter which the Boers and the Indian

Swarajists may have in common, if the old doggerel does not to-day malign the Boers, viz., the habit of giving too little and asking too much. The phrase is in some cases a barren truism; in others absolutely false.

PROVINCIAL AUTONOMY

"Autonomy" a most Equivocal and Unhappy Term—Question one of Degree of Independence permissible to a Subordinate Government

This is a phrase that is glibly passed round. It originated in the impatience of the old Presidencies of Madras and Bombay against grandmotherly control by the Government of India, and the large sums which that Government demanded for its own expenses. The phrase has, in fact, nothing to do with the form of government, which may be autocratic, bureaucratic, or democratic, and simply expresses a relation between a subordinate government and a superior one. As time has passed the powers of the various local governments have been increased and assimilated *inter se.* Autonomy is a bad word, it may be too limited, viz., to the legislative field, or, in broader senses, it may be too much expanded, until it becomes a synonym for absolute independence. Absolute independence in the provinces is impossible either in India or under any federal system. In that broad sense no province or sub-state in any country can have complete autonomy, but the word is now flying about India as a synonym for democratic government in the provinces, a meaning which is entirely outside the scope of the word autonomy. I would, therefore, like to drop the word and merely discuss the degree of independence from the control of the Government of India which can be permitted to the provincial governments. There are three fields concerned, legislative, executive, and financial, but it is admitted by all that the central government must be master in some central fields. Since the reforms, local governments have enjoyed a largely increased measure of independence, but the price that their people have to pay for this greater independence is not inconsiderable. The finances of the local governments have indeed improved, but their citizens have to pay a corresponding additional sum in the shape of Customs and Income Tax, in some cases at higher rates than before, because the expenditure on central responsibility had to be made good from somewhere when a large share of the resources from which it was partly met was relinquished to the provinces. What the provinces have gained the taxpayers have lost. If the provinces, who have begun to live up to their new incomes, want still larger resources, they must obtain them from fresh provincial taxation, and the central government naturally cannot permit any taxation which will jeopardise their own resources for their own central expenses. In the executive field, the central government has relaxed its power of supervision and control over the transferred departments. On the reserved side these powers still continue. In the legislative field, the provinces already enjoyed a considerable degree of independence, even before the reforms, and the changes made have not been very important.

Now the Swarajist party do not worry very much about the legislative field. It is the financial and executive fields that they long to exploit. These are the real spoils of office, the power given by the purse and the purse given by the power, and to what use will they put the purses and the powers? If the purse is going to be used for strengthening the power, and the power for filling the purse, the case for the grant of both will depend upon who is going to receive the contents of the purses, and who is going to pay for keeping them full. Are they going to be the same people in each case, or will some be in the first category and others in the last? Here you have the whole communal, religious and caste questions epitomised in a sentence. What the political clique mean by "provincial autonomy" is "responsible government in the provinces," and what they mean by "responsible government in the provinces" is self-government "under popular control," and what they mean by "popular control" is control by their clique and its Press for the benefit of their clique. Can ministers, many of them themselves well-meaning men who wish to be honest, resist the control of the clique? I am afraid not, certainly not for long. These same ministers, protected from the clique, will act one way; under the power of the clique, in another. Or, if they stand out against the clique, they will be replaced by creatures of the clique. The provincial autonomy of the Swarajists is impossible because the control suggested by the nomenclature will not be the control in actual fact. If, in the domain of local self-government, where the voters have more chance of seeing the results, the spoils of office are manifest as the incentive to the candidate, what can be expected in the larger spheres of which 90 per cent. of the electors have no real cognisance at all?

There are other reasons than this, however, for reserving to the central government not constant interference, but the power of supervision and control which it has enjoyed since the Mutiny. Crime and lawlessness do not recognise provincial boundaries; they overflow them at all times, and they migrate from one to the other wherever the hope of plunder seems most promising. If each province is independent both of the central government and (as it must be) of its neighbours, who is to intervene when neighbouring provinces under totally independent authorities either do not co-operate or even thwart one another? This is impossible to any extent under All India Services (though one has seen, even under the existing system, little feuds between the police of two neighbouring provinces). If the Services were provincialised this tendency would spread. The police of one administration might take bribes from the criminals of its neighbour, and be slow to assist in their capture. A slack province would attract criminals from others, and we cannot tolerate the springing up of Alsatias in different parts of India. The King's writ and the magistrate's warrant must run from end to end.

Again, provincial boundaries are fixed but upheavals are peripatetic. A contempt for law in one province may cause outbreaks of crime to be imitated in others. The people who genially advocate a transfer of power to unstable control grasp neither the strength of the impulses to disorder nor the weakness of the restraints upon them. It is prestige that keeps the people law-abiding; not the prestige supposed to be a synonym for arrogance, but the prestige of a wholesome awe by the law-breaker of the law and its power to punish, and a wholesome confidence by the law-abiding in the law and its power to protect. These two corollaries are the secret of the internal peace of India. Disorder, like epidemic diseases, requires co-ordination and co-operation to check its spread. If these be lacking, the danger of one becomes the danger of all. We are not here dealing with the affairs of some petty townships, but of the large states of a subcontinent. To transfer law and order to the "popular control" of the politicians in each of these would be to sap the prestige of the law and lay the train for the eruption of those subterranean fires which are smouldering beneath a seemingly-peaceful crust. Catastrophes sometimes arise from an apparently trivial genesis.

SITTING ON THE SAFETY VALVE AND DRIVING DISCONTENT UNDERGROUND

Principles which Govern the Policy that should be followed—Strategy depends on Accurate Diagnosis of Trouble

This is a favourite phrase, always used by people who deprecate what they are pleased to call "repressive measures." The phrase is applicable in certain circumstances, but inapplicable in others. The whole penal code is a repressive measure, but we are not afraid of driving the discontent of criminals underground. The particular laws, however, which are deprecated are those which stifle the expression of a grievance and thus drive discontent underground. A government is always in a difficult position, for a decision whether to repress or refrain from repressing vehement agitations depends upon whether the grievance is real or artificial. An accurate diagnosis is necessary to find out whether the patient is suffering from a malady or is malingering, at his own instance or that of others, and this requires intimate knowledge of the mentality of the people concerned and soundness of judgment as to the root of the grievance. I quite agree that if the grievance is real, or even if not serious in reality is serious as sentimental, the best endeavour that you can make to redress the grievance is the wise policy. Here you must not close down the safety valve on any account: but if you can feel sure that the grievance is artificial and the sentiment behind it quite spurious, the safety valve argument does not apply at all. Or again, the sentiment excited may be real but built on false surmises, or deliberately false rumours, or statements set about by mischief makers. Here you must contradict, but repress if the contradiction does not readily find acceptance. In the course of a long career in India, among credulous and excitable people, you meet with all these variations, but the false grievances are far more numerous than the real ones. If you do not apply these very simple rules, you make a mess of things. If you have been correct in your diagnosis, all goes well. But the rules that are applied depend upon the psychology of the people concerned. British psychology is quite different from Indian psychology, because both the character and education of the British people induce a commonsense which rejects foolish extremes; even if it momentarily loses its head, commonsense soon reasserts itself. In India the case is different. You have people so gullible and excitable that the most preposterous rumours gain credence and arouse violence. And if you wait for commonsense to reassert itself, great damage may have been done and many innocent lives sacrificed.

Again, the idea that keeping the safety valve open is the wise policy, even though the grievance is plainly artificial, depends once more upon the character of the people concerned. You may allow Communists to declaim at street corners in England who, if they declaimed in Indian bazaars, might do an infinity of mischief. In this case there is no safety valve at all. It may be all gas, but it is poisonous gas, which suffocates the minds of the victims and may turn quiet citizens into raging murderers. This is exactly what has happened in Bombay, and it is especially insidious, for during the last few years it masquerades as an industrial dispute. The rule is that where the vast majority of your people have acquired immunity to the virus, you can afford to neglect it; when they have not, you must stamp it out. The store-room of the British public mind contains asbestos with just a few damp squibs; the store-room of the Indian public mind is crammed with petrol and explosives. It is obvious that the rules about people going about with torches in store-rooms must be different in the two countries.

And, last of all, the subterranean danger is exaggerated as compared with the dangerous movement to which full license has been allowed. Compare the effects on the minds of the masses in Bengal of anarchy burrowing underground on the one side, and of the non-cooperation movement flaunting itself over the whole country on the other. How did the masses regard these? They saw clearly in the first case that the secret agitators were afraid of the Government. They interpreted the open non-cooperation license as a sure proof that the Government was afraid of the agitator. The whole matter does not depend on phrases at all, but upon correct diagnosis first and sound moral strategy based on that diagnosis afterwards.

CHAPTER XXV

COMMUNAL ELECTORATES AND THE REDISTRIBUTION OF PROVINCES BY LINGUISTIC AREAS

Premature attempt to introduce Democracy creates necessity for Communal Electorates—Futility of Reserved Seats on General Electorates—Redistribution of Provincial Areas by Languages absolutely useless

BOTH the Nehru Group and the Ceylon Commissioners take the line that communal electorates being incompatible with democracy, therefore away with communal electorates! Other people may think differently, and say: "The necessity for communal electorates, while it lasts, renders democracy impossible of introduction; therefore, democracy must wait." I am assuming that what both sides desire is that democracy should be real and genuine, and not merely a fabric on paper. The real truth, at least as I see it, is this: It is only the attempt to create democracy out of unripe and incompatible elements that has made communal electorates a necessity. Homogeneous people are willing to be governed by majorities, provided that the majorities have sufficient sense to govern at all. Heterogeneous peoples are not willing to be governed by such majorities, unless their own section is in a majority over the rest, or, if not in a numerical majority, has some other extraordinary advantage which they feel sure will give it full control over the others. The advocates for abolishing communal electorates urge that their continuance will postpone for a long time, if not indefinitely, the introduction of democracy, because it will encourage the people to think communally instead of nationally. They consider that the abolition of such electorates will soon teach them to think nationally instead of communally, and so make of them a single nation instead of a collection of jealous races.

It all sounds so plausible. It is a very soothing plea to enable puzzled constitution-makers to get over their difficulties by just ignoring them. Here we are in England and Scotland, Wales and North Ireland, and we had continuous parliamentary institutions for many centuries before we consented to be governed by a bare majority of the whole nation. The coming General Election, indeed, will be the first occasion on which we have tried this experiment right out to its final limits. Surely we should be rash fools in assuming that we can anticipate centuries of slow political development in England and force on the peoples of India, with entirely different traditions of government, a different outlook on life, with 93 per cent. of the population illiterate and ignorant, a system which we never ventured to introduce amongst ourselves until we had at least 90 per cent. of the people literate, and did not carry to its full limit until all except prattling infants were able to read and write, until, also, universal primary education had been compulsory throughout the country for fifty-seven years. But this is not nearly all. Here we are, with the exception of South Ireland, thoroughly settled down to our coalescence into a single nation. Two things have enabled us to do this—education and intermarriage, so that vast numbers of our people have somewhere or other in their ancestry, English or Scotch or Welsh or Irish blood. And we have also to a great extent, Ireland excepted, so assuaged our religious differences, again as the result of the same two causes, that we can manage to get on without any violent strife. Yet even amongst ourselves some difficulties of that nature are still possible. For example, if at a future date the influx of Irish Catholics into Protestant Scotland became so great that the members of Parliament for Scotland were almost entirely Irish Catholics, an awkward situation might arise. At any rate, the history of Ireland should warn us how dangerous it is to the rights of minorities if political arrangements ignore racial and religious antagonisms that are still active and not extinct volcanoes. The danger of this policy of ignoring such differences must clearly be greatly intensified if the two great solvents of them—education and intermarriage—are virtually unavailable. The object lessons available at our very door should warn Parliament of the dangerous road in India that it may be invited to take. And yet this is not all, for we are asked to do this in a country of social exclusions, where the distances are so great and areas so vast that if you cut out of India a piece of it equal to the size of the British Isles the remainder would still be seventeen times as large as they are. To ignore the necessity for communal electorates in India is to ignore facts simply because the democrat finds them inconvenient to his preconceived scheme.

There is still another point. The advocates of abolition say that communal electorates keep up communal strife and that their abolition will allay it. This is another comfortable assumption which again overlooks facts. Communal electorates do not create communal strife, which exists independently of them, and will become still more violent if they are abolished. Surely if two Mahommedans contest a seat, or two Hindus, there is more chance of an election on the merits than if the two candidates were one a Hindu and the other a Mahommedan. Each will then make his strongest appeal to his co-religionists, and the issue at once becomes religious and communal. The friends of the defeated candidate are likely to break out into violence against the other party. If, on the other hand, the minority of the Mahommedan or the Hindu, as the case may be, is so small that the contest is hopeless, then the bitterness of exclusion will make itself felt the more strongly. If the Irish Loyalists in the South of Ireland had all along enjoyed a communal electorate of their own, they might not have been crushed almost out of existence, as they were, in the troublous times that preceded the Irish Treaty. They were left voiceless and absolutely at the mercy of their opponents, yet they too had a great stake in the country. That is not the fate to which we should consign the minorities in India. All the easy anticipations that the ballot box without communal electorates will bring communalism to an end are absolutely falsified in Ireland, and will be falsified everywhere where racial and religious antipathies are radical and deep-seated. It is at this moment being falsified in Europe, and, even as I write, the antagonism between the Croats and the Serbs in Yugo-Slavia have become so vehement that their democratic institutions have broken down and been suspended.

RESERVED SEATS WITHOUT COMMUNAL ELECTORATES

This is a sort of compromise which is sometimes suggested as a *via media* between communal and general representation. The Nehru proposals, in despair of unanimity between Hindus and Mahommedans, clutched at this device for those provinces in which Mahommedans are in a hopeless minority, and for non-Moslems in the frontier province where the Moslem preponderance is overwhelming. All other minorities are entirely disregarded. This idea was suggested by Lord Morley at the time of the Morley-Minto Reforms and was rejected. The grounds are obvious. The representatives of a creed, or race, or section are to be chosen by the opposite creed, race, or section, and the class in question will therefore in most cases be represented by its renegades. Suppose that in Ireland the Protestants were nearly all Loyalists and were in a very small minority, and the Catholics were practically all Home Rulers, and in a large majority, and that a few seats had been set apart for Protestants, in proportion to their numbers, but the electors were Catholics and Protestants. There would be a few Protestants in favour of Home Rule, and these would clearly be elected by a general electorate in preference to Loyalists. What earthly use would these reserved seats have been towards securing Loyalist representation in a Parliament of South Ireland, or Home Rule representation in Ulster?

An even more glaring example can be given in regard to India. Suppose that under a principle of a few reserved seats, a few seats here and there had been reserved for Europeans on a general electorate. These might be contested by people like Mrs. Annie Besant and her British satellites, or by British Communists, and on a general electorate the small minority of genuine European interests in the country might not be represented at all. The Swarajists would canvas, cajole, and threaten the ignorant people in favour of the Communists, while the genuine European representative would be quite unable to get in touch with the electorates in the bazaars and the back lanes, and the interests of Europeans in the country would find their only representatives in its parliament to be Communists or Besantites. In like circumstances, the wealthy Parsees of Bombay might find themselves represented by a Saklatwala elected by deluded mill-hands. Representation by your renegades is worse than no representation at all. The device is useless.

THE CREATION OF PROVINCES BY LINGUISTIC AREAS

In the hope of stilling the clamour of minorities which refuse to be stilled by the democratic Pundits of Allahabad and their followers, all sorts of people, wise and unwise, interested or disinterested, have proposed a rearrangement of provinces by language as a solution of the communal question. The question must first be asked whether the advocates of this system envisage India as a single nation as their goal, or as a federation of different nations, or an India split up like Europe into a large number of independent nations. If they wish the first (and that is what the Nehru constitution contemplates) and are bent upon the foundation of a single Indian nation which All-Indian politicians loudly declare to be in existence, then the segregation of her racial component parts in watertight territorial compartments is the very last thing that they should be aiming at. For if it were to be secured that India was divided up into separate national states by language and race, it would be a solid step towards her complete disintegration. These states would have to be "autonomous," and would, as His Highness the Aga Khan has pointed out in the *Times*, require their own military forces to protect their frontiers from invasion by individual princes or by grasping neighbours. The problem was to have been a national one, but it at once becomes international. Segregation by racial and linguistic elements will not serve to unite a country of heterogeneous peoples but only to put them further apart, and where some community of interests between different classes of people was slowly forming under many years of provincial administration, it would be forcibly disrupted. Constitution makers, like Mr. Lionel Curtis, may quote with approval the words used in a representation made by European and Indian co-signatories to Mr. Montagu in 1917, who thought that the redistribution of areas in this way only required "nerve and foresight." It would certainly require "nerve," in the slang sense, but "foresight" is a complete misnomer. The people who airily proposed this plan have never thought out the concrete difficulties that would arise. The casual marking off of areas on the map with a blue pencil is quite easy; the administrative execution of this project would cause storms of fury over the length and breadth of the land, and if these were forcibly quelled, the desired aim would be just as far off as ever. A few people might exult for a short time, but many more would become sullen and discontented for a long one. Mr. Montagu was wise enough not to attempt this problem, or try to make separate nations out of separate races. Few people think out such schemes to their logical conclusions. His Highness the Aga Khan did not pursue his own scheme of the division of India into Free States in full detail—he only gave some illustrations. He is quite right about Burma, but when he proposes to divide Bengal into two separate states, an Eastern or Mahommedan State and a Western or Hindu State, he would at once arouse furious opposition. The whole agitation about the first partition of Bengal was over this very division, and the Bengalis, whom the agitators always regarded as Hindus, would be cut in two. As regards Maharashtra, he seems to contemplate that the Mahratta princes and the Marathi-speaking districts of Bombay, and the C.P. and Berar, should combine into a new Free State, thus mixing up large portions of British India and several Native States into a single unit. He also contemplates a Mahommedan State in the North and North-West, to embrace Sind, the Frontier Provinces, and the Punjab. He makes no suggestions about Madras or the United Provinces, but he would not object to single small states, such as Guzerat. For the welfare of Mahommedan minorities in states mainly Hindu, he depends upon the influence of adjacent Mahommedan States, but since he emphasises that these states must be fully independent of each other, each having armed forces of its own, it looks very much as if such influence would end in armed conflicts between them. He provides for no central government in India, and looks to the British Crown as the bond of union between them, but having no local force on the spot whereby it could stop wars between the new Free States. The bones of contention that might arise would certainly be as numerous as the new states. He has in mind the model of Bavaria, which Sir Valentine Chirol, an authority on European politics, condemns as unsuitable. One can foresee a great conflict between the Nizam and the Mahratta Princes over Berar, which both would certainly claim. There seems to be no peace in the scheme.

The Nehru Report makes up its mind only about the sub-province of Sind, which it desires should become a separate province. The report leaves over financial difficulties. Will Sind be self-supporting, and, if not, who will support it? All the rest of these difficult problems are left to be examined by a Commission as soon as the new Commonwealth has been proclaimed. The report contents itself with indicating the special linguistic areas which are demanding independence from the provinces to which they are now attached without counting the cost at all, either to themselves or to their neighbours. In order not to bore any reader with all the geographical and racial details affecting a redistribution of territory between Indian provinces in this search for linguistic areas, I have relegated to Appendix III. a note on some of the obstacles which might be interesting to those who have local knowledge of India. I will here only discuss some other general considerations which affect the question. The first argument used by the "re-distributionists" is that the present provincial divisions are due to mere administrative accidents of British rule, but do not correspond with linguistic and historical facts. History has been the determining factor in settling the boundaries of races and nations, and all claims of nations to territories in the possession of neighbours are based on historical grounds. It is on similar grounds also that their right to retain their own territories must necessarily depend. When you are talking about history you cannot just wipe out the events of nearly two centuries and say that they do not count. There is hardly any history in the present; it is divided between the past and the future. You cannot alter the past and you can only anticipate the future, which may prove to be quite different from your anticipations. The history of British India is a distinct period in the history of India; not very long, but very important, and it cannot be ignored. For British India has a history longer than that of the United States, since they became established as a national unit. The present provinces are, therefore, the product of events since British rule became a reality. It is true that particular areas were joined to or detached from other areas for administrative, even sometimes linguistic, reasons, while certain states annexed by, or ceded to, or escheats to the Crown, had to be fitted in with the arrangements of British India. Still, these are all part of history. Administrative arrangements may be local history, but they are history. In the course of all these years a decided provincial patriotism has been springing up. The people have become accustomed to a particular capital, to resort to a particular high court, and to send their sons to particular universities. Vast sums have been spent on railways, roads, and buildings, having relation to the connection of different parts of a province with its own particular capital. The people are very conservative; they hate changes, and they think a great deal of vested interests, as everybody knows who attempts to redistribute even district areas. Even over the exchange of villages between two districts there is sometimes much dissatisfaction. The "re-distributionist" does not heed these things. "Linguistic areas" seem an admirable objective round a table, and the old Indian habit of adopting attractive phrases and leaving awkward facts for the future asserts itself. If you took up an "Ancient Atlas" of our school-days and tried to restore the territorial areas of 2000 years ago, you would cause serious upheavals among the people living there to-day. Dispositions made in British India must be regarded as the modern history of the country.

Again, the re-distributionists just mention but do not examine the financial difficulties that might defy adjustment. In the majority of countries in the world there are prosperous areas and poor areas, and the total revenues of the country are pooled, the poorer portions benefiting from the greater wealth of the richer ones. If these all be split up into new combinations, poorer areas will find themselves unable to support the equipment to which they have become accustomed, and have therefore either to wait for humbler institutions of their own or to repair to their neighbour's courts, markets, and universities. The richer provinces so formed are not going to give up the revenues of their own territories, old or new. Therefore the new and poorer administrations must make up their minds to deficits or rigid economies, or extra local taxation, for the central government is not going to subsidise from its own barely sufficient resources a number of new poor relations and dependents. If people have to go outside their provinces in search of justice or education, the linguistic advantages are not gained, for it cannot be expected that courts and universities will maintain bilingual or trilingual arrangements, which it was the object of the whole scheme to render unnecessary. Lastly, in any case the scheme, however put into effect, will not cure communal or religious troubles, which stand in the way of democracy, so that all the disturbance, administrative and financial, and the vast expense of carrying it out, will after all be thrown away.

In the last hundred years or so people from various parts of India, though no longer migrating in masses, have spread themselves about so much that there are now numbers of people speaking one language in a district speaking another. The question of Hindu and Mahommedan minorities will not be solved, for nothing is really gained by turning one community from being a majority into a minority and the other from being a minority into a majority. So the question of minorities will still remain. In no way is it possible to split up a province such as the Punjab in such a way as to get rid of Mahommedan, Hindu, and Sikh difficulties. The rendition of the frontier province to the Punjab may be desirable or not on general grounds, but the Mahommedan ascendancy in numbers over Hindus and Sikhs would merely be increased. An attempt to create linguistic provinces would thus cause much more discontent, while its objective, to allay communal and religious strife, would not be attained.

Suggestions have at times been made for reconverting British India into Indian States, under Indian princes. Where, as in the case of Benares, there is a great Zemindar holding compact domains, popular with the people on his estate, and of an old aristocratic family, the Government may be able to turn the estate of a feudal laird into the state of a feudatory raja. This was done with great success in that case. On a large scale it would prove impossible, as it was in the case of Berar, where these assigned districts, though part of the Nizam's sovereignty, have been for seventy years under British administration. The majority of the inhabitants are Hindus, and dislike being handed over to a Moslem ruler. The time for reconstructing British India by turning it into several Native States has long since passed, unless indeed we abandon India and let the princes and Pundits fight it out.

CHAPTER XXVI

INDIA AS A SELF-GOVERNING DOMINION, INSIDE THE BRITISH EMPIRE

Absurdity of comparing India with Great White Dominions—India cannot fulfil any single test

THE Nehru Report devotes a good deal of space to the question whether the words "responsible government" do or do not coincide in meaning with what is called "full Dominion status." Sir Malcolm Hailey, in a famous speech delivered in the Assembly, drew a distinction between the two. The Nehru Report quotes references in subsequent Royal Proclamations and in the Sovereign's Instrument of Instructions to Governors, to show that the goal contemplated was a status similar to that of the great British Dominions. For years the Congress has been talking about "Colonial Swaraj," or "Swaraj on the Colonial System," or "Home Rule," or, since the announcement, "Responsible Government," but the definite demand for "full Dominion status" has been of more recent growth, and has been taken up more loudly since the famous declaration of principles made in London at the Imperial Conference of 1926. I am quite willing to leave to constitutional theorists as experts in constitutional terms the decision as to which view is correct, but as neither "full responsible goverment" nor "full Dominion status" is within practical politics, the question for the present is purely academic. One thing, however, is certain, that the definition to which the Nehru Report alludes, pronounced in 1926, could not have been present to the minds of Lord Curzon or Mr. Montagu, or the Coalition Government which accepted their formula, when they drew up the terms of the announcement in the middle of the war nine years earlier. The full status of 1926 was defined in popular rather than in legal terms; it related to Dominions which had been in being for many years and had clearly attained to their full stature; they were all full democracies in being; they were all federations of states; for a great many years they had been preserving their own internal peace, and together they had expressed their self-determination as democracies, when they flocked to the help of the mother country in the crisis of the war.

To grant to India *in her existing circumstances* the same degree of independence in her constitution is, on the face of it, absurd, and nothing of the kind was ever promised. What was promised was an increasing share to Indians in every branch of the administration and a *gradual* development of self-governing institutions with a view to the *progressive* realisation of "responsible government." This progress was only to be achieved by "*successive stages*," and the British Government and the Government of India were jointly to judge of the time and measure of that advance, which was also to depend upon the degree of co-operation received and the sense of responsibility displayed. The Statutory Commission, which was to examine and report at the end of each decade, might recommend restriction as well as the maintenance or the further development which should characterise the new stage.

If Pundit Moti Lal Nehru, as a skilled lawyer, can claim that Parliament will be breaking a promise if it does not grant full Dominion status in 1929, then words have no meaning.

The Swarajists may say, and they do say: "We don't like your Act; we want it altered in accordance with our demand." They can say that if they like, but they cannot say that Parliament has broken any promises or will break them if it does not accede to this new demand. Nor can they say: "We hold you to your announcement, but we refuse to accept it, and demand something else that you did not promise, and that we demand this by such-and-such a date, or we will bring you to your knees and paralyse your Government in India." And this is just what they are saying. As suitors, they are entirely non-suited; as intimidators, they must be treated as such.

The Swarajist party, claiming to represent these millions of people, have either to make good their ultimatum, which no self-respecting nation or parliament could accept, or else withdraw it with apologies and press their suit as suitors, within the four corners of the Act and its preamble which embodied the announcement. But so far they have refused to lay their case before the delegates of Parliament; they have not withdrawn their ultimatum, in fact they go on repeating it. But Parliament will presently find that these spokesmen do not represent the millions and have no authority for this ultimatum. It will, therefore, go on with its work, as it always intended to do, and these self-appointed spokesmen and their demands will go by default. If they proceed to carry out the threat in the ultimatum, they will be trying to overawe the Governor-General in India, and the King, the Lords, and the Commons in England; they will be breaking the law, and must take the consequences.

There are some arguments, however, put forward in the Nehru demand for Dominion status which deserve scrutiny; although they are irrelevant, they might find some hearing among those who do not know the land and its people. It is contended that the Colonies had self-governing powers before they were made responsible for their internal defence. But the Colonists were all settlers of British or European stock; they were accustomed to some form of constitutional government, and not to centuries of undiluted autocracy; their territories were vast; their numbers few, and there was no real disunity in their own ranks. Both the French in Quebec, and the Dutch in the Cape Colony, had accepted their position in the constitution. In South Africa those Boers who did not like the Government had trekked further north to the Orange River and the Transvaal. And they, too, were afterwards to come in. All these people were democratic and capable people, and they did not depend on extraneous aid for keeping order among themselves. What is the comparison between these Dominions, when they became either partly or fully self-governing, and India of to-day? In the Union of South Africa, in 1926, there were a little over 1½ million whites. In New Zealand to-day they number a little under 1½ millions. In the Commonwealth of Australia the population is 5½ millions. In all Australia there has never been a battle, except the incident of the Eureka stockade, merely the mutiny of a mining camp. In South Africa there have been wars with the black races and between the British and the Dutch, but these are now of the past. In New Zealand there were the conflicts with the Maoris, but these too have now long since settled down as citizens. Canada was formally ceded by the French in 1763, and its present constitution was granted in 1867, after a hundred years of constitutional development all their own. In Australia, South Africa, and New Zealand they had citizen forces with universal training; in Canada a militia and a reserve militia, behind the small permanent forces that are maintained. What is the resemblance between India and these? Again, in these Dominions all the institutions and developments which they enjoy have been of their own initiative and execution, while in India these same institutions and developments have been initiated and executed by or under the guidance of the British, or, if started by Indians, they have been copied not from their own history but from our exemplars.

Lastly, these Dominions are bound by those loyalties of blood, language, religion, history, and literature to the mother country. The most populous of the dominions, Canada, with her 9½ millions, has just one-thirtieth of the population of India, and all the dominions put together contain only 18 million whites. Contrast any of these conditions with those of India, and he must indeed be a hardy optimist who thinks that Indian soil is ripe for a constitution similar to theirs.

Not one of the problems discussed in the first part of this

book exists in them. They were always democracies *in posse*, they have long since become democracies *in esse*.

India is not yet nearing the stage of a democracy *in posse*. If the Simon Commission or Parliament were to make her a democracy on paper, she would be a democracy *fainéant*. The chance of her becoming a democracy *in esse*, is in the womb of distant history. She can advance only on her own Eastern lines at present; on Western she will be a complete impostor.

When the Pundits talk of Turkey and Persia, they talk of countries that bear no resemblance to their proposed Commonwealth. These are countries, one under a dictator, one under a king, whose representative pillars are just ornamental. The Egyptian imitation of "responsible government"—and that is the Oriental country nearest Europe, its big cities almost cosmopolitan, traversed by the thoroughfare of all nations, and containing only 13 millions of people—has had to be suspended because it will not work. Japan is the only exception in Asia, and is quite unique from it; she is the Asiatic counterpart of Great Britain, an island empire, a martial and maritime nation, self-contained, of one race and language, but even she is only just feeling her way towards democracy.

Look at all those pictures and then look at the Indian one. There is no resemblance between her and them, and the essential differences are patent. Indian disqualifications are many, but three stand out:

(i) Without British help, India cannot defend her frontiers either on land or sea.

(ii) Without British help she cannot maintain law and order within her own boundaries; and

(iii) As she cannot do either of these two things without British help; therefore without that aid she cannot maintain her financial stability, on which her credit and her prosperity depend.

No thesis on paper constitutions can get over these three awkward facts. They are beyond the power of the Simon Commission to circumvent, even if that body were so to desire.

CHAPTER XXVII

THE CLAIM FOR COMPLETE INDEPENDENCE

IF BRITAIN SHOULD ABANDON HER TASK IN INDIA.
THE ALLEGORY OF "LETTING IN THE JUNGLE."
"THE BITTER *KARELA*"

SOME few hundred people in India, with a chorus behind them of a few thousand students and a few more immature thinkers, not yet out of the learning stage, loudly proclaim their goal as "absolute independence," and the Swarajists, as a whole, do not put this out of court. They indeed approve of activities taken in pursuit of it. They actually take credit to themselves for not going quite so far, but qualify that credit by pointing out that the two are really indistinguishable, except for the link with the Crown. As they say, "the real difference between the two is merely a difference in the executive. It is possible," they add, "to lay down general principles governing the entire constitution without deciding at that stage the question of the executive." That question is their mental reservation. The proposal to adopt a formula of full responsible government was therefore accepted with the clear understanding that those who believed in independence would have the fullest liberty to carry on propaganda and otherwise work for it. I am glad to read these words, for they are the most candid and true to be found in the Nehru Report. It was more than twenty years ago that in addressing the Government of India, in Lord Minto's time, I pointed out that the demand for colonial Swaraj, then recently adopted as the Congress cry, whether right or wrong, was in effect a demand for complete independence. The sentimental reasons which maintain the tie between the dominions and the mother country are all lacking in India, and if India were really able to maintain herself as a dominion, governing herself and defending herself, the one remaining tie that binds the other dominions to the empire, viz., self-interest, would also be lacking in India. For while the dominions, with their few millions of inhabitants, could not alone resist the attacks of powerful external enemies, India with her 300 millions, forming a compact and an efficient nation or union, would easily keep at bay a world at arms. In other words, were India really qualified with all her vast population to be a true and full dominion state she would "cut the painter." If a white Australia had 100 million people she might do the same, only her sentimental ties might still keep her within the family.

Pundit Moti Lal Nehru and his son, whose able arguments he praised, both really have the same thing in view, but the father, being more cautious, dissembles. On the other hand, he is rash when he openly encourages his friends, who do not wish to dissemble, to carry on propaganda for depriving the King-Emperor of his sovereignty over India. I cannot say what the dignities and conventions may be of the Legislative Assembly, but suggestions to this effect are openly discussed across the floor of that House without any rebuke from the Speaker of the Chamber.

To demand independence, however, must be a separate issue, for the declaration in Parliament, whatever it did or did not promise, did not contemplate this, for whether wide or too narrow, or clear or too dim, the promise only related to India "as an integral part of the British Empire." India might at some date, long distant, have the power to secede but not the right.

It is not superfluous to depict (for vast numbers of the British public do not realise them) the inevitable happenings that would occur in India if the British nation were to weary of their task and declare that they were tired of all this Indian agitation and this Indian ingratitude, and would take at their word those boasters who say: "Remove your white soldiers! Take away your white Civil Servants! Come chaos and anarchy! Anything is better than British rule!

If the British nation decided on this and carried it out, it would certainly give the politicians the "opportunity of learning by their mistakes," but alas it would also subject the vast masses to the certainty of sufferings untold and unmerited misery for the sins of the politicians. The things that I am about to describe are not just the fervid imaginings of a retired bureaucrat, but the prophecy of the Radical statesman, Lord Morley, who predicted "Anarchy and bloody chaos," of which the sound would begin to reach the ears of the departing British as the last man stepped upon the last ship.

In Rudyard Kipling's *Second Jungle Book* is told that wonderful story, as only he could tell it, called " Letting in the Jungle," the finest pen-picture of the rapidity of the onrush with which the " Jungle moved," when Mowgli, the youthful wolf-man, with "the master word " called in the Jungle, to destroy the village from which he had just rescued his human parents with the help of his foster-mother, Mother Wolf. For the villagers were intent on their torture and murder for suspected witchcraft, and had also attempted Mowgli's own life. So, at the master word, the Jungle began to move, and presently the village began to be surrounded by the deer and the pig and the "nilghai," [1] and the wild buffaloes from the swamps, and these ate up all the ripening crops, and the flesh-eating animals caused them to stampede over and over, and so trample upon and tread down the corn, and cut flat the banks of the irrigating channels. So the villagers began to eat up their seed stores, and the village grain dealer began to think of the prices he would be able presently to levy for his well-filled grain bins. But these too were cut under the sharp tusks of the elephant, and demolished, and the assault on the village itself began. In Kipling's own words:

" The more they kept to their village, the bolder grew the wild things that gambolled and bellowed on the grazing grounds by the river. They had no time to patch and plaster

[1] Blue Bull.

the rear walls of the empty byres that backed on to the Jungle; the wild pig trampled them down, and the knotty rooted vines hurried after and threw their elbows over the new won ground, and the coarse grass bristled behind the vines like the lances of a goblin army following a retreat. The unmarried men ran away first and carried the news far and near that the village was doomed. 'Who could fight,' they said, 'against the Jungle, or the gods of the Jungle? when the very village cobra had left his hole in the platform under the peepul-tree.' So their little commerce with the outside world shrunk as the trodden paths across the open grew fewer and fainter. At last the nightly trumpetings of Hathi (elephant) and his three sons ceased to trouble them; for they had no more to be robbed of. Native fashion they delayed their departure from one day to another till the first rains caught them and the unmended roofs let in a flood, and the grazing ground stood ankle deep, and all life came on with a rush after the heat of the summer. Then they waded out—men, women, and children—through the blinding hot rain of the morning, but turned naturally for one farewell look at their homes."

The last scene was yet to come, for the elephants now began in mad earnest to destroy all the habitation. A rebounding beam hurt one of the elephants. "He needed only this to unchain his full strength, for of all things in the Jungle the wild elephant enraged is the most wantonly destructive." And then Mowgli issued an order, and the elephants began again with renewed efforts to smash the outer walls.

"The four pushed side by side; the outer wall bulged, split, and fell, and the villagers, dumb with horror, saw the savage clay-streaked heads of the wreckers in the ragged gap. Then they fled, houseless and foodless, down the valley as their village, shredded and tossed and trampled, melted behind them.

"A month later the place was a dimpled mound, covered with soft green young stuff; and by the end of the rains there was the roaring Jungle in full blast, on the spot that had been under plough not six months before."

This wonderful picture of the creeping and the crashing desolation that will accompany the assault of the jungle when it moves upon the fields and hamlets once so smiling, affords an allegory on which to ponder if we think what it would mean suddenly to call off the forces of order from India and let the forces of disorder begin to move, the unbridled passions of ignorant masses so long held under restraint. In the story the village Brahmin and his prayers to his deities had been of no avail, so he went out with the rest. The old Gond adviser, the aboriginal of the land, was called in to appease the jungle deities, and he did nothing but pick up a traii of the *Karela*, the vine that bears the bitter wild gourd and "lace it to and fro across the temple door in the face of the staring red Hindu image. Then he pushed with his hand in the open air along the road to safety and went back to his jungle, and watched the jungle people drifting through it. He knew that when the jungle moves, only white men can hope to turn it aside."

It was the sign, neither the highest nor the humblest could do aught when the jungle moved. "There was no need to ask his meaning, the wild gourd would grow where they had worshipped their god, and the sooner they saved themselves the better."

And then Mowgli sang his song against people, of which three verses are reproduced below:

I will let loose against you the fleet-footed vines—
I will call in the Jungle to stamp out your lines!
The roofs shall fade before it,
The house-beams shall fall,
And the *Karela*, the bitter *Karela*,
Shall cover it all!

In the gates of these your councils my people shall sing,
In the doors of these your garners the Bat-folk shall cling;
And the snake shall be your watchman,
By a hearthstone unswept;
For the *Karela*, the bitter *Karela*,
Shall fruit where ye slept!

I have untied against you the club-footed vines,
I have sent in the Jungle to swamp out your lines!
The trees—the trees are on you!
The house-beams shall fall,
And the *Karela*, the bitter *Karela*,
Shall cover you all!

And so would be re-enacted over the vast areas of India the story told in this allegory. Before any new government could gather the reins into its hands, the master word of the jungle of disorder would be passed with amazing rapidity from town to town and from village to village from one end of the land to the other. The handful of people who thought to establish a new heaven upon earth in India would be assailed with as many messengers of calamities as poured in upon the patriarch Job when the Almighty set free for a time the powers of Satan. The commissions and the committees designed to solve all India's problems, the hordes of clerks designated to draw up electoral rolls for 120 million men and women now to be enfranchised, would alike be suffocated and strangled by the *Karela*, the great bitter gourd of human passions and human greed, before they could set themselves to their task. Like the famous *Chupatties*, before the Mutiny, mysterious signs would be passed from hand to hand, as the red chillie is passed from village to village by the aboriginals of India, the signal that the barriers of law and order have burst, and that revolution, red revolution, calls every man together for the strife. Dacoits so long repressed would break out under their several leaders, and their plundering gangs would spread devastation, while the custodians of the peace, after half-hearted efforts to restrain them, would find it the easier way to join the plunderers. The money-lenders hiding under their cots would be dragged out and murdered by the men whose lands they had taken, and by the victims of their usury; all the ancient feuds and grudges of every countryside would be fed fat with the red blood of slaughter at the bidding of the Mowglis issuing the master word. The Mowgli of the story spared the lives of the villagers, for he would not shed the blood of the "man pack" to which his mother belonged, but the Mowglis of this human jungle would have no such scruple. The great town mobs would set free the prisoners from the jails, and together they would plunder the rich temples of all their jewels, and the burnings and the massacres would have none to stay them when the jungle began to move. The Afghans and the tribal warriors would pour over the great plains of the Punjab, and the Sikhs would be up to dispute their old conquests with the Pathans of the borderland. From the great cities the Marwaris, collecting their portable valuables, would flee back to their desert homes where but few would arrive. The business of the great cities would stand still in awe and amazement, and the credit so long built up by the British peace would totter and crash in the panic. The great princes and chiefs would raise their standards and collect their forces, and the soldiers of the Indian army would flock to their banners, each to each as they belonged. The Nepalese would bethink them that they must not be left behind, and rich Bengal, rich and intellectual Bengal, yet powerless to save herself, would be the common theatre of countless invaders, grasping at and fighting for the spoils. The courts that had functioned so tranquilly under the Pax Britannica now departed would function no more, for there would be none to execute their decrees and the voice of the pleaders would be no longer heard. The Moplas, like hill torrents, would flood over peaceful Malabar, bringing death and desolation to the helpless Hindus. Sikhs, Mahrattas, Rajputs, and Mahommedans would be locked in the death grapple for the mastery over the lands that each claimed from the rest.

And when the country, tired of its chaos, and its bloodshed, and its anarchy, was once more seeking the way back to sanity, there would be an India divided into many parts, as its peoples had clustered for protection or gathered for the fray under the standards of the leaders that seemed to them best. It would be an India divided, not by linguistic areas.

but by new conquests and the power of the strong right arm. The commonwealths, the constitutions, the franchises, and their framers would be heard of no more—

> For the *Karela*, the bitter *Karela*
> Would have covered them all.

CHAPTER XXVIII

THE SACRED TRUST

The Meaning of the Great Proclamation of Queen Victoria—We must not betray so sacred a trust

THE politicians of India say—and I have heard an Indian in a responsible position so inform a British audience—that the trust is imaginary, that it never existed, that it has become an exploded theory. And those who seek to oust British rule entirely are less polite, for they say that the theory of the trust was a hypocritical invention under cover of which Great Britain has been exploiting India. Where is the trust deed? Who is the *Cestui-que* trust? cry these politicians with an air of forensic triumph. Neither history nor facts can be so easily disregarded. The trusts that exist between many multitudes and their rulers are not drawn up like private deeds in a lawyer's office; they do not depend upon stamped contracts signed by the executants and attested by two witnesses. They come into being from the protection which the sovereign can give and from the willing allegiance of the subjects. How did this trust arise? It came on us, it crept on us, gradually, as we assumed protection over more and more of the peoples of India, and as more and more of the peoples of India sought that protection or accepted it when given. The East India Company started under a great trading charter and ended by becoming trustees for the Crown of England and for the British nation, and were definitely so declared by Act of Parliament in 1833. After the great mutiny of Sepoys, supported by some of the population but opposed by a great many more, who helped in its suppression, Queen Victoria issued in her noble words the great proclamation to all the Indian princes and peoples, and she confirmed that trust in language the most solemn, with an appeal to the Almighty for His aid to help her faithfully to discharge it. It began:

"Whereas for divers weighty reasons we have resolved by and with the advice and counsel of the Lords Spiritual and Temporal and Commons in Parliament assembled to take upon ourselves the government of the territories *heretofore administered in trust* for us by the honourable East India Company.

. . . . . .

"We shall respect the rights, dignity and honour of Native Princes as our own, and we desire that they, as well as our own subjects, shall enjoy that prosperity and that social advancement which can only be secured by internal peace and good government.

"We hold ourselves bound to the natives of our Indian territories by the same obligations of duty which bind us to all our other subjects, and these obligations by the blessing of Almighty God we shall faithfully and conscientiously fulfil."

Then came the great clause regarding the religious freedom guaranteed to all creeds, the great charter of religious liberty in India, and the proclamation went on to say:

"It is our further will that, so far as may be, our subjects of whatever race or creed be freely and impartially admitted to all offices in our service, the duties of which they may be qualified by their education, ability, and integrity, duly to discharge.

. . . . . .

"When by the blessing of Providence internal tranquillity shall be restored, it is our earnest desire to stimulate the peaceful industry of India, to promote works of public utility and improvement, and to administer its government for the benefit of *all* our subjects resident therein. In their prosperity will be our strength, in their contentment our security, and in their gratitude our great reward."

And then the amnesty was announced to all those who had taken part in the rebellion, and the great act of clemency to all who had not themselves committed the murder of British subjects.

This great and sacred trust, with all its mutual rights and obligations, translated into all the principal languages, announced by the Governor-General and the Governors in great public assemblages, accepted by the princes, acclaimed by the people, required no lawyers, no stamped deeds to make it binding on the Crown, the British Parliament, and all the princes and peoples of India, until such times as the princes and the peoples and the Parliament and the Crown by their common consent release all the parties from their mutual rights, obligations, and allegiances thus solemnly created and interchanged with the world as witness and with the blessing of the Almighty invoked.

The great promise made to the peoples and the princes of India has been faithfully kept, and these millions, save only for a few rebels and renegades, have also faithfully observed their allegiance. Only in one single matter it has been said that the promise has not been completely fulfilled, in respect to the offices thrown open, and the words "as far as may be" used in that clause, reproduced above, have been the subject of controversy. What did that qualification mean? It was not meant as an equivocal reservation by means of which the promise could be broken; it simply meant consistently with "the internal peace and good government" by which alone the desired prosperity and social advancement could be secured. The promise of the proclamation by the Queen "for the benefit of *all* our subjects," constitutes a sacred trust for all alike. It includes the intelligentsia and the ignorant, the richest noble and the poorest ryot, the proudest Brahmin and the humblest Sudra. Authorities in this world may have the will to protect and not the power, or the power and not the will. Only the paramount power in India has both, and no section of the people, least of all the poorest and most defenceless, can be handed over to the custody of another unless there is complete certainty that the section to whom it is handed over has the same will and the same power to protect all alike. That is the sacred trust.

An old Indian proverb says that all the people of India

are divided into two classes, the oppressor and the oppressed. But the people discovered in the British Raj a third set of persons who tried to be impartial and were ready to check the oppressor and protect the oppressed. And that is the whole basis of their allegiance. The school of Mr. Lionel Curtis may tell us that it is for the good of the people that we manufacture new constitutions and properly chasten them for their good, in order that they may learn to protect themselves. We cannot thus boastfully assume the role of the Almighty, for the school that tells us to do this has not the foreknowledge of the Almighty that it is for their good. The Swarajists may protest, some honestly, some recklessly, and some dishonestly, that they will protect them all if we leave them to their charge. Some may honestly have the will, but they will not have the power, and when the "jungle moves" they too will be overwhelmed by the stranglehold of caste and the resurgence of tyranny. And so I say to my fellow-countrymen, do not, I implore you, do not betray this sacred trust.

CHAPTER XXIX

THE DILEMMA DISCLOSED

The True Nature of the Dilemma Examined

We have now reached the true dilemma in front of us, we are in sight of the two horns. It is not merely the rate of progress or the actual step in front of us. On the one horn is inscribed "The Breach of Mr. Montagu's Announcement, 1917"; on the other, "The Betrayal of the Sacred Trust, Queen Victoria's Proclamation, 1858." If we keep the trust do we also keep the pledge made by Mr. Montagu? Or, if we keep Mr. Montagu's pledge, do we commit a breach of the sacred trust? If we can keep both the pledge and the trust we have escaped from the dilemma; if we cannot we are impaled on one or other horn. The Swarajists insist upon the Nehru constitution; if we accepted that and gave them what they demand we should be impaled on both horns, because if that step were taken it would become impossible for either pledge or trust to be fulfilled. We cannot give a gift which disappears in the giving. A man may wish to give an egg to his son, but if the egg in the recipient's hands transforms itself into a scorpion he has failed to give the egg. In that case the pledge and the trust are both broken, for the scorpion will breed so many scorpions that it will slay both the Swarajists and the people. As already urged, an Indian Dominion status breaks up in the giving. We are not pledged to grant the Swarajist demand, and have not promised that any such gift should be made immediately. All we promised were stages in progress, as time renders possible and their own behaviour will justify. There is no time limit to the promise, but their own co-operation and sense of responsibility would be a factor in speeding the pace, and the absence of these is a bar to progress. So far as the Swarajists are concerned no question of further progress arises, because they have refused all co-operation and have shown no sense of responsibility. I do not dwell on the point that the pledge contained no reference to a Dominion, in any definite shape, for nobody could pierce the veil of the future and say exactly what that shape would be. And so the technical term "responsible government" was used in its place. At any rate, on the British side the pledge has been honoured. Indians have been *increasingly associated* throughout the administration; *a substantial step forward* was taken in the general direction of developing gradually free institutions, and the next step forward is being investigated by the agency provided in the statute. The opinion commonly expressed that in any case some further step must be taken is expressed by people of whom the majority have studied neither the terms nor the conditions of the announcement made. The Swarajists were bidden to the feast, but they declined the invitation and have begun one and all to make excuses. It is time that we thought of the people in the highways and hedges. The rest of the people include, first those of the intelligentsia, who are ready to co-operate and would have done even more if the others had let them, *e.g.* the Council of State and a few Hindus and a good many Mahommedans; secondly, the vast illiterate masses, who are ready to help us if they only knew how. We have to see how we can keep both pledge and trust in respect of these two classes.

After the close analysis of principles that has gone before I invite my reader's acceptance to the following:

1. "Responsible government" is a condition incapable of being conferred from outside; it can only come into existence if developed from within.

2. "Responsible government," however it may be defined by constitutional experts as a term of art, cannot come into existence as a living organism until certain conditions are fulfilled. These are:

(*a*) That the executive is responsible to the legislature;

(*b*) That the legislature is responsible to the people who choose it;

(*c*) That the people who choose it should be a majority of the whole people, and that the majority of the choosers should be fit to exercise a choice.

If this tribunal of the people is from ignorance quite irresponsible, then the persons elected by them become responsible only to irresponsibility, which is the negation of commonsense. The voter may vote for A. instead of B. because he is a Brahmin or non-Brahmin, or a Hindu, or a Mahommedan, or because somebody has cajoled him or intimidated him, or even because a collection of boys will applaud him if he votes for A. and jeer at him if he votes for B. While 90 per cent. of the people are in this helpless condition all talk of responsible government by them is futile. The ignorant voter who recorded two votes, one for the King-Emperor and the other for the Viceroy, was merely guided by his good angel to record an opinion that was really his, but he, obviously, knew nothing of responsibility or what he had to do at the polling booth These helpless people have a profound belief in the benevolence of British rule and in its power. They have been told on all sides that it is this government at whose order they are voting. The only people to choose are the people who talk English, and these are the people in whom they have no trust. Still, as the benign government has ordained "democracy," they think they must express their approval, and their spokesmen with a little English ask for Dominion status or a Free State, and at the same time call for undiminished British supremacy and for the same British district officers whom they have always obeyed. In effect they say:

"Ave Caesar morituri te salutant,"

but save us from those men who, when we are prostrate before them, will turn down their thumbs.

There is not a single section in India who believes in or is anxious for democracy. The nearest approach to it is the mob rule, liked by the howling proletariat of the towns which the communist in his malice, and the seditionary in his blindness, are combining to produce in all the large cities. The only people who consistently throughout India acclaim a pure democratic constitution are the Brahmins, for they think that even if a Brahmin's hereditary astuteness should not by itself suffice to secure him a monopoly of power the Brahmin's religious curse will supply the deficiency. The Irish priest in a small Catholic community in Ireland never wielded more power than the Brahmin in India. The non-Brahmin Hindu in the West and South knows this well; the non-Brahmin in the North and East fancies himself the intellectual equal of the Brahmin, and thinks to hold his own. He is mistaken; it is only by British help that he has so far succeeded, and, further, he has not reckoned with the Brahmins' curse. That is why the Brahmin pretends that democracy, namely, to be governed by the Sudras of India, is his dearest wish.

The following further principles emerge from all the problems and discussions that have gone before:

(i) Democracy in India is not wanted, now or in any future that our limited vision can peer into.

(ii) The first essential to democracy in India is lacking—the existence of a united Indian nation, and therefore Indians cannot combine in a joint government, and between different nations single democratic unity, as proved in Europe, is impossible.

(iii) The union of these different races in India is possible only with British control. If that be withdrawn the country breaks up into units that will be at war with each other, to the destruction of its progress and the waste of its resources, while its system of government will not be democratic at all. Therefore

(iv) A purely Indian Dominion as a vague goal is merely a dream.

(v) If Indians want to be governed by themselves or by other Indians they must abandon all idea of a single government and face the consequences (No. (iii) above).

(vi) Therefore, the only kind of dominion that can be kept as a goal is a dominion in partnership or an Indo-British Dominion.

The Brahmin oligarchy and their rash following will make wry faces at this goal, but their ambitions have no connection with democracy nor with any form of government that could be called "responsible" within the contemplation of the enactment of 1919. On the other hand, the vast majority of the intelligentsia would feel much safer with this goal, and the masses would receive it happily in so far as they would comprehend that the protection which they receive from the British Government will not be taken from them.

The late Lord Sinha, in the last conversation that I had with him before his death, said that he could see no future before India except on the lines of an Indo-British partnership.

We have now to see how, with an Indo-British Dominion as a peak in the distance guiding our direction, we may still pursue the policy announced by Mr. Montagu and yet save a breach in the great trust. That trust was committed to us by Providence, history, or fate—some may prefer one name, others another, to describe the great causes that have linked the destinies of Great Britain and India. I think that most Christian people will prefer to regard it as a task committed to our nation by a Divine Providence, and I know that large numbers of Indians hold that view.

CHAPTER XXX

THE WAY OUT—AN INDO-BRITISH DOMINION

The Extent and Foundation of Great Britain's Rights in India—The True Path of Co-operation—An Appeal to the New Intelligentsia

THIS is the appropriate point at which to lay emphasis on facts of cardinal importance not hitherto mentioned. The Indian demand assumes that the British have no rights in India at all, and that at the request of the Indians they will quietly clear out, bag and baggage, while those British who remain in the country will remain on Indian sufferance. Those few who may care to accept such terms as the Swarajists choose to offer may remain on in public offices or commerce, if their continuation there is held to be beneficial to India, the Swarajists, of course, being the sole judges.

The Nehru Report contains no recognition of British rights, except a promise of some compensation to those actually in service, civil or military, who are not retained or do not wish to stay on when this great upheaval takes place this year or next.

The British rights in the country are solid and incontrovertible. The whole of British India is British territory, while the Indian States are a political entity in the British Empire. Bombay came to the British Crown in 1661, Calcutta was founded by Job Charnock in 1690; Fort St. George in Madras had been founded even earlier in 1639. British rule over large areas of the country took its more definite shape after the Battle of Plassey in 1757.

These rights were acquired by cession, by conquest, by occupation, and by prescription, fortified in each case by the ready acceptance of the inhabitants and by treaties and engagements with the princes.

The three great cities thus founded received their large

populations and their growth from those who flocked in themselves for protection or for the profitable trade which they offered. These three were the creations of British rule, and formed the *nuclei* of the great commerce of to-day.

It may be that the number of British who have actually settled in India is small, but there are settlers in those parts where climatic conditions allow, and there are some 125,000 Anglo-Indians related in blood to the British; but the army, the Civil Services and commerce have drawn a constant chain of British to the country in unbroken succession from the time of the first factories of the East India Company up to the present day. Among the vast population of India their numbers have been small, but their importance to the country has been of paramount extent. Their presence there has given India the gifts of unity, peace, prosperity, justice, education and opportunity, communications, financial stability, and credit. The British Raj has secured all these benefits in the country itself, but because it has this great responsibility and this trust it has done even more. Great Britain has given hospitality and training to Indians in the motherland; she has thrown open facilities there for learning in medicine, law, science, mining, agriculture, and industry, and she has represented and protected the interests of Indians by her consular and diplomatic Services all over the world. Her navy has protected India's coasts, and her army its land frontiers. Her commercial men and her capitalists built her great trunk railways and started most of her large industries. Many British citizens have lost their lives in her service, and the graves of many British men, women, and children may be found throughout the land.

As India has advanced in education the British Parliament has been ready to grant political facilities by which Indians should more and more acquire knowledge and experience and so become more and more associated in the day-to-day government of the country. To its legal rights and its political rights, which both India herself, the British Empire, and the whole world have recognised, the British nation has added every moral right that any nation can acquire to the allegiance of any peoples and lands. Her position is not only one *de facto*, it is also one *de jure*, acknowledged by the princes and chiefs, and by all but a handful of India's 320 million. The Montford Report and the Act of Parliament never contemplated an entirely Britonless India. Until secondary education has advanced far and wide, until racial and religious feuds have become ancient memories, until that ancient land has acquired Western political wisdom, the only possible goal is that of partnership, or an Indo-British Dominion. We must diffuse that education; we must further the acquisition of that political wisdom, and these two together will gradually soften these asperities and feuds, racial, religious, and social, which make unity impossible. And all these things depend on education, and education depends on financial resources, and financial resources depend upon unity, and unity depends upon the British Raj. Politicians may deny these facts or ignore them, but they cannot alter them, and any political arrangements made in defiance of them will simply bring down the whole edifice, old and new, in a common ruin. The whole illusion arises from forgetfulness that the power wielded by the politicians in the legislature is based not upon the mandates of the people but simply on the courtesy of British authority. The politicians are busy hacking at the bough on which they are supported at a point between themselves and the trunk, and ask us to help them in their hacking. If they succeed their fall will be catastrophic.

I hear it said: "Oh, but every country is governed by its intelligentsia." I invite a reference to Chapter VI, in which the peculiar circumstances of the political intelligentsia in India are discussed, and to Chapter I, which should make it clear that what the wisest men in Ireland cannot achieve and the wisest men in Europe cannot even attempt must be beyond the power of even the wisest men of India to attain.

But with all this I do not want to do injustice to the political intelligentsia, and I hope that I have already done justice to all the non-political part of it if it be left to follow its own inclinations. The political intelligentsia are the product of the learning that the British Government freely and quite rightly put at their disposal. They also are of the trust, for we do not fulfil our trust by obstructing the light. I try to put myself in their shoes. If I were an Indian I should probably ask, as some of them do, why having brains and capacity and learning should we require the support of foreign control? It is not as men that I have been inveighing against the politicians; many of them have been friendly to me and I still number friends among them, though many have passed over as we have grown older together, and as seas have divided us. I acknowledge as men their great ability, their many private virtues, their kindness and sympathy in trouble, and their hearty wishes in good fortune. It is not the men themselves, with the virtues and failings that we all share alike, it is their politics and their policies which I so unceasingly condemn. For their aspirations that are worthy have politically degenerated into ambitions so vaulting that they have overleapt themselves and are falling on the other side. But to them I would say: If you deplore the actual facts as they are, you must find out the causes that exist and must examine them fairly; you must let in not merely those rays of light which are pleasing to your ambitions, but also those which reveal the obstacles which stand in the way of their realisation. If you deliberately shut off part of the light you will certainly stumble and fall over the obstacles which you so persistently hide that you forget that they are there. If you preferred it you might split yourselves into many portions under old hereditary leaders, the Rajas and the Maharajas and the Nawabs, and some score of you might still stand behind their thrones and advise them, but the unity of them all would have gone, and, with this unity, peace, and with loss of peace progress. Without all these essentials your resources would fail, your children would grow up on lower standards than you yourselves enjoyed; you would find yourselves gradually slipping back into those old grooves of Oriental government out of which you had emerged, and your retrogression would be sure. Therefore, revise your programme, accept the proffered hand of friendship, accept the idea of partnership, and let us go forward together, the British people and yourselves, in a steady march of progress, slower than you may have in your enthusiasm pictured, but safer and infinitely more sure; co-operate where you have opposed, freely acknowledge what is good in us, and we shall all the more readily acknowledge what is good in you.

If you revise your outlook you will be able to give a more patient scrutiny to the steps which lead forward to an Indo-British Dominion.

CHAPTER XXXI

THE SUGGESTED ROUTE FOR ADVANCE

(i) IN THE PROVINCES
(ii) THE GOVERNMENT OF INDIA

A Durbar of the Indian Empire, the Amalgam of the Old and the New

No one man, however experienced, can propose a complete new constitution for a whole sub-continent of so varied a character. He can only sketch out the framework around which, if it be found suitable, the details can be built up. The evidence that I have tendered in the chapters that have gone before points to the following conclusions:

(i) That territorial electorates give unrestrained power not to the voters or their true representatives but only to a clique of politicians.

(ii) That if we wish the different classes of the people to be represented on the councils in some proportion to their relative interests and importance, we must ensure that the constituencies adopted will fulfil that test.

(iii) That the desired training which the present system was designed to give merely confirms people in their errors, for the ignorant electorate are too ignorant to perceive cause and effect, and the elected who are not called to account use their powers mainly for the aggrandisement of their own class.

(iv) That this system, instead of providing "the richer life" of the Montford Scheme, is merely producing the Dead Sea fruits of strife, intrigue, and corruption.

(v) That the longer this system is continued the greater is the demoralisation that will set in.

We must not blame the people for this. From time immemorial, when a man wanted anything, and could not get it for the asking, if strong he took it, if weak he got it by bribes, if poor he went without. And this same rule will continue until the whole people have learnt a lesson which only education can teach them in the course of many generations.

Since councils have been established and electorates have been created I have always been in favour of a franchise to those who had some knowledge or shrewdness, in order that from amongst themselves they might be able to find spokesmen of their poorer brethren. The franchise given is narrow, but the men that it puts into the councils are not the true spokesmen of their poorer brethren but the gramophones of the politicians, who advise the ryot to his ill, the labouring man to his loss, and the young of their own class to their eventual complete destruction. They build nothing, they destroy everything. They are neither fit to be given Swaraj nor able to retain it if given to them. Therefore, let us keep to the franchise with such small adjustments as may be necessary, but *change the constituencies.*

The great classes and interests are well defined. Of these the urban intelligentsia is one, and as such entitled to its fair share, but it must not be allowed to grab the whole. These great interests are:

(i) The Land; the most important in numbers, for some 90 per cent. of the people live in villages.

(ii) Commerce.

(iii) The Professions.

The people are now suffering under the third class, for the lawyers and journalists overpower the other professions; they overpower the land, and they even dwarf the power of commerce. The land cannot find proper spokesmen of its own, except the few great landholders, and such men as they can supply will often be men who may spoil the case for want of knowledge, who may know what their brethren want but do not know the best way to get it, and are at the mercy of any clever agitator. For three classes, therefore, we must rely upon nominations to the councils. These are the ryot, the labourer and artisan, and the submerged fifth or the untouchables and outcasts.

Further, under the three main heads of Land, Commerce, and Professions, we must provide such sub-divisions of race or creed as are required to keep a balance of power in the councils between those who are contesting together as to which should govern the rest. We must also provide for those small but important minorities who, small in numbers, have contributed to the civilisation of the country to a degree infinitely greater than their numbers alone would suggest.

Finally we must insure that for the three great interests representatives are returned who are not professional special pleaders, but genuine members of the great class whose interests they are to voice. The present system has resulted in pleaders acting for imaginary clients, and urging not what their supposed clients want, but what they want themselves. Our task is to turn imaginary clients into real constituents, and pleaders of their own advantage into genuine representatives. There is no room for the "carpet-bagger" in India.

So much for the people; now for the government.

I spoke in Chapter XXIV. of the impossibility of any full sense of responsibility being created between voter and elected so long as the voter, whether he can read or not, is so crassly ignorant that the elected can claim the credit of any success for himself and throw the blame for the tax, or the disaster, or the strife, upon the great White Government. The ambitious will say: "Of course, that is why we commend the removal of the great White Government. If that were only out of the way, this wonderful 'responsibility' would soon take its place." If this were really true, we could abdicate. But it is not "responsibility" that would succeed to the throne, but "an abomination of desolation," accompanied by the destruction of all those seeds of "free institutions" which Mr. Montagu's voice committed the British nation to sow and to weed and to tend, until the harvest was ripe for the garners. The great White Government must stay until that day comes, and while it stays it must govern, for a government that cannot govern is not a government at all. If the Government, therefore, is to govern it must have the means of doing so. It has the means in its army, its police, and its executive, and it has the obedience of the voiceless millions, but if it puts itself at the mercy of the talkers on the council it cannot use its own means. Under the peculiar structure that it has been busy creating the position has come that it has to persuade. It must, therefore, be given the means to persuade, but if the majority on the councils are irreconcilable it has lost even the means to persuade. It must then either surrender and become a puppet or it must over-rule. It cannot canvas; it cannot put up candidates for the electorates; it cannot as a candidate address the electors, so it must be enabled to choose its own fitting representatives, as all sections of the people are allowed to choose their own. If not, it is bound hand and foot. It must therefore be able to select a substantial body of the representatives on the Council, which it can only do by nominating representative men.

The framework of the provincial councils is now complete; the provinces all differ, as the ratios of these principal interests towards each other may vary, and no cast iron model can suit them all, but the main principles must be the same throughout.

Only a specimen can be put forward to illustrate these principles.

Take a specimen council of 100 members, and let us see how it should be constituted.

We might make 65 elected and 35 nominated. Next we have to divide these 65 between the land, commerce, and professions, and those small minorities that are competent to vote. I suggest for that distribution, 30 to the land, 10 to commerce, and 20 to the intelligentsia (the professions). And these seats will be distributed as may seem fit in each province between Hindus and Mahommedans in the case of the land; between Indians and Europeans in the case of commerce; while the professional intelligentsia, being enlightened, should require no communal electorates. The land representatives will represent the country, and the commerce and the professions the towns.

There remain five seats for election to be distributed among those interests which are in numbers small but are clearly capable of electing their own men. Among these will come Europeans and Anglo-Indians.

Next, I come to the nominations. There are 35 seats in all. We must have 20 for officials and 15 for non-officials. We must represent the ryot, the labourer and artisan, and the depressed classes, and of the 15 seats we may give 9 for them. And this will leave 6 free seats for those eminent Indians who have a stake in the country or have won special distinction, but whom age and status deter from the rough and tumble of an election. Out of the 20 official seats the Government will be able, if it sees fit, to nominate some of its officials, British or Indian, from the ranks of the district and settlement officers, or the agricultural or co-operative departments, men who are specially qualified to voice the interests of the voiceless. For among these are to be found the truest champions of the poor, those who know best their real needs, and yet can distinguish between policies that are practical and policies that are not. For representatives that merely cry for the moon are only futile.

And now I come to the constitution of the provincial government, and again I sketch the framework.

There will be the governor and his cabinet, of four in the small provinces and six in the large; all members of the cabinet will be called ministers. "Responsible government" has no monopoly of the name of "minister," for every government, despotic or constitutional, must have its ministers. With the principle of a partnership government before us, half must be European and half Indian; half official, half non-official; half of the nominated portion, half of the elected portion of the Legislative Council. Where an Indian holds an official seat in the cabinet, a European will hold one of the non-official seats, for the European non-official community must make some sacrifices if it wishes to enjoy its share in the government of a province. The reservation of half the seats in the cabinet to the nominated portion of the council must continue until after long experience of the councils and the cabinets a different distribution has proved itself to be justified. Dyarchy must go, ministers cannot be left in the position which they now occupy, liable to be shouted down for doing their duty and applauded for failing to acquit themselves like men. If they are selected from minorities they are holding only by the support of the reserved side of Government, or else, when selected out of the obstructive clique, they are behind the scenes the bitterest opponents of their colleagues on the reserved side. How can a governor carry on with two camps in his inner counsels, the one for ever opposing the other, in which one set is thinking only of the interests of the people and the other set, however honest, however well-intentioned they may wish to be, yet forced to obey an oligarchic Press? If the electorates do not like these elected ministers under the scheme that I have sketched, they can do as they do in other countries and reject them next time at the polls. When there are no policies and no parties and ignorant electorates who know not what they do, when the wreckers and their clique dominate the chamber, the talk of "responsible ministers", as the constitution-makers of the West intended them to be, is sham and hypocrisy.

When ministers are part of a single government they will be protected from the menace of a pressure which no man living can stand against, for his resignation would be forced by a clique of his opponents and in his place they would thrust a creature of their own. When parties join and part like the figures of a kaleidoscope, and policies change their colour like the chameleon, nothing can be safe and nothing certain.

The over-ruling power of the governor must still remain in the background, but if the councils are better balanced and better equipped with sweet reasonableness he will not often require to use them.

The Government of India as the central government must have its powers of supervision and control intact in the background. Let it delegate its authority as much as it chooses, and in as many departments as it can, but with power to withdraw that delegation if it finds the authority it has given is misused. Constitutional safeguards are always essential to provide against possible constitutional breakdowns. That is the degree of autonomy possible and permissible in India.

Some will say, here is no constitutional advance, we want full responsibility. It is an advance. We are not back at the Morley-Minto stage; we have the enlarged franchise; we have the larger councils; and the larger preponderance of elected members therein; we have one-half of our cabinet from elected members, and we have a greater independence in the powers delegated by the central government, powers that it can enlarge or contract according as the provincial governments show their fitness for true responsibility. We are not back at the Morley-Minto stage; we have changed our destination; we have made a great advance on a new route, the route of partnership government, in place of the old route which had led us into a quagmire. We have tried the other system of full responsibility in the domain of local self-government, but it has done no good. People who cannot use their powers wisely in the lesser sphere cannot surely ask for more powers in the higher. They were given their talent, they can show neither ten nor five, and the one talent they were given they have not even buried, they have thrown it away.

(iii) FRAMEWORK FOR THE GOVERNMENT OF INDIA

The third proposition contained in the Montford Report, and reproduced in Chapter XVI, page 174, has not been satisfied. We must satisfy it now.

In the central government we are not giving "responsibility" at all, for the Legislative Assembly has committed political suicide, and the electorates, except the European, cannot call anybody to account, for the attitude of their members is entirely beyond their ken and the proceedings of the Assembly beyond their comprehension. The requirement is not a parliament but a house made up partly of delegates from the provinces and partly of enlightened persons, versed specially in those wide and greater subjects with which the central legislature of this great sub-continent must deal wisely and well if it is to help the British nation in the discharge of its responsibilities to the 300 millions whose interests are held in trust. Indirect electorates of the classes and the interests involved are the best way in which this wide knowledge and experience can be secured. Not even the constitution builders intended their term of art, "responsibility," to extend to large electorates incompetent to judge. The behaviour of the assembly as it has existed has been sketched in Chapter XX, and was summed up in Sir Basil Blackett's last speech. It is certain that no government can perform its great duties when a legislature half-filled with Swarajist lawyers is a millstone round its neck. The remodelling of this chamber into a house of delegates is an essential element in any new constitution. Its composition should, as in the provinces, include the due proportion of the three principal interests, land, commerce, and the professional classes, distributed, the first among Hindus and Mahommedans, the second among Indians and Europeans, while the third requires no communal element. I would sketch it as follows:

Having regard to the urban interests involved, the great interests of trade and commerce, and the customs and the maritime interests, the special charge of the central government, I would give the great corporations and the port trusts of Calcutta, Bombay, Madras, Karachi, and Rangoon the right to send a separate delegate to represent these important interests. There would thus be ten representatives in all from these seaport towns. Delhi and the other provincial capitals would each send a commercial representative, as well as the capitals of minor administrations that have no councils of their own. These would be Patna, Allahabad, Lahore, Nagpur, Peshawar. Bangalore, Ajmere, to which would be added the following trading centres and great cities, Ahmedabad, Lucknow, Cawnpur, Amritsar, and perhaps Madura or Calicut, and Quetta. European commerce should be represented by six members from different parts of India on a distribution between the chambers as decided from time to time by the Associated Chambers of Commerce. Assam with no great city should send a representative of its tea.

The general interests of the major provinces would be represented by six, five, four, or three members according to their size. The distribution of these would take into account as far as possible different linguistic areas within a province, so that each of the important ones might find one delegate at least for the legislature of the central government. Thus Bombay might distribute its membership between Sind, Gujerat, and Maharashtra; Madras between its Telegus, its Tamils, its Malayalams, or its Canarese; the landholders of Agra and Oudh would have their separate representation, and the Hindus, Mahommedans, and Sikhs of the Punjab theirs; the Hindi-speaking people of the Central Provinces, and the Urya-speaking people of Orissa, could all be provided for, and among these representatives the landholders and the professions would have their proper place, the landholders and the Mahommedans with their special electorates, and the remaining provincial members as delegates of the provincial councils. . .

On the scheme that I have sketched classes and interests would each have some share, and communal misgivings would be allayed, while all the minor administrations would find a place there through the representatives of their capital cities. If we allow 39 members in all for the 8 major provinces we shall have a total of these elected seats of 70 members. To these we must add, say, 50 nominated seats, to make up the chamber of 120. Of these 25 should be official seats, including the members of the Governor-General's Executive Council, constituted as at present and having their places *ex-officio*. That will leave the Governor-General 25 seats to be filled by nominated non-officials. It is very difficult in some parts to find electorates for scattered interests, such, for example, as Europeans, Anglo-Indians, and Indian Christians, but having regard to the composition of the elected side of the council, after the elections had been held, the Governor-General would always be able to nominate from any class that seemed to have been left out in the cold. There are certain special interests connected with the central subjects for which representation might be found in this way. All Companies' railways might jointly designate a panel of two or three representatives, out of which the Governor-General might select one for nomination to his legislature. Nominees would also be required for the voiceless people and charged with looking after the interests of the ryot, labour, and all depressed classes.

So much for the new central legislature, by whatever name you may call it, assembly, house of delegates, or house of representatives. It is still left to consider whether there should be a second chamber, or, if not, what should take its place. The Council of State has done very well, and performed most useful revisional functions as a second chamber, but on the proposed constitution of the new central legislature, as I have sketched it, a great many of the elements of the Council of State would find their place in the new chamber. While we hitherto have had two chambers, in the larger of which extremists preponderated, it was absolutely essential to have a second chamber with a majority of moderates. But if the larger chamber is revised as in my sketch then the necessity for a second legislature, much of the same kind, is no longer so urgent.

I have some other proposals to make.

It is surely right that in a country like India, with all its aristocratic and hereditary traditions, with 95 per cent. of its peoples (except for better locomotion) living in the thirteenth century, there should be some meeting of the twain —the 95 per cent. of the thirteenth and the 5 per cent. of the twentieth century. Surely in this great Oriental country we should not imitate too slavishly these new-fangled

Western models, and leave entirely out of our constitution everything that is Oriental. What is missing in this amalgam of East and West, medieval and modern, is some kind of institution resembling in its character, on the one side the House of Lords and the Privy Council, and on the other side the Durbar of an Oriental Emperor. To meet these requirements I propose that the Viceroy, as the representative of His Majesty, should be provided with a Durbar of the Indian Empire. Upon this Durbar the following elements, drawn from both British India and the Indian States, would find a place.

(1) Hereditary princes and chiefs, members of this Durbar by hereditary rights, but nominated for office therein by their own order.

(2) Ex-dewans and ex-ministers of great Indian States who had earned their inclusion by the distinguished talents they had shown to be selected by the Viceroy in consultation with the Princes.

(3) The great landholders and members of the old aristocratic families of the country.

(4) The most distinguished men in various walks of life, such as retired judges, ex-executive councillors, ex-ministers, captains of industry and commerce, men specially distinguished in the law, or medicine, or literature, or learning, heads of great religious orders or great social movements, great leaders of thought. In this category the poet Tagore, the great scientist J. C. Bose, men like the late Lord Sinha or the late Mr. Gokhale, Sir Rajendranath Mukerji, aye, even such as the "Mahatma" Gandhi, if only he would drop his political campaign and stand for those beneficent principles which he advocates but for ever mars by his impracticable admixture of calumny directed against the benevolence of the British Government.

(5) Retired Indian public servants, or European if any have settled in India, whose valuable experience in responsible posts that they have held is now lost to the country.

Over this Durbar the Viceroy himself would preside, whenever necessary, and its functions would be advisory and deliberative, like the council which the French Government have provided for the Governor-General of Algeria. The business would be divided between some of the component parts of this great body, according to the subjects with which it had to deal. If these matters concerned British India alone, classes (1) and (2) would not participate. If the matters concerned Indian States alone, classes (3), (4) and (5) would stand aside. If the matter was one of common interest to British India and the States, then all the Durbar could participate in the discussion. The Commander-in-Chief and two of his heads of military departments, the chief representative of the navy, all the members of the Executive Council, and the Foreign and Political Secretaries would *ex-officio* be members of the Durbar. All members appointed would be appointed by His Majesty the King-Emperor for life; the nominees of their order selected by the princes themselves would be members of the Durbar by hereditary right.

Now this Durbar would not be by itself a legislative body, but an advisory one, and it would appoint a special legislative committee to take into consideration all Bills passed by the central chamber and specially referred to the Durbar by the Governor-General. This legislative committee would submit its report to the Durbar; on the advice of the Durbar, the Viceroy, as Governor-General, would signify his assent to the Bill, or the desire of the Durbar to return the Bill with amendments, or would refuse assent. And the same procedure would be followed in the case of Government Bills thrown out by the chamber below, which the Governor-General none the less felt it necessary to certify. All persons appointed to the Durbar, except the princes, who already have all the titles they can desire, would be designated by the title Right Honourable.

In fact the aim of this sketch is to obtain a body of "elder statesmen," each with a large stake in the prosperity of the country, representing all the best elements of the aristocracy, the higher intelligentsia, and all the best men of light and leading that India can produce. It is not even essential that every member should know English.

The Durbar could be convened at any time by the Viceroy, and not merely when the legislative chamber was sitting. Its legislative committee might sit continuously whenever the work before it was of an urgent nature. It would have its rules of business and its quorum, which should be large enough to ensure that its opinions were weighty and representative.

Suggestions have been made before for advisory councils, privy councillors, and such like bodies, but the sketch that I have ventured to put forward is a more complete enumeration of the composition and functions of such a body so as to make it worthy of a definite place in the constitution of the whole Empire. When the matters before it were of a confidential nature its proceedings would have to be confidential too; otherwise, if the matter was of the legislative order, its proceedings would be published abroad. There would be here no star chamber, for the consultations that were confidential would only be those that all cabinets have to keep confidential until the decisions are announced. This is the body, partly Oriental, partly Western, partly medieval, partly modern, that I would put forward as representing the different centuries, the different Princes, peoples, races, languages, and classes, the different interests, aristocratic and popular, in a manner far more suitable to India than a machinery slavishly modelled on the legislative chambers and senates of modern Western States. These latter can only be built up, rising from the foundation, and gradually fulfilling modern "responsible" notions, as education filters down to the masses of the people, and the masses of the people rise up in their intelligence on the new strength that education has given them. At any rate I put forward this scheme for consideration for what it is worth, and the germ of it is partly derived from the unsophisticated proposals of the artisans, which suggested placing aristocratic life peers into an upper chamber to combat "the tyranny" of elected members because these poor people have no trust in a new and exotic intelligentsia.

Surely when we take a bird's-eye view of the vast panorama of India, her hoary antiquity and the wonderful varieties of humanity of which her teeming millions are composed, it must seem the height of folly to select a narrow section, drawn from a few clerical classes, to be the sole successors either of the Oriental dynasties which preceded British rule, or of the paramount and beneficent authority of the King-Emperor's Government, when we know, first, that these few people, though they may have acquired by rote the phraseology of the West, have not in them the spirit of free institutions; and secondly, that in the absence of our military and moral support any authority that we may give them would be overthrown as soon as given by the revolt of the vast number who are steeped in Oriental traditions, and will not for a moment accept the pretentions of this class to rule the rest.

CHAPTER XXXII

LAST WORDS

THE situation in India is approaching a crisis.

Even since the last chapter was written strange things have been happening there. The Statutory Commission has completed its local investigations, and the Swarajists, and even the so-called Liberals, have, to the last, refused to hear the voice of Sir John Simon and his fellow charmers, charmed they never so wisely. A dastardly bomb outrage has been perpetrated within the Chamber, and the passage of the Public Safety Bill has been obstructed. Lord Irwin has been compelled to issue an Ordinance to counter the dangerous situation which the Indian politicians would neither recognise nor deal with. The inconsistency of these people is demonstrated anew with each thing that they do. The President of the Assembly first swallowed a camel by ruling that when certain prosecutions had been launched a Motion to discuss the policy of these very prosecutions would not raise issues that were *sub judice*, and later on strained at a gnat by holding that the passage of the Public Safety Bill, which had been before the House for a long time, would involve discussion of cases under judicial investigation. He was good enough to add that if Government would withdraw the prosecution he would remove his embargo on the Bill.

In respect to the bomb outrage the Swarajist leader in one breath spoke lightly of it as the act of some "hare-brained youths," and in another breath solemnly adjured Government that they were confronted with the alternatives of "Balraj" or Gandhi, unless, of course, they meekly accepted all the demands of the Swarajists. "Balraj," the cult of physical force, and Gandhi's non-violent programme of mass disobedience, or "soul force," are really one and the same thing, for what virtue is there in the soul force if, each time that its chief apostle raises a voice pleading for non-violence, somebody's blood is shed? This is what happened before, and this is what will happen again if the disseminator goes forth unrestrained to sow his dangerous seed of incitement. When Lord Irwin, after almost inexhaustible patience, has found it necessary to use his special powers because his constitutional auxiliaries failed to help him in an emergency a so-called *moderate* Indian journal demands his recall. These are the people who seek to impress the world with their capacity for governing. The irresponsible Indian Press has now claimed a new recruit from the stronghold of commonsense, for *The Pioneer* trips cheerfully down the easy slope to Avernus, forgetful in its blindness of the bottomless pit. It has thrown over its old friends, will it keep its new?

If accounts in the Press are correct, the Madras Government has recommended complete autonomy in that Province, the control of law and order to be placed in ministerial hands. Has it asked, I wonder, of its British Collectors and Police Superintendents how many will wish to serve under Ministries at the mercy of men who seek not to administer the law but to obstruct it? Has it considered how it will replace these officers if they do not wish to serve on? Has it, I ask, paid any heed to the cry of the Sudras, and of those untouchable classes who have suffered under the tyranny of the Brahmins, most of all in Madras? I do not know. There may be some explanation. Perhaps the points in its Confidential Memorandum which found their way somehow into the Press do not do it full justice. But if it feels itself too weak to enforce law and order, and has decided to throw up the sponge and leave it to the Central Government to clear up the wreckage left by the horse-play of Swarajists and the hay-making of communal intrigue in the police offices and the magistrates' courts, it will deserve the fate of disintegration into four minor Provinces which the Nehru Constitution has foreshadowed as the solution of its linguistic rivalries.

In *The Hindu* of Madras of 2nd March, 1929, is published an article by an old Brahmin friend of mine, Mr. C. Vijayaraghavachariar, under the title "The National Demand—an appeal to the League of Nations." The writer has thrown his article into the form of a dialogue between himself and a friend called "*K*." My old friend is an honest man, but an ardent idealist, and he too has succumbed to the fatal facility of making the facts suit his ideals instead of basing his aspirations on the facts. In order to show the trend of thought of those who call for immediate Dominion status I include his article as Appendix IV for separate study by any reader who cares to study it. It is, as such articles go, a temperately-worded statement of his views. He is in no sense hostile to Englishmen as such, and I know that, unlike some of the rabid school of young Swarajists, he has a genuine regard for them. But he begs question after question in stating his views, and the deductions that he proceeds to draw lose all their cogency because they are based on postulates which are nothing but incorrect assumptions. His argument is that as the people of India have the sole right to determine their own form of Government within, or for the matter of that without, the Empire, the British Parliament and the British people have nothing to say to it any more than the Indian people could claim a voice in determining British political institutions. That being the case of course the labours of the Simon Commission are superfluous, and the decision of the British Parliament irrelevant. As India will not accept the authority of the British Parliament he is afraid the British people and the Indians must come to blows, a contingency which he regards with genuine aversion. The only method of avoiding it, in his opinion, is a reference to the League of Nations.

I need not follow the writer into his disquisitions upon the right of the League of Nations to decide between the Swarajists of India and the British Government. He bases this view of its right and authority upon the course which it followed in registering the Irish Treaty, and in settling the rival claims of Finland and Sweden to the sovereignty of the Aland Islands. But the Irish Treaty was not made by the League of Nations or under its influence, whereas, in the case of India, according to the writer, the League would have to make the settlement itself. As to the Aland Islands, which were the subject of dispute between two independent states of Europe, they can offer no parallel at all for the affairs of India. The rights and obligations of the League of Nations *vis-a-vis* its Members are a question for jurists. My friend is, however, so sanguine as to think that the Hindu-Moslem question in India might also be referred to the League for settlement, and that the League should further investigate the economic and social difficulties and the sanitary conditions prevailing in India, indeed presumably all the problems which arise in the sub-continent, and pass appropriate decisions upon them. It is, of course, just possible that the experts of the League of Nations might come to findings unpalatable to the Swarajists, in which case it is not made clear what course should be followed, either by the Swarajists or by the British Government. The strange thing is that Mr. V. Achariar, who is a most industrious reader, can make the assumptions that he has made. He assumes that India consists of one nation, of which the crowd of people who throng the Congress precincts—many of them irresponsible students or self-appointed delegates all of one party—are the duly accredited representatives, and that what the Congress decides upon, after heated discussions lasting into the small hours, represents the considered opinion of the inhabitants of India. He also assumes that the country is daily becoming poorer, and that its inhabitants are slowly dying out, since the expectation of life of an Indian is steadily being reduced. For these assertions he offers neither facts nor figures, nor does he stop to ask himself what is the explanation of all this lamentable decline in wealth and health. If all Western efforts to provide schools and hospitals to combat disease and overcome famine, to introduce better midwifery, and encourage infant welfare, to construct waterworks and drainage schemes, to open up the country with roads and railways, have only had the effect of reducing wealth and increasing the death rate, then my friend and his political associates are surely wrong in asking for Western nostra which have these deplorable results. He should not be advocating Western institutions on Oriental soil, but a return to the simple life, to the old régime, in fact to Gandhi's Arcadia, to the old beautiful relations of *Raja* (King) and *praja* (people) of which Indian idealists love to discourse as the delightful memories of a fabled golden age.

One of the advantages which leads the writer of the article to prefer Dominion status within the Empire to complete independence is that it will enable self-governing India to retain British in the Public Service, on account of the valuable help that they can give after Dominion status has been established. Yet, if the association of British administrators has hitherto been merely productive of evil, how is India to be advantaged by their retention? His own explanation in his own words is contained in the following extract from the full dialogue reproduced in Appendix IV:

" The next advantage (viz. from Dominion status) is that we require for many a long year the co-operation of Englishmen in the Services, Civil and Military (including Aerial and Naval). It is best to be frank and honest in the eternal interests of ourselves. Long, long ago, say a thousand years ago, we lost our capacity and disciplined habits for running a free government with all its necessary institutions, while the Englishmen have been these eight hundred years developing all the qualities of head and heart which are most necessary for progressively maintaining free institutions. We sadly but imperatively need their association with us in maintaining and developing our newly-won free institutions on the soundest practical principles tested by their long experience.

"*K*. But we have all along been crying against the Bureaucracy and have wished to get rid of them.

"*C.V.* There has been confusion of thought in this particular. The present English Bureaucracy in India have all along been our political rulers as well, charged by law and conventions to run and maintain the most selfish autocracy solely in the interests of Great Britain and even her possessions beyond the seas. Stripped of all their present political and other special powers and privileges they would be most valuable merely as constituting a definite and appreciable portion of the great Services of the new régime along with our own countrymen. I believe that it is far more difficult to preserve internal peace and carry on the administration in and by every Department satisfactorily than to ordain our defence against external aggression."

I have no doubt that my friend has persuaded himself to believe in the correctness of these arguments, but his very honesty shows that he does not recognise the limitations of the situation. He assumes that the Indian races once had a capacity for free institutions and disciplined habits which they lost roughly a thousand years ago.

He assumes that pending the growth of these free institutions British military and civil officers will serve contentedly under a Brahmin oligarchy.

He assumes that British Civil Servants, deprived of all political authority, will be able to achieve what they could not do when they had the power to make their influence felt. His facts appear to be wrong. He will have to go back to the dim recesses of many centuries before he can find the existence of those ideal relations between the Raja and his subjects to which he refers, and even then will find edicts of benevolent monarchs rather than free institutions of a democratic people. His reasoning is also at fault. He will not perhaps admit the Brahmin oligarchy, but in the absence of British rule, in the absence of the long lost capacity for free institutions, in the absence of the restoration of old Indian Rajas, what can there be but a Brahmin oligarchy or

Mahommedan rule over Hindu India? Even the Brahmin oligarchy would have to be kept in power by British troops and dry-nursed by a modicum of British Civil Servants. He forgets that it is not the character of a public service that moulds a nation, but the character of a nation that moulds its public service.

The Hindu commends this article to the careful attention of its readers as one deserving their consideration. I do the same, though not for quite the same reason. That article represents the views in his own words of an honest Swarajist who has at least kindly feelings to British Civil Servants, and is most anxious for a peaceful settlement. But among the political intelligentsia men like to him are not numerous. They mostly consist of persons inspired by anti-British feelings or of ambitious hot-heads. I have cited one piece of evidence from an ex-President of the National Congress who supports the demand for immediate Dominion status. I will next cite as a witness a Parsee gentleman with experience both of journalism and of membership of the Legislative Assembly, Mr. Naoroji Dumasia. The following letter over his signature was printed in the *Times* last year, under the title "An Indian Warning—The Extremist Menace":

"The approaching departure of the Simon Commission impels me to offer some observations on the present grave situation in India.

"During my stay in England this summer I have heard expressions of good-will for Indian aspirations from all classes of the people. Some, like myself, do not believe that democracy is suited to India; yet Englishmen are resolved to give a patient trial to the experiment launched in consequence of the pledge of 1917. While the British Parliament has appointed the Statutory Commission under the chairmanship of an eminent Liberal statesman for the purposes of revision the Indian political leaders have failed to respond to the generous gesture. I am glad to find that the British public does not take their puerile performance seriously. The melancholy daily news of the implacable hostility to

British rule of self-seeking professional politicians, who claim to speak in the name of the people of India, fills me with sorrow. But, I am sure, Englishmen will not fail to discriminate between loyal India and the vapourings of a few.

"No one is better qualified to speak for India than the Maharajah of Bickaner, whose timely assurance of staunch loyalty to the Crown and British connexion reflects the true opinion of Indians, who have immensely benefited by British rule. Were Englishmen to clear out of India, everyone who has any stake in the country would follow them. Unfortunately most of the loaves and fishes secured under the reforms have gone to political agitators, who seek to destroy the reforms, while the law-abiding members of the minority communities, who believe in fitness as the test for office, who have enormous stakes in the country, and have made tremendous sacrifices for consolidating and upholding British rule have had the least consideration. If the democratic idea of "One man, one vote" is pushed to its logical conclusion there will be no safety, still less any political influence, for minorities. Hindus and Mahomedans will cut each other's throats for political domination.

"The Simon Commission will fail in its purpose if it omits to examine the credentials of self-seeking political agitators, the measure of their stake in the country, and their title to impose their authority on us. What tradition of ruling authority have they got? I, for one, will refuse to acknowledge their authority, and there are millions who hold to my view. Indian Princes will refuse to have anything to do with these false gods of democracy. Englishmen have changed the face of India and raised it to the position of a modern civilized country. But they are doing irreparable harm to India and to the Empire by dangling before immature minds democratic theories, the application of which would imperil India. Indian literates form only a fraction of the population; and the politically minded are only a part of the fraction. Will your idealists deny that power without education is a danger, and liberty in the hands of ignorant masses is bound to degenerate into license?

"England has produced great Empire builders. Englishmen have established interests of vital consequence to the Empire by their connexion with, and sacrifices for, India. Their stake in the welfare of my country is enormous. Will that Empire-wide interest be safe under the Bolshevist *régime* which we may expect when, and if, British authority is reduced to a pale shadow? The Indian Princes mostly come of martial races. When their authority is challenged by the Swarajists civil war will shake India to its very foundation. But what of the British Indians who have stood by Englishmen and who look to them for protection? On what grounds of statecraft are we to be forsaken and thrown to the wolves? Indian patriotism is not a Swarajist monopoly. Those of us who have drunk at the fountain of free institutions of your country, in which the roots of liberty have struck most deeply, certainly are not less patriotic. We believe that patriotism consists in making one's country happier and more prosperous and peaceful. That condition is fulfilled under the British rule, which, as the late Mr. Gokhale aptly said, though foreign is our own Government.

"That the new school aims at confiscation of lawfully acquired rights of Englishmen is shown by the recent debate in the Assembly on a private Bill for the reservation of the Indian coastal trade to Indian firms. Thus, while the European Chambers of Commerce have furnished evidence of their good will by recommending full provincial autonomy under certain safeguards of doubtful adequacy, the Swarajists have responded to their generous instincts by confiscatory proposals. Recent proceedings in the Assembly make painful reading. Recommendations for any further reform must be made to depend upon a good-will so far lacking in the major political party towards British interests, and due consideration for the rights of minorities like Moslems, Parsis, Jains, Anglo-Indians, and the depressed classes. I yield to none in the patriotic desire to promote the political freedom of India. It would be wrong to deny that we are suffering from a number of grievances. But we do not live in Utopia. The freedom of religion, speech, and writing and security against external aggression which we have enjoyed for 150 years of British rule can only be had at a price. That price we must pay. The political agitators would evade payment.

"The beginnings of Parliamentary institutions in India have placed a heavy burden on the taxpayer and an excessive strain on the Civil Service. Moreover, they have not obliterated but sharpened racial bitterness. The major political party considers these institutions worthless. Their best fruits have gone to the Swarajist President of the Assembly, who more than once has openly challenged the Government on the floor of the House to withdraw them. As a former colleague of his in the Assembly and as a journalist I have a right to ask:—" Is the deliberate move to punish honest members of the Press Gallery for criticizing the President's rulings a foretaste of the kind of liberty of the Press we are to enjoy in the Swarajist *régime*?" At any rate, the "satanic" Government has never hampered the liberty of expression of opinion of its severest critics.

"I am well aware of the sturdiness of the British character. I am sure Englishmen will not willingly set back the clock of political progress in India. But here we are in a dilemma. The Swarajists do not believe in the reforms; they are pledged to destroy them. If they do not want them, let the reforms be suspended, and make the Swarajists responsible for the step. I guarantee that the non-cooperation movement will then vanish like the mist in the sun. But if Englishmen fail to grasp the meaning of the rapid development of racial bitterness, if they fail to understand the import of the opposition to the Public Safety Bill, then I do not hesitate to say that a rude awakening is in store for them.

"NAOROJI DUMASIA."

If any reader is so strong in his faith in the suitability of British institutions for all peoples, nations and languages, that he throws this book aside as the prejudiced view of a sun-dried bureaucrat lacking political sagacity, let him study these two examples of what highly-intelligent Indians have said on the one side and the other.

The whole fabric of a self-governing India, holding itself together in unity, is only what the Hindus themselves call *Maya*, or illusion.

Why is it that Englishmen can think of no model save that of Westminster as a school for the Oriental populations that the Empire contains? Is not France a democratic nation? Has she not liberal ideals and free institutions, and how has she been governing Algeria, and Tunis, and French Indo-China, and Annam, all these years? Has she attempted to set up local democracies in any of these countries? She has for certain purposes kept them as if they were part of France. In Algeria, the nearest of these, the non-Mussulman Services are under the French ministries at Paris, and the Local Services under the Governor-General at Algiers. It is he who frames the Budget; the Budget is passed by the aid of the Superior Council, consisting of high officials and a few elected members, and it is assisted in this work by three delegations, of which the delegates represent respectively the French Colonists, the French tax-payers other than Colonists, and the Mussulman natives. They have neither given nor promised a local "responsible" government, and it is the French Chambers alone that have the right of legislation for Algeria, and all difficulties about democracy are got over by allowing Algeria to send its own group of delegates to the Chambers in Paris.

India is larger, 2½ times as large as Algeria, and her population 50 times as numerous. Her distance from Great Britain requires her to have some local Legislatures of her own, though the British Parliament has ever retained its own super-legislative power. Even this power it is required now to give up under an ultimatum delivered by the Scribes and Pharisees of India, and all because those who laid the foundations of the new reforms building neither counted the cost nor examined the materials available. They were, like the architect from England, fresh to the country, who designs roofs fitted to keep out snow in the torrid Indian plains. We can only honour the pledge of 1917, inconceivably rash as it was, by setting before ourselves and India something durable and held together by good British cement. But for that cement in its composition even the United States of America could not have stood so long together and become the nation that they are to-day. South America proves it. That same cement has been necessary to keep a unified India, and that cement will be more than ever necessary if she is ever to become a Dominion. A thousand voices with discordant cries assail the ears of the Statutory Commission. Will it listen only to those voices it can understand, or will it strive to catch the faltering whispers of the masses below?

I have completed the task that I set before myself. I have endeavoured to explain one by one the formidable obstacles which make an Indian Nation impossible and Democracy there a dream. I have endeavoured to show how political progress in India has gone off the rails, and how legislative bodies created by ourselves in undiscriminating generosity have been mistaken for Parliaments created *suo vigore* by the people concerned. I have tried to show that the Indian *demos* has neither the power nor the wish to govern itself. Its only desire is that it should be " godly and quietly governed " and not placed under the heel of a few oligarchs of high caste. We have been accused of dividing to rule—the charge is untrue. While we governed we united. Since we began to relax our governing we are dividing ; if we cease to govern the numberless fragments that we have pieced together would fly apart. I have sketched a rough framework for a constitution of partnership in the hope of thus maintaining a balance of power between the races, and creeds, and classes that we have found in India, without abandoning entirely the direction sketched out in Mr. Montagu's announcement.

It is now for the Statutory Commission to mature its proposals and for Parliament to decide. It is not a case of placating Swarajists, that is a false scent to follow. If we followed it we should merely be putting another coat of paint on a whited sepulchre. We must devise something that will endure for a long period, and that will give reasonable scope to the ambitions of the few, but compatibly with the safety and security of the many.

The situation calls for great firmness. The trained emissaries of Soviet Russia are corrupting the simplicity of the Indian worker, the sophistries of Gandhi are applied to exploit the credulity of millions of peasants, and the Swarajist agitators are encouraging the former and making a decoy of the latter to further their own ambitions. If we are not careful the factory workers will be turned into a mad proletariat and the peaceful peasantry into no-rent agitators. We cannot be supine while the programme of civil disobedience is being insidiously developed. We must show that we at least can learn by our own mistakes of the former Non-Cooperation period, and suppress treason at its source before it can extend its tentacles over the land and the people. An association to organise a general strike must be declared illegal. Only by this means shall we retain the confidence and support of all loyal and moderate men amongst the educated, as well as the trust of the illiterate millions.

Above all, we must insist upon the maintenance of our British Services in full security, for their value is known from one end of the land to the other. The Ex-President of the National Congress, whose remarks I have quoted, and the voices of the unsophisticated, are one in recognising this necessity. The Swarajist bluff must be called; if it is called they will throw in their hands.

If the British in these Services were to be banished as a sop to the Swarajist agitators, or forced to resign their charges rather than become the unwilling instruments of corrupt administration, they might rightly exclaim with Coriolanus when he heard his sentence of banishment:

> " Let every feeble rumour shake your hearts!
> Your enemies with nodding of their plumes
> Fan you into despair! Have the power still
> To banish your defenders; till at length
> Your ignorance (which finds not till it feels)
> Making but reservation of yourselves
> (Still your own foes) deliver you
> As most abated captives to some nation
> That won you without blows ! "

APPENDIX I

COMPARISON OF THE COUNTRIES OF EUROPE WITH THE PROVINCES AND STATES OF INDIA

EUROPE.			INDIA.		
Country.	Area in sq. miles.	Population in millions.	Province or State.	Area in sq. miles.	Population in millions.
Germany -	182,000	63·18	Bengal - -	77,000	46·69
			Bengal States	5,000	0·90
			Sikkim - -	3,000	0·08
			Central Provinces and Berar - -	100,000	13·91
			C.P. States -	31,000	2·06
				216,000	63·64
France - - -	212,000	40·74	Madras - -	142,000	42·31
TOTAL, France and Germany -	394,000	103·92		358,000	105·95

Europe.			India.		
Country.	Area in sq. miles.	Population in millions.	Province or State.	Area in sq. miles.	Population in millions.
Italy - -	120,000	38·75	Behar and Orissa -	83,000	34·00
			Orissa States -	29,000	3·95
				112,000	37·95
Spain - -	190,000	21·34	Bombay - -	124,000	19·34
			Bombay States	63,000	7·41
				187,000	26·75
Portugal -	34,000	5·54	Gwalior -	26,000	3·19
			Baroda - -	8,000	2·13
				34,000	5·32
Netherlands -	13,000	7·53	Nizam's Dominions -	83,000	12·47
Belgium -	12,000	7·46			
Luxemburg -	1,000	0·26			
	26,000	15·25			
Total, Western Europe -	582,000	121·62		558,000	124·80

Europe.			India.		
Country.	Area in sq. miles.	Population in millions.	Province or State.	Area in sq. miles.	Population in millions.
Scandinavia :			Burma - -	262,000	13·21
Sweden -	173,000	6·07			
Norway -	125,000	2·65			
Denmark -	16,000	3·43			
	314,000	12·15			
Finland -	133,000	3·36	N.W.F. States	25,000	2·80
			Beluchistan States -	80,000	0·38
			Beluchistan -	54,000	0·42
				159,000	3·60

Europe.			India.		
Country.	Area in sq. miles.	Population in millions.	Province or State.	Area in sq. miles.	Population in millions.
Poland	150,000	29·58	Punjab	100,000	20·68
			Punjab States	27,000	4·62
			N.W.F. Province	13,000	2·25
				140,000	27·35
Austria	32,000	6·53	United Provinces	106,000	45·50
Hungary	36,000	8·48	U.P. States	6,000	1·13
Yugo-Slavia	96,000	12·22			
Czecho-Slovakia	54,000	13·61			
	218,000	40·84		112,000	46·63
Bulgaria	40,000	5·48	Coorg	2,000	0·16
			Mysore State	30,000	5·97
				32,000	6·13
Roumania	122,000	17·39	Rajputana States	129,000	9·84
Greece	50,000	6·60	Assam	53,000	7·60
Albania	17,000	0·83	Manipur	8,000	0·38
Turkey in Europe	13,000	1·20			
	80,000	8·63		61,000	7·98
Latvia	24,000	1·80	Ajmir	3,000	0·49
Lithuania	32,000	4·80	Central Indian States	52,000	5·99
Esthonia	18,000	1·11	Madras States	11,000	5·46
	74,000	7·71		66,000	11·94
Switzerland	16,000	3·95	Kashmir	84,000	3·32
Grand Total	1,911,000	313·89		1,819,000	318·44

APPENDIX II

THE STORY OF THE COW THAT SHIED

ONE afternoon in the rains I received an order from my district magistrate to repair to the town of Katwara, some fifty miles by rail from the headquarters of the district, and investigate a case which was pending in the court of the Tahsildar (sub-magistrate and revenue officer). It was all about a cow, and Hindu-Mahommedan feeling had been aroused. As the only European assistant in the district I was directed to make the investigation.

The unfinished record of the case was sent to me and appeared on the surface to be an ordinary case of simple theft, with which the Tahsildar was quite competent to deal. It seemed that some days previously the district magistrate had received a telegram from the Mahommedans of Katwara that two of their co-religionists were being arrested on a false charge and that the Mahommedans were being subjected to grievous oppression. The district magistrate had then despatched an experienced Mahommedan inspector of police to go to the spot and report what it was all about. Some days later a second telegram was received by the district magistrate—this time from the Hindus—that the Mahommedan inspector was causing a reign of terror in the place, and that the Hindus were being grievously oppressed. It was upon this second telegram that I had been ordered to go. I left that night and arrived at Katwara at about 10 p.m. There were a number of people to receive me, clustered round a dark object on the dimly-lighted platform, which on further scrutiny proved to be the hide and horns of the cow (for the poor creature that had convulsed the town and was the chief exhibit in the theft case had in the meantime died). I spent the next two days in unravelling the case, and examined a large number of witnesses, and this is the true narrative of events.

In a village about twelve miles from Katwara a Hindu cultivator sold two ancient cows to a Mahommedan called A., who re-sold them to his friend, also a Mahommedan butcher, B., for the sum of Rs. 6. B.'s small son was driving the cows through the town to his father's house when something coming the other way made one of the cows shy, and it shied right into the open verandah of a house which belonged to the orderly messenger of the Naib (assistant) Tahsildar. The messenger was a Brahmin, who at once took the line that as the cow had taken sanctuary in his house from a butcher it would be sacrilege for the Brahmin to surrender it to the butcher's boy. He accordingly tied it up. The boy then drove the other cow on to his father, B., and told him what had happened. B. then came along and demanded the release of his cow, but was met by a refusal. For some days the butcher went about the town interviewing this man and that and entreating them to use their influence to get his cow back. At last he went to the office of the Naib Tahsildar, and tried to get two Mahommedan clerks employed there to move the Naib Tahsildar to order his messenger to return the cow. The clerks, being Mahommedans, did what they could, and a small conference took place with the Naib, who was a Brahmin like his messenger, and some other people who were interested in the episode. It was then suggested by the Naib that a few Hindus in the town should subscribe two or four annas each and make up a sum of two or three rupees to pay the butcher as compensation for the cow, which he agreed could under no circumstances be restored to the butcher by any Brahmin. Some of the Hindus seemed willing, but the butcher expressed high indignation. He said he had paid six rupees for that cow, and six rupees he would have or the cow, whichever they liked. The Hindus said that two rupees was all they were prepared to pay, and if he didn't like it he could go without. The butcher, after having entreated everybody in the place in vain to get justice done to him, then said he would go and report at the police station that his cow had been criminally misappropriated by the Naib's messenger, and have him arrested. He waited a day or two to see if his threats would have any effect, but as they had none he then laid his formal charge at the police station. The police officer in charge, a sub-inspector (who was also a Brahmin), when B. made his report questioned him as to where he had bought the cow, and he mentioned his friend A., who had bought it from the Hindu cultivator. A. was sent for, and to the intense surprise of A. and B. they found themselves both arrested, A. for theft and B. as the receiver of stolen goods in respect of a cow belonging to the Naib's messenger. The Hindus had not been idle. The villager denied all knowledge of the sale, and the Naib's messenger declared that the cow was his long-lost cow which had been stolen from him two years previously, and that the cow had not shied at all but had merely recognised its old place and entered the verandah. The two men were accordingly placed before the Tahsildar on the charges named; the Tahsildar was also a Brahmin. The Tahsildar was in a quandary, and after recording a very little formal evidence, adjourned the case "for want of time." The Tahsildar must have known that the case was totally false, for he could not have failed to hear the story which had set the whole town agog. The negotiations over the price of the cow had actually taken place in the room next to his court, and in front of his own assistant. On the next day fixed for hearing he again wrote "press of work" as a cause for adjournment, and on the next occasion "a touch of fever" was the pretext, and once more "the extreme heat of the weather." In the meantime the Mahommedan inspector sent by the district magistrate had arrived and pursued his enquiries. The cow, which had by then been transferred to the pound, was invoked as a witness, and was slowly driven down the street to see whether it would again turn into the house of the Naib's messenger. This rather futile experiment ended in nothing. The Mahommedans said that it did not go in; the Hindus declared that Mahommedans armed with sticks had stood in the way and frightened it. In any case the experiment could have proved nothing, for the cow had been admittedly tied up there for several days and might naturally have gone into a place where it had been fed. The next experiment was to drive the two cows to the outskirts of the village from which the butcher said they had been bought, and let them loose at different points to see whether they would go back to the cowshed of the alleged former owner. Now the landlord of the village was also a Brahmin, and every man, woman, and child in the village had been coached to declare that the two cows were not the cows of the villager, and as proof of this they stated that these two cows had horns which turned upwards, while the horns of the cows that the villager had sold to someone else had turned downwards. Anyhow, the one cow did apparently find its way to the neighbourhood of the villager's house, but the other cow failed to go there because the regular path had been completely blocked up by someone by a barrier of thorns. In these foolish ways did these Hindus combine to defeat justice and support a false charge. Then occurred the tragedy, for the exhibit cow, being very weak and ill after its long march for twelve miles in the drenching rain, collapsed, and had to be carried by men on an improvised stretcher twelve miles back to Katwara, and on arrival there it died. The hide and horns were removed, and it was at this time that the enquiries of the Mahommedan inspector frightened the Hindus and induced them to send their telegram which had brought me on to the scene. Several Hindu witnesses, including the richest Hindu contractor in the town, swore that they recognised the cow as having belonged to the Naib's messenger, and that they knew nothing about the negotiations as to the compensation to be paid to the butcher. This, although one amongst them had actually offered to subscribe four annas. When I arrived at Katwara station for the investigation of the case these two Mahommedans had actually been in the under-trial lock-up for seventeen days! After hearing all the evidence I discharged the two accused and reported all the circumstances regarding the conduct of the officials to my chief. The Tahsildar, a magistrate with powers up to six months' imprisonment, and the chief officer of the local area, had been afraid to throw out the case for fear of offending the Hindus, and, after the Mahommedan inspector arrived on the scene, he was afraid to convict in case the facts came out, so he resorted to the subterfuge of gaining time by futile adjournments. His assistant, the Naib, personally knew the case to be totally false, yet allowed two innocent men to be kept in lock-up, though he could have given evidence of their innocence. His messenger committed gross perjury. The case was got up by the Hindus of the town in collusion with the Brahmin sub-inspector of police. He was the worst culprit of all, for he prosecuted on a charge which he knew to be false. He was, however, beyond the reach of punishment, for, having in the interval been called away to a distant dacoity case, he had contracted cholera and died. The other officials named were punished in various ways and transferred to distant places. I had in fact recommended their dismissal. The butcher was, of course, partly to blame, for he stated that he had paid six rupees for the cow, when that was the price he had paid for both. It is possible that if he had only claimed three the Hindus might have put up that sum. But the fact remains, that if there had been no British district magistrate, to whom the Mahommedans of the town could appeal, these two Mahommedans would almost certainly have been convicted and sent to prison on a charge not only false but actually known to be false by the police and magistrate. If the Mahommedan inspector had not been sent to the spot the information about the negotiations would have been completely suppressed, and evidence would have been given that the story about the cow shying was an invention of the butcher's. The facts would not then have come to light.

APPENDIX III

NOTE ON THE LINGUISTIC PROVINCES OF THE NEHRU CONSTITUTION

The Conference which accepted the Nehru Report laid it down that a Commission should be appointed by the new Government of the Commonwealth of India, as provided in that scheme, which in addition to the separation of Sind from Bombay as a separate provincial government, should take all necessary steps:

(*a*) To separate off Karnataka and Andhra into separate provinces.

(*b*) To constitute a new Uriya province by collecting from other provinces their disjointed Uriya parts.

(*c*) To report on the C.P. Hindustani districts, Kerala, and other linguistic areas which would like to be constituted into separate provinces.

(*d*) To resettle the boundaries of Assam, Bengal, Behar, and Orissa, C.P. Hindustani districts, Kerala and Karnataka in accordance with the principles recommended by the Nehru Committee.

Now the principles were, first, the wishes of the majority in the different linguistic areas, and, secondly, administrative and financial reasons were not entirely to be neglected but were to be quite secondary to the wishes of the majority and to linguistic conveniences.

A very brief examination will show the effect of dismembering the existing provinces in the manner suggested:

Bombay. Loses Sind, Guzerat, North Canara, so that Maharashtra only is left.

Madras. Loses Ganjam, Vizagapatam, and all its Telugu areas of the Godavari and Kistna; also Malabar and South Canara. It thus becomes a Tamil province with a provincial capital shorn of a great part of its territories.

Bengal. Takes Sylhet, its richest part, from Assam, and a strip of Chota Nagpur, the best mineral area of Behar and Orissa. But Eastern Bengal, with its Mahommedan majority—and under the

Nehru scheme that majority should prevail—will certainly demand its complete separation from Western Bengal, as His Highness the Aga Khan, speaking on behalf of Mahommedans, has publicly testified.

Assam. Will be relegated to its two great valleys unless, indeed, under this wonderful test of self-determination, the one should demand separation from the other.

United Provinces. Oudh will certainly want to shake off the dominance of Allahabad, and Agra and Allahabad will then raise covetous eyes to the C.P. Hindustani districts, of which more anon.

The Central Provinces and Berar. The Marathi districts of the C.P. and Berar should, on this linguistic basis, be joined on to Maharashtra in Bombay, as a compensation to that presidency for the territories of which she has been deprived. But Nagpur is 520 miles from Bombay, and the Eastern limit of Marathi-speaking Bhandara is yet another 120 miles further off. But there is one more trap in the linguistic idea. The Nizam has still the sovereignty of Berar, and Berar divides Nagpur from the Bombay border by some 200 miles of foreign territory. The Nizam agreed to lease these districts to the British Crown, but he will never consent to handing them over to any commonwealth of politicians. The first act of the Nizam on the establishment of the commonwealth would be the re-occupation of the leased districts of Berar. And so poor Nagpur, shorn of its northern districts that speak Hindi, will be left a poor little province, of four districts only, with perhaps two or three little strips of the southern base of the Satpuras.

The C.P. Hindi districts are likely to lose Nimar, which is half Marathi and borders Khandesh of the Bombay Presidency. The Hindi districts would remain a forlorn collection of peoples, touching the U.P. only by a narrow isthmus in the north of Saugor, but otherwise completely shut off from Agra by Central Indian States, Bhopal and Gwalior, and from Allahabad by the large State of Rewa. Of the nine districts to be provided for, three are fairly rich in parts, but the other six are poor, and contain a large percentage of aboriginals. When the politicians were seated round their table they forgot entirely the name of Gondwana. These districts would be too poor to make a separate province, and they would be connected only by a thread with the Province of Agra.

There still remains a distinct linguistic tract in the C.P., known as Chhattisgarh. It is quite different from all the rest. It defies incorporation with its neighbours. Linguistically it is not part of Nagpur, and it is divided from its other neighbours by vast tracts of hills and jungle and numbers of small States. It does not speak a word of Marathi, and its main cultivators are Satnami Chamars, who revolted against Brahminism in the last century. It, too, has its own distinctive pride, the traditions of the old Hai-Hai Bansi Dynasty which governed Chhattisgarh for a thousand years before the Mahrattas came. It has its pride, but it would be only a poor relation, and it could not finance itself as a separate province.

Behar and Orissa. Orissa has gone; it has collected its scattered portions and has formed itself into a new province, requiring its own new capital, its university, and its high court. Then what is to happen to Chota Nagpur? Should it try to join itself to Chhattisgarh? No, because Uriya and Hindi States intervene, and miles of jungle. It will have lost some of its richer portion to Western Bengal. Are we to make of it an aboriginal province? And then what is to happen to Behar itself? Would some of it be wanted by Agra or Oudh, or would it itself demand some of the southern districts of the U.P. on both banks of the Ganges?

The Punjab. For the Punjab there is no scheme provided. Its Sikhs, its Hindus, and its Mahommedans will have to fight it out between them.

All this comes of sitting round a table without exact local knowledge and trying to make policies without studying the facts. As has been stated in Chapter XXV, to which this is an Appendix, the Committee and the Conference have wiped out the history of 150 years.

APPENDIX IV

(An Article in *The Hindu* of Madras of March 2nd, 1929)

THE NATIONAL DEMAND

Appeal to the League of Nations

MR. C. VIJIARAGHAVACHARI'S VIEWS

The following conversation took place recently between Mr. C. Vijiaraghavachariar and a friend of his on the problem of the political future of India, in the course of which Mr. Achariar propounds a solution which will be found as striking as it is original:

K. You will remember the request personally made to you by me on your return from Calcutta, early in January last, regarding your own considered views on the present political situation as disclosed by the decisions reached in Calcutta by the Congress and Convention during the last Congress week. You were somewhat reluctant, I thought, to freely express them then. In the light of the speech of His Excellency the Viceroy in the Legislative Assembly, the other day, do you think you can now comply with my request?

C. V. I shall make an endeavour. I should like to say at once that the speech of His Excellency the Viceroy, made in opening the proceedings of the Legislative Assembly the other day, does not much alter the very acute political situation reached, notwithstanding that he therein made some refreshingly original statements which, in my humble opinion, entitle him to the country's gratitude.

K. I am greatly surprised at what you say. I fear that you are yourself original in your opinion. Pray tell me what in your view are the statements which are to be found in that speech which can secure him our grateful thanks.

C. V. Well, I do not know if I am original in my judgment on the speech in question. I trust that you remember the historic pronouncement of the 20th August, 1917. While that announcement does contain a pledge that the destiny of British India is responsible government as an integral part of the British Empire, it is impossible to conceive a more diplomatic device to lull a subject people into fancied security and hopes and consequent political inactivity. The real author of that idea was Lord Curzon. It does not at all recognise the right of self-determination or anything approaching it on the part of the people of this country. On the contrary, the promised responsible government was to be gradual, was to be achieved by successive stages, and that Governments at home and in India were to be the exclusive judges both as to time and measure of each advance! The people of this country have not been deceived by this extraordinary political device. It simply shows that Englishmen are not good judges of character. Now, for the first time, His Excellency the Viceroy has interpreted it as an honest promise of responsible government on the one hand, and on the other that the people of this country must have a voice in determing the arrangement to be finally reached. He admits that the solution of the present political situation is possible only by the mutual agreement between Great Britain and India. He admits too that it would be short-sighted policy on the part of Parliament if it tries a solution of the present impasse which would not carry the willing consent of the people of this country. These admissions, imperfect as they are, of the right of the people of this country to ordain their own system of government, are almost if not quite new in the history of authoritative proclamations and pronouncements, pledges and promises made from time to time in reference to India.

K. Are you quite sure that this view of yours is absolutely correct? Does not the Great Queen's proclamation of 1858 recognise such a right?

C. V. I am pretty sure that I am correct. At all events I should be glad if you would correct me and refresh my memory. No doubt the Great Proclamation of 1858 contains a pledge that the sovereign of the British Empire would henceforth observe no distinction between the white and the Indian subjects of the Empire, and that she held herself "bound to the natives of our Indian territories by the same obligations of duty which bind us to all our other subjects; and those obligations, by the blessing of Almighty God, we shall faithfully and conscientiously fulfil." But it is very doubtful whether at that time, notwithstanding it was some sixty-five years after the French Revolution, with its gospel of universal fraternity, liberty and equality before the law, the Great Queen fully understood and recognised the principle of political sovereignity of her own subjects, and that all authority, legislative, executive and judicial, emanates from them. It must be remembered too that this was some three years before Abraham Lincoln enunciated the divine principle of the government of a people by the people for the people. Apart from the possible implication of such a principle in the Great Proclamation, I am aware of no express statement authoritatively made by British statesmen admitting the right of the people of this country to self-government. I omit from all consideration vague statements made in this behalf now and then in the course of the Great War.

K. I admit I am not in a position to say that you are not correct. But why do you say that the statement of His Excellency the Viceroy on this vital point is imperfect?

C. V. I say so because His Excellency does not admit the right of self-determination of the people of this country to its fullest extent. He would give the right of determing the constitutional government of this country both to the people of this country and to the people of England.

K. Has not the Parliament a voice in the question?

C. V. By the right of Parliament you mean the right of the people of Great Britain, for the British Parliament as such has no right as against the people of this country apart from the people of Great Britain. And the people of Great Britain has not joint voice with us in the exercise of our God-given and inalienable right of self-determination or sovereignity any more than we have a joint voice with the people of Great Britain in ordaining their own political institutions.

K. Have you no other criticism to offer on the speech?

C. V. I have a great deal to say. But it is not quite necessary to traverse the whole of the speech for the purpose we have in view. I would allude to one or two points. His lordship does not find his way to say what the people of this country should do if a solution is not reached by mutual agreement. He takes good care to say, however, Cromwell-like, that Government would ever keep the powder dry for the purpose of maintaining law and order in the country. Reading between the lines it is clear that while he is prepared to do his best to interpret our wishes to the Parliament, and to co-operate with us in reaching a mutual agreement, he necessarily implies that if any such agreement is not reached we should remain content with what we might get eventually from Parliament. But if, on the other hand, we take to non-co-operation in view to secure full responsible government at once, not to say absolute independence, the British Government would take good care to maintain law and order, that is to say, to use all the available force to prevent the success of the movement of non-co-operation. Here we are.

LORD IRWIN'S OPPORTUNITY

K. Quite so. But what in your opinion could His Lordship do in all the circumstances?

C. V. Why, he can make history, the most glorious chapter of it, if he likes and if he would have the necessary courage. The present situation in the relations between the United Kingdom and India presents a strong parallel to the Canadian situation ninety years ago as found by Lord Durham, who saved that rich colony to Great Britain by his bold and wise recommendation that it should be allowed to have immediate responsible government; Lord Irwin has a unique opportunity of becoming a second and even a greater Lord Durham in the British Empire if he would only summon courage to rise equal to the crisis. But I believe that every indication points to the contrary direction, even ignoring his threat that the powder would be ever kept dry for the maintenance, in the chronic formula, of "law and order."

K. What, then, is the course which the people of this country should adopt, assuming that His Lordship would not sieze this golden opportunity to follow so brilliant and historical an example?

C. V. Before I attempt to answer your question it is better that you let me do some spade work in view to find out what exactly is the present political situation in our country. The problem is exceedingly complex. I think I can here take up the Calcutta decisions of both the Indian National Congress and the All-Parties' Convention for a rapid consideration.

THE DECEMBER DECISIONS

K. I should be very glad to have your criticism of these decisions, especially the better to know how these resolutions of those two bodies would enable us to find out what exactly is our political problem.

C. V. I venture to think that an examination of these resolutions would much assist us in understanding the problem we are called upon to deal with. The most prominent of these decisions is, of course, the adoption of the demand for the immediate establishment of Dominion Status for India. The All-Parties' Convention following the recommendations of the Nehru Committee, adopted the resolution without any qualification. But the Congress, in adopting the same by a majority vote, tacked on a condition in the nature of an ultimatum that it should be established in one year or the agitation in the form of non-co-operation would be renewed for the separation and absolute Independence of India from the British Commonwealth of Nations.

The manner and the circumstances under which this resolution was passed in the Congress are most remarkable in its history, and conclusively show the present phenomenal political mentality of the people of this country, especially the rising generation. This resolution was sent up by the Subjects Committee—the All-India Congress Committee—as the result of a compromise between the two wings of the Congress, the party for the absolute independence and the party for Dominion Status respectively. Yet this resolution was most vehemently fought out in the Congress, and the debate was hot and prolonged till the small hours of the night, when it was finally decided by a majority on the side of the right wing, that is, for Dominion Status. You will thus see that the compromise arrived at by the "leaders and thinkers" was not accepted by the followers, who were determined on having a voice. They resented the existence of the smaller inner cabinet among such leaders and thinkers, whom some of them irreverently designated as a "driving team" which ordained all the resolutions of the Congress. The whole situation was grim and ludicrous. Of these revered leaders and thinkers some were silently asked to step aside, while all the rest without exception were respectfully but firmly asked to descend from their lofty pedestal to the plane of their followers. While Messrs. S. Srinivasa Iyengar and Subhas Chandra Bose wisely recognised that it is occasionally the duty of the leaders to allow their followers to lead them, several of the older leaders who could not see eye to eye with the youth of the country were discontented and grumbling.

K. I see this is your view about the most important resolution of the two political bodies. What say you about the other resolutions of the Congress?

C. V. I do not think I need traverse the rest of the resolutions for the purpose we have in view. But I must say that the programme of work ordained by the Congress resolution should not have included social problems, even those which are admittedly urgent and need immediate solution. On the one hand, the solution of these problems has little to do with our political salvation. On the other, it has furnished the enemies of Indian political reform, especially in England, with a handle similar to the weapon furnished by the infamous book of Miss Mayo, to be used in the arrest of the urgent processes for the political and economic freedom of India.

ADJOURNMENT OF THE CONVENTION

K. By the way, I read in the papers that you were against the adjournment of the All-Parties' Convention. Can you kindly tell me why?

C. V. I was. I cannot understand why that course was sprung upon the Convention at all. It was against the resolution of the Madras Congress of which the Convention was the creation. Besides, it was in my humble view most injudicious. It would have been quite in public interests at this crisis that the Convention should have finished its labours and published an agreed constitution; in any event the resolution moved by Dr. Besant that a committee be appointed for considering what further work should be done by the Convention should have been allowed. Such a committee with a more comprehensive reference than Dr. Besant expressed in her proposed resolution was most necessary in this national crisis. Such a committee, with power to co-opt experts and experienced men, is most necessary for investigating the present deplorable economic condition of the country, if only to show to the world the great necessity there is for the immediate establishment of Swarajya Government for India as a Dominion of the British Empire on elastic lines, capable of healthy conventions from time to time as they obtain among the existing Dominions.

K. Pray, how would such a report help us in solving the complex political problem?

C. V. I will tell you. And here I believe I am entering on new ground. I agree with those of our countrymen who are pessimistic and who believe that the British Parliament would not, in the near future at least, establish Dominion Government in India. I need not here state their reasons and mine for this belief. The speech of the Viceroy in the Legislative Assembly is alone sufficient for warranting such a belief, not to mention the statements and observations which Sir John Simon now and then makes.

APPEAL TO THE LEAGUE OF NATIONS

K. Then what is the course which at all is open to us?

C. V. The only course open to us now is an appeal to the League of Nations to save us. And the League of Nations can save us. Nay, more. The League of Nations is the only resource open to us to save us now both from ourselves and from our rulers and establish Dominion Status with financial stabilisation and economic prosperity. For this supreme purpose the League of Nations can start an enquiry into the present political and economic conditions of our country and recommend the immediate establishment of Dominion Status in it under letters patent of the King-Emperor.

K. I am most agreeably surprised. Is not your idea quite new, I dare not say, startling? It is now nine years since this great institution was started. How was it that during all this time nobody suggested an appeal to the League of Nations for help to achieve our freedom?

C. V. I don't know if my idea is new. But, however, I venture to say that an appeal to the League of Nations can be legally made for the high purpose we have in view. I am further satisfied that if, on technical grounds, the League of Nations declines to help us we shall still be the gainers, because we shall have then gained the sympathy of the world in our struggle to gain our freedom, and our process of non-co-operation will be better appreciated in the opinion of the world as the only weapon open to us. So it would be the easier for us to reorganise this movement with efficiency, and the Government in using force against us under the name of law and order will stand condemned at the bar of the world's public opinion.

HISTORY OF THE LEAGUE

K. Do please briefly tell me how you have reached this remarkable conclusion. I am getting more and more interested in your proposal which, I would repeat, appears to me as quite original.

C. V. I will begin with a brief history of the League of Nations. If Grotius was the father of modern international law, Woodrow Wilson may be truly said to be the father of the machinery for doing international justice. We all know of the famous fourteen points which he laid down in his address to the Congress in January, 1918, as his programme for achieving the world's peace, and we know that, of these fourteen points, the last and the most important was his conception of the League of Nations. He went to Paris at the head of the United States Delegation, and there under his immediate auspices the League of Nations was established in January, 1920. And the greatest institution of the world has been in incessant operation ever since. Its constitution is embodied in a Covenant, and it became Part I of the Treaty of Versailles.

K. Was this constitution entirely the work of President Wilson?

C. V. Not quite exactly. The entire idea and the leading principles embodied therein were his, but they were adopted after a good deal of discussion as to the plan and details with English and other European statesmen and General Smuts of South Africa. And it is worth while to remember that the English Foreign Office had a good deal to do with the drafting of the Covenant.

K. Then kindly tell me how many nations have accepted and adopted the principles of the League of Nations and become its members?

C. V. The very vast majority. I believe that there are now fifty-five Nation-States who are its members, and there are only about twelve more left. The members of the League of Nations have been recruited in reference to their attitude towards the Great War. The first set of members, called "Original Members," were "the Allied and Associated Powers" who were the signatories to the Peace of Versailles. And these "Original Members" invited thirteen neutral members also to join them and become "Original Members." Then other nations could only become members when the Assembly of the League of Nations admits them by a majority of two-thirds. In this way the League of Nations consists of all the three classes of members.

K. Is there any distinction in rights and privileges or duties between one class and another? I believe there is none.

C. V. None whatever. There are but two conditions. The first is that every one of the members should be fully self-governing, it does not matter whether it is called a State a Dominion or a Colony; and the second is that every one of them should undertake the duties and obligations arising from the membership, and guarantee to carry them out.

K. If so, can you explain how India, which is not fully self-governing, if it is self-governing at all to any extent, has become a member of the League of Nations? Is it not a very curious circumstance?

C. V. It is the only one among the fifty-five members of the League of Nations which is not a self-governing State or Dominion. And this very anomaly is our hope. We fully expect the League of Nations to get rid of this strange anomaly and raise India really and in fact to the level of the other members as she is now theoretically and technically occupying the same status with them. We must remember that India is among the first class of members, namely " Original Members," who signed the Treaty of Versailles. She was one of the "Allied and Associated Powers." Among these there were also the Dominions of Canada, Australia, South Africa, and New Zealand. Absolutely no distinction was made in the nature and prestige of the status, rights and privileges and duties between India and any of the other Member-States. And this position was accorded to her with everybody's eyes wide open. I have already told you that English statesmen and General Smuts took part in the discussion and framing of the Covenant of the League of Nations, and that the English Foreign Office was chiefly responsible for the actual drafting of it. No attempt was at any stage or anywhere made to restrict India's power or privilege under the Covenant. As an ally and as one of the "Allied and Associated Powers" it would have been impossible.

THE LEAGUE'S RESPONSIBILITY TO INDIA

K. It is clear that it was not by accident that India became a member of the League of Nations co-equal in status and in everything else to all the other members. Yet do you think you can account for this strange phenomenon? Why was she made a signatory to the Treaty of Peace at all?

C. V. I believe I can state one or two reasons. In the first place the whole world knew then and the United Kingdom and the Dominions then fully appreciated without any reserve the tremendous sacrifices which India made during the Great War in men and money, indeed more than and earlier than the self-governing Dominions of the British Empire. Nextly, the principal "Allied and Associated Powers" were then full of the rights of self-determination for every country, and generally English statesmen then genuinely meant to allow India to get into her Dominion Status soon after the War. It must be remembered too that the solemn pledge of the people of the United Kingdom to let India have responsible government within the Empire, notwithstanding the somewhat disquieting language of the pledge diplomatically inserted in it by Lord Curzon, was made some two and a half years before the Covenant of the League of Nations was born and even several months before President Wilson announced his famous Fourteen Points. Therefore, everybody believed and expected that India was, for all practical purposes, as good as a fully self-governing Dominion as she was soon bound to be one. I submit, therefore, that the League of Nations is not only entitled but bound to call upon the United Kingdom to carry out the sacred pledge made expressly to the people of India on the one hand and, by necessary implication from authoritative conduct, to the League of Nations itself on the other. This argument of mine is greatly reinforced by the attitude of the United Kingdom in reference to the Kellogg Pact. When the British Government accepted the proposed Pact, the United States suggested that the *British Dominions* be invited to sign the Pact. The Pact was signed a few months ago, in August 1928, and India was among the signatories. This Pact is justly regarded as supplementing and fortifying the Covenant of the League of Nations. Here again the British Government and the other high contracting parties made no distinction between India and the other parties to it.

THE ALTERNATIVE

K. Do kindly tell me how we are to proceed in order to make this appeal to the League of Nations, and what exactly we had better do for the purpose.

C. V. We must remember that under the Covenant the activities of the League may be divided into two principal spheres, namely, those relating to the preservation of international peace and avoidance of war on the one hand, and, on the other, those relating to the promotion of health conditions and economic prosperity of the world. I may add that, as a sort of corollary to its two sets of activities, another sphere has been added, namely, the protection and guarantee of the rights of minorities, whether racial, religious or linguistic. I venture to think that the League of Nations has jurisdiction to interfere in the affairs of India just at this crisis from the standpoint of every one of its three spheres of action. First and foremost, the League has jurisdiction to interfere on the one supreme ground which is the essence of its very existence, namely, the preservation of peace and prevention of rupture and war and anarchy. There can be no doubt whatever that, if Dominion Status is not forthwith established in India, the people are resolved to take to non-co-operation, including non-payment of taxes to Government, and they are bound to take to it as the only weapon open to them. And this method to achieve their salvation is sure to lead to a rupture between the United Kingdom and even its Dominions on the one hand and the people of India on the other. The speech of His Excellency at the Legislative Assembly leaves no doubt on the point. But we really required no threat or menace on his part to induce us to believe that a serious rupture, little short of a war, would surely be the result.

TWO INSTANCES OF THE LEAGUE'S INTERVENTION

K. Let us then assume that the League of Nations has jurisdiction to interfere in view to the solution of the present political situation in India and that it is its duty to help us in reaching the solution. What do you think the probable attitude of the United Kingdom in this behalf would be?

C. V. Well, I can only speculate. Her first and foremost objection would be the denial of the League's jurisdiction to interfere. She would probably plead that the question of the settlement of the relations between her and India falls within her "domestic jurisdiction" within the meaning of clause (9) of Article XV of the Covenant, and, therefore, that the League has no jurisdiction. I venture to submit that the objection would not hold. The relation between India and the United Kingdom is clearly international. Otherwise she could not have been her ally and one of the "Allied and Associated Powers" for the Great War and Peace, and it is impossible to conceive that it could be a domestic business of the latter country. It is too late for her to deny India a status in the League equal to that of any other member, deliberately assigned to her in collaboration with herself (United Kingdom) from the start, for which India has been paying but too handsomely, and that she (India) has been ever accorded equal rights of participation and voting in the activities of the League. It must be remembered that the Covenant of the League is designedly vague and elastic, and that its full and varied jurisdiction has to be determined and ascertained in relation to its actual activities in view to achieve its high purposes. I would take two instances of its activities, those relating to the Aaland Islands and the Irish Free State, as most germane to the point in question. A serious dispute arose between those islands and Finland after the late Russian revolution when Finland became an independent republic. The people of the Aaland Islands, who are ethnically Swedish, wished to seize this opportunity to separate themselves from any part of Russia and become absorbed into Sweden. Sweden naturally enough sympathised with them, but Finland claimed sovereignty over these islands as part of herself. A serious rupture was thus imminent. The British Empire, acting under clause (2) of Article XI of the Covenant, exercised her "friendly right" and brought the matter to the attention of the League in view to her interference in the interest of peace. Sweden was a member of the League but Finland was not. But the League invited her to become a member thereof under Article XVII of the Covenant for the purpose of settling this dispute between her and the islands. She consented and became such a temporary member, but she at once raised the plea that this was her own domestic concern and that the League had no jurisdiction to interfere. The League, however, entered on an investigation of the state of relationship, found that Finland had sovereignty over the islands, but yet she claimed and exercised jurisdiction on the ground that otherwise the rupture would be serious and disturb international peace. So she made several recommendations, including full autonomy for the islands. Finland obeyed, and carried out the recommendations, and the Aaland Islands are now enjoying a Dominion Status so to speak. Let us next take the case of the Irish Free State. We must remember that under the preamble of the Covenant clause (2) the relations between any two nations should be open and honourable, and that under Article XVIII thereof every treaty or international engagement between any two nations, both or one of them being members of the League, should be forthwith registered in the Office of the League Secretariat and published by it. Otherwise such a treaty or engagement shall not be binding. The Free State of Ireland, after she had secured her treaty with the United Kingdom under which she became a fully self-governing Dominion, but before she became a member of the League of Nations, applied to the League to have the treaty registered and published. Great Britain objected on the ground that it was a matter of her domestic concern and that the League had no jurisdiction. The plea was disallowed by the League and the treaty was registered and published under the Covenant on the ground that it was an international engagement within the meaning of Article XVIII. These two instances are sufficient conclusively to dispose of the possible or probable objection of the United Kingdom in our own case. It requires no argument to show that, if the doctrine of "domestic jurisdiction" is carried too far, the one supreme aim and object of the League of Nations, namely, to avert danger or threatened danger to the world's peace, would be frustrated. If the League of Nations had existed at the time when the Wars of the Roses in England and the War between the North and South of the United States of America took place, could jurisdiction have been denied to her if she tried to avert those great and sanguinary wars, on the ground of "domestic jurisdiction?" It is clear from the actual operation of the Covenant of the League that the principle of domestic jurisdiction ousting the jurisdiction of the League is subject to the far more important vital principle of maintaining the world's peace, and the phrase "domestic jurisdiction" has to be confined to comparatively petty disputes in which the outside world has no concern or interest. If the great authors of the League of Nations meant that countries under one sovereign cannot invoke its jurisdiction under circumstances which would warrant the exercise of its jurisdiction if such circumstances would affect the countries under separate sovereigns or were separate republics, nothing would have been easier for them or more necessary than to have said so in several Articles of the Covenant where such a statement would be most relevant, such as Article XV where it might and ought to have expressly declared that in spite of the Annex No. 2, which allows self-governing Dominions and Colonies to become members of the League with equal status and rights and duties with the rest, they are all one and the same with the Empire within which and of which they are Dominions and Colonies for the purpose of "domestic jurisdiction." It would be strange indeed if the great authors of the League meant that the relation between the United Kingdom and India were domestic and not international they would have laid upon the latter such a heavy contribution to the budget of the League and that on the application of the test of her own resources and populations and not in reference to the combined resources and population of the two countries if at all. For the Colonies do not contribute a penny at all to the 105 units out of 937 which the British Empire pays. India like them should not pay anything, whereas she pays 56 units, and she is the fifth among the fifty-five members according to the extent of the sums paid by each.

It is worth while observing that Professor Keith hesitates to accept the British interpretation of the Covenant in this important particular. He characterises its attitude in the significant words, "the claim is hard to substantiate." It is needless to argue the point further. To put such a construction upon the Covenant would be not only to defeat the one great object of the great institution but also to hold out a premium to the people of India that in view even to secure their political and economic freedom as a Dominion within the Empire with the aid of the League of Nations, they shall have to declare their absolute independence of Great Britain, and start or seriously threaten a rupture that would disturb the world's peace. May merciful God save us all from such an interpretation of the principles and provisions of the constitution of the greatest and most humanitarian institution of the world.

THE METHOD OF APPROACH

K. I am certainly inclined to agree with you in this view. Please tell me how we are to proceed in order to bring the matter to the attention of the League.

C. V. This question is easily answered. It is the duty of the Governments of Great Britain and India, under Article XV, to submit the matter to the Council of the League; either of them may give notice of the existence of the dispute between them to the Secretary-General of the League. If neither of them would do its duty, a not unlikely event, then any other Member-State of the League may invite its attention to the subject matter by exercising its "friendly right" under clause (2) of Article XI just as Great Britain did in reference to the dispute between Finland and the Aaland Islands. If the people of India, by means of any one of their innumerable organisations, do not succeed in persuading one of the remaining fifty-three Member-States to act under this Article, a most unlikely contingency, still, I submit, there are other ways open to us. If a single member of the League can start its jurisdiction in this important particular, then it does not require the genius and statesmanlike outlook of a Chief Justice Marshall to infer a necessarily implied power on the part of the corporate institution itself for exercising *suo moto* its supreme function. I venture to think that, on credible information before it, the Assembly or the Council of the League can set the whole process of the Covenant in motion for the purpose of the investigation of the dispute, and taking all such actions as the Covenant commands and warrants. The course adopted by the League in the matter of the Upper Silesian frontier problem in 1921 furnishes a very good precedent for showing conclusively that its jurisdiction to settle a dispute can be started by agencies other than those expressly mentioned in its Covenant. The duty of tracing and fixing a frontier between German Upper Silesia and Poland in accordance with the provisions of the Treaty of Versailles devolved upon the "Principal Allied Powers." But the Supreme Council of these powers after strenuous endeavours failed to reach an acceptable solution, and hence there was imminent risk of a dangerous rupture between Germany and Poland. Thereupon, Briand, President of the Supreme Council, wrote to Viscount Ishii, President of the Council of the League of Nations, inviting his attention to the gravity of the situation and soliciting the prompt intervention of the League. Viscount Ishii complied with the request of M. Briand, and summoned a meeting of the Council of the League forthwith. In his report, Viscount Ishii said ". . . . that it is not only the right but also the duty of the Council to accept the rôle which, in the spirit of the Covenant, it has been asked to assume, and in the fulfilment of which its liberty of action and authority will be fully guaranteed." And the members of the Council of the League unanimously decided to accept the invitation of the President of the Supreme Council. A satisfactory solution of the problem was eventually reached, but for our purpose it is unnecessary to describe the steps taken by the Council in this connection. The point is that neither the Supreme Council of the Principal Allied Powers nor its President had any status in the League of Nations under the provisions of its Covenant for the purpose of starting its jurisdiction for settling a dispute. And Viscount Ishii hit upon the doctrine of the spirit of the Covenant. This view is even better than the principle of implied power which Chief Justice Marshall would evolve under the circumstances. It is thus clear that the people of India have the right and power to submit their case to the League of Nations in view to its investigation and settling our dispute with the British Empire in regard to our political emancipation. The President of the Indian National Congress or of the All-Parties' Convention, for instance, not to mention other non-official public organisations such as the Hindu Maha Sabba or the Muslim League, can, like M. Briand, invite the attention of the League of Nations to the very acute political situation in India, calculated to lead to a dangerous rupture with the British Empire, and effectually start its jurisdiction for the exercise of all its powers under the Covenant for reaching a satisfactory solution in the interests of peace. Besides, this power is within the letter and spirit of Article XI, clause (1) of the Covenant which makes it obligatory on the part of the League to take any action that may be deemed wise and effectual to safeguard the peace of nations.

K. You told me a little while ago of the jurisdiction of the League in matters of national health, economic prosperity, and also for the purpose of protection of the rights of the minorities. May I ask you kindly to tell me how far the present state of India in reference to these points would justify the interference and action of the League.

C. V. The Great Powers that drew up the League, and the several treaties of peace at Paris in 1919 imposed upon the League of Nations the duty of safeguarding the rights of minorities in the several countries in Europe, whether racial, religious or linguistic. To the several governments affected, protesting against this proposal, M. Clemenceau, on behalf of the Great Powers, explained the purpose and declared that the duty of protecting the minorities would be entrusted to a body representing all the nations and in a purely judicial manner. The Council of the League is the authority to which complaints from the affected minority should be made. The Covenant itself, apart from these treaties, contains no provisions expressly conferring jurisdiction upon the League for protection of the rights of minorities. But such a jurisdiction may be conferred on the League by declaration by the minorities affected. Above all, the League has power to intervene for this purpose if the circumstances affecting the question are such as to threaten to disturb the peace. In our own case the several minorities and majority can agree to refer the whole question to the League. The Hindu-Moslem problem has been found to be too tough to be settled by the people of this country. Past experience shows that it is not easy for us to solve it in the near future. On the other hand there is no near chance of the powers that be enabling us to reach a satisfactory solution. Without a solution of this important problem it is admittedly impossible to establish Dominion Status, much less absolute independence, in our country, and to successfully maintain the same. Judging from its hitherto very satisfactory activity in this behalf in Europe the League of Nations is the best and perhaps the only tribunal that can settle this question to the satisfaction of all parties in India. For this purpose any minority in India can move the Council of the League to enter into an investigation of the subject, and even the Hindus can do so, as they are in a minority in some provinces. Besides, they are most interested in satisfactorily and permanently securing a settlement of the claims and disputes relating to the rights of all the minorities in India in order to reach the political and economic freedom of the whole country. Our Muslim brethren throughout the country can possibly have no objection to this course, but on the other hand they should welcome the suggestion. It must be remembered that Persia is one of the Member-States of the League, and they can have no reason to entertain any fear that the investigation and decision of the League of Nations as to their rights as a minority would not be thoroughly impartial and satisfactory.

K. Cannot some political body, such as the Indian National Congress or the Muslim League, take the initiative in the matter?

C. V. It can, I should think. But the best body is the All-Parties' Convention which stands adjourned *sine die*, as that is more representative than the Indian National Congress as regards the varieties of political views. And for another reason, too, which I shall state presently.

INTER-DEPENDENCE OF POLITICS AND ECONOMICS

K. Is it necessary that we should invite the League of Nations to enter into an investigation of the health and economic conditions of our country now? Is it not enough if it settles the constitutional problems and the question of the rights of the minorities as incidental and even essential for that one purpose?

C. V. I am clearly of opinion that they should all be treated and investigated as constituting the one complex problem confronting us. On the one hand, it should be emphasised times without number that politics includes economics, and that our political and economic freedom are interlocked and cannot be conceived the one as separate from the other. A sound and lasting constitution for a country cannot be constructed without a due regard to the economic conditions obtaining therein, and to the prospects of their improvement. On this important aspect of our duties I dwelt at some length in my address to the delegates of the Madras Session of the Indian National Congress over a year ago. The present deplorable economic condition of our country is admitted by the most impartial observers. There is any amount of very good evidence on the point taken by the Royal Agricultural Commission. There are also the statements of Major-General T. H. Symons, President of the Tropical Diseases Congress at Calcutta, and of Sir Daniel Hamilton, made only the other day, the exact truth of which cannot be challenged. While we cannot agree with them in their views as to the causes and remedies suggested, we cannot but be grateful to them all for the accurate and masterly picture of the frightful fact itself. In the light of all this unchallenged and unchallengeable and conclusive evidence it is unnecessary for us to discuss this aspect at any length here. Briefly stated, the notorious facts are that the present-day Indian is gradually deteriorating physically: he is unable to resist diseases to any degree anywise approaching the capacity possessed by the people of well-governed modern states, or even by our ancestors up to some two centuries ago; that this capacity of his has been gradually shrinking; that his average age has been diminishing and is now very low, being about a half of the average age in England or Japan, and even very much lower than that of our neighbour the Afghan, not a citizen of a most well-governed state as yet; and so, too, the condition of the cattle and of the soil have been steadily deteriorating.

THE LEAGUE TO INVESTIGATE

K. Quite so. But after an investigation of all these questions what use can the League of Nations make of the result?

C. V. The League of Nations has to consider what is the exact structure of the mechanism of the Government that is most suitable to our country in reference to all these facts; to find out what form of government would be the cheapest and yet at the same time the most efficient for starting institutions and policies for the gradual removal of all these fatal aspects.

K. But cannot the investigation of these questions be made by ourselves, say a non-official commission of the Congress, and then the result placed before the League of Nations?

C. V. This can be done. But I must say that, on the one hand, such an investigation would not be most satisfactory, and, on the other, the League would not act on it with the confidence with which it would accept the report of a committee of its own experts. We cannot secure the services of such experts. But it would be desirable that we should make such an investigation as well as we can and place the result before the League of Nations to show that it is necessary for it to enter into an investigation of this aspect as well. In my view the All Parties' Convention is more suitable for this purpose, as its authority would be better appreciated as being more representative than the Congress. If the Nehru Committee is deemed still to exist on the ground that it can only expire with the All-Parties' Convention which has been adjourned it can and ought to undertake this important work. If it does not exist, either the Convention should at its next meeting appoint a committee for the purpose, or the All-India Congress Committee should appoint a committee of its own.

K. I should like to ask you one question in this connection. Cannot all the information relating to the economic condition of the people of this country be collected from the published records, and if all of them have not been published can they not be secured from Government? Is it necessary for a committee to make enquiries anew?

C. V. No; a good deal can be secured in the way you suggest. But Government have not as yet investigated this question thoroughly and in all its aspects. For instance, I am not aware that the question of the diminishing average age of the Indian has been investigated, nor the question of the incidence of taxation with due regard to national and individual incomes, nor again the question how far the incidence is responsible for the growing poverty of the people and deterioration of cattle and soil. Besides, the whole financial policy of Government in all its aspects, namely, taxation, public expenditure, currency, exchange, and banking should be examined by the best and unprejudiced experts which the League of Nations alone supply. The committee we can employ can only do work sufficient to convince the League that the field is worth exploring by great experts in view to the reconstruction of the whole system of government for our country.

K. But are we sure that the abnormal mortality and the low average age among us are not also due to social evils such as child-marriage?

C. V. No doubt child-marriage of girls and premature maternity are somewhat responsible for the high mortality, especially infant mortality, and for the low average age. But this factor is exceedingly small if not negligible when the question is considered as affecting the people of the whole country. This social custom obtains only among a small class of Hindus, and the custom is gradually being discredited. To show that this social custom has very little to do with the vital statistics of India, let me allude to one important fact. The infant mortality among the Muslims of Bengal is 15 per cent. more than the same for the Hindus.

K. Strange phenomenon this, is it not?

C. V. I don't think so. The true and substantial causes are economic and not social.

INDEPENDENCE AND DOMINION STATUS

K. There is one important aspect of the whole problem to which I must call your attention. You will remember that the volume of opinion in favour of absolute independence of India is increasing, and that the Congress in its resolution for Dominion Status has recognised this growing opinion in accepting the ultimatum attached to it. Assuming that Great Britain won't let us have full Dominion Status this year or in the near future, do you think the country should ask the League of Nations for the establishment of mere Dominion Status and not for absolute independence? What would be the attitude of the League of Nations if we ask for absolute independence?

C. V. A complete answer to this question would be very long indeed. In the first place the League would not entertain such an appeal, as being beyond its jurisdiction. The Covenant says that, provided its members are fully self-governing, it is immaterial whether any such member is a State or Dominion or a Colony. Prof. Laski says, and rightly in my view, that the League has no power to ask Great Britain to quit India. No doubt if the world's peace is menaced by an attempt on the part of India to secure complete independence it has jurisdiction to interfere, but it has also another essential principle to follow at the same time, viz., international justice according to the Covenant; and the Covenant having deliberately limited its activities on well-expressed principles, the League would not and could not assist us if we try to secure absolute independence. On the other hand, if we decline to accept its recommendations in view to conciliation it would leave us severely alone, or perhaps it may use all the powers it possesses to restrain us in our attempt in view to the world's peace. In the second place, I believe most conscientiously, as I have ever done all my life, that independence is undesirable in our interests, and perilous too to aim at absolute independence for our country.

K. Surely you may be right as regards your view that the League cannot entertain our appeal for total independence, but I am simply surprised that you maintain the extraordinary position that our independence is undesirable in our own interest. How can it be? Would you be against our independence even if Great Britain withdraws or if we can win it by peaceful means?

C. V. I have no hesitation in answering your questions in the affirmative. The first contingency would never happen, and the latter hypothesis won't arise at all, and we shall not be able to win independence by peaceful means, or by bloodshed even. In the next place, Dominion Status has in substance all the advantages of absolute independence without its disadvantages. You must remember that from very ancient times one of the chief factors of lasting political independence of a country has been powerful and loyal allies. Isolated independence is precarious and is becoming more and more so. The late war could not have been won but for the association of very powerful allies. Dominion Status means that India has several allies who are bound to stand by her in case of external danger, just as India is bound to stand by them all in such an emergency. It is impossible to exaggerate the vital aspect of the entire question.

K. I fear that you attach undue importance to the system of Government called "Dominion Status." Prof. Keith says that the Dominions are after all dependencies of Great Britain. Yet you seem to think that such a Dominion Status is even better than thorough independence. It is quite a new form of Government. Is it not?

C. V. I admit that I am partial to this kind of political status for our country. I fear that there is considerable misapprehension as to the nature and the capacity for sound development of this form of Government. Its history should inspire confidence in us although it is quite true that it is a very modern institution, and unknown to political philosophy. The ideals and the word "Dominion" in this sense are of Canadian origin. They were taken from the 8th verse of Psalm No. 72, "He shall have dominion also from sea to sea." The British Parliament accepted the word and the doctrine, and the British North America Act of 1867 was framed in accordance therewith. The Imperial Conference of 1907 appreciated the new political conception and extended the use of the appellation to all other self-governing colonies of the Empire. This modern polity is as elastic in its evolution on sound lines as it is unique in origin, due chiefly to the successful rebellion of the thirteen United States of America. The self-governing Dominions of the British Empire are content and prosperous, and Canada is even proud of her status and is most happy in inventing and developing conventions in the way of national prestige and national advancement. Canada is in substance as independent as the United States of America, and with much less responsibility and expenditure for the defences of the country. If we would but compose our domestic quarrels arising from religion or caste, and adopt the wisest course as Canada did, we shall also have our dominion from sea to sea and from sea to mountain and become as free and as prosperous and as proud too as Canada.

I may here invite attention to the very melancholy state of affairs in China and Afghanistan. Both are independent countries, and political reform there should be easy of achievement. Yet what do we find? Instead of hailing King Amanullah as another Peter the Great, not only the unthinking masses and tribes and ignorant priests but also the chiefs and several of the upper classes are unrelentingly opposing the great Prince. God alone knows whether he will succeed in establishing a lasting free constitution. In China the noble attempt of the patriots to convert the ancient regime into a free and modern Government has been opposed by the Governors of the huge provinces from personal ambition and under the selfish abetment of the foreign exploiters. Let us remember, too, that these two independent countries cannot become self-governing Dominions. But India can ; and thereby escape the dangers that are sure to overtake us so soon as we set up independence. And India is more apt than Afghanistan or China to cause disturbances in our way. Its innumerable tributary princes and religious and racial sections would all be exploited to oppose the national patriots. No, British-India should not at this crisis think of absolute independence, whatever the provocation given to us by Great Britain. The establishment of a sound constitution as a self-governing Dominion within the Empire under the auspices of the League of Nations, with its organs for the continued protection of the rights of minorities, is by far the best instrument for effecting and progressively maintaining our constitutional freedom. Let us not forget that the embittered relations between minorities and ruling Powers in Europe brought on the Great War, as the Rt. Hon. Sir W. Dickinson says.

ADVANTAGES OF DOMINION STATUS

K. Well, be it so. But even in that case we shall have to fight and win Dominion Status by non-co-operation, as Great Britain won't let us have it peacefully. What becomes of the ultimatum of the Congress resolution then?

C. V. Yes. Nothing should provoke us into a rebellion, even a peaceful rebellion for the sake of technical independence. It would be really perilous. While Dominion Status would be much more easily won by us, even if we fail to secure the intervention of the League of Nations, as I have already explained, it is best for our country. I am not one of these men who believe and assert that we cannot defend ourselves against foreign aggression. Besides the advantage just mentioned of being associated with Great Britain and her Dominions for purposes of defence against external aggression there are two other very great advantages in our becoming a Dominion, and that with the assistance of the League of Nations. Let us not forget that as soon as we become a Swarajya nation, whether as a Dominion or as an absolutely independent State, financially we shall be on the brink of national ruin. The story is too long and painful to tell. India is fast losing international credit. The appalling and growing poverty of the people tells the same dismal tale. So we need the assistance of the League of Nations to save us from this ruin as she saved Austria soon after the War. But for her lead and assistance the ruin, financially and economically, of Austria would have been certain and complete several years ago. So we should do everything in our power to secure and retain the League's sympathy in working out our salvation both politically and economically. With her assistance alone can we hope to make our rupee as stable as the Australian crown now is.

The next advantage is that we require for many a long year the co-operation of Englishmen in the services, civil and military (including aerial and naval). It is best to be frank and honest in the eternal interests of ourselves. Long, long ago, say a thousand years ago, we lost our capacity and disciplined habits for running a free government with all its necessary institutions, while the Englishmen have been these eight hundred years developing all the qualities of head and heart which are most necessary for progressively maintaining free institutions. We sadly but imperatively need their association with us in maintaining and developing our newly-won free institutions on the soundest practical principles tested by their long experience.

K. But we have all along been crying against the bureaucracy and have wished to get rid of them.

C. V. There has been confusion of thought in this particular. The present English bureaucracy in India have all along been our political rulers as well, charged by law and conventions to run and maintain the most selfish autocracy solely in the interests of Great Britain and even her possessions beyond the seas. Stripped of all their present political and other special powers and privileges they would be most valuable merely as constituting a definite and appreciable portion of the great services of the new régime along with our own countrymen. I believe that it is far more difficult to preserve internal peace and carry on the adminstration in and by every department satisfactorily than to ordain our defence against external aggression.

ANOTHER POSSIBLE ENGLISH OBJECTION

K. One more question and I have done. Would not, in case of our appeal to the League of Nations now, Great Britain urge that the intervention of the League would be premature at this time as the Parliament is considering the whole question of Indian Reform?

C. V. It may. But it won't hold. On the one hand, the reform undertaken by Parliament is limited and narrow in aim and scope, and does not include economic and financial reform, without which the political reform, even if Dominion Status is established, would be most inadequate and unsatisfactory. Great Britain would by no means reduce the huge and costly services, civil and military, nor adopt the soundest financial policies in every direction solely in the interest of India. It is the League of Nations alone that can, with the assistance of disinterested experts, tackle with all the aspects of the complex political problem of our country in a satisfactory way. Again, if this objection should be entertained, then after the disposal of the question by the Parliament the objection would be that the intervention is too soon and that the reform effected should be allowed a chance.

K. If the League of Nations intervenes now, then the labours of the Simon Commission and all the associated committees would all go in vain.

C. V. Yes, they would. I am not quite sure that the Commission and the Committees, I mean the personnel of them, would not warmly thank the League of Nations and ourselves too in that event. And I imagine that their thanks would be the warmer the sooner we enter this path for achieving our national salvation.

K. So let us prayerfully aim and work.

C. V. I think I can most appropriately close our talk with an apt quotation from the speech of His Gracious Majesty the King-Emperor, whose recovery from his dangerous illness has filled the hearts of the teeming millions of India with joy and gratitude to Providence, delivered on December 22, 1927, proroguing Parliament:

" I have watched with profound sympathy and satisfaction the steady growth in influence of the League of Nations and the increasing part which it plays in composing international differences and preserving peace. The recent meeting of the Council at Geneva marked a further stage in this progress. My Government will continue to base its policy on loyal co-operation with the League."

Let us mark and inwardly digest the ideas embodied in this passage, especially in the last sentence, and do prayerfully hope as we go to perform our duty.

INDEX